T0305089

Risk Management and Corporate Governance

Risk Management and Corporate Governance

Interconnections in Law, Accounting and Tax

Edited by

Marijn van Daelen

Tilburg University, The Netherlands

Christoph Van der Elst

Tilburg University, The Netherlands
Ghent University, Belgium

Edward Elgar
Cheltenham, UK • Northampton, MA, USA

Published by
Edward Elgar Publishing Limited
The Lypiatts
15 Lansdown Road
Cheltenham
Glos GL50 2JA
UK

Edward Elgar Publishing, Inc.
William Pratt House
9 Dewey Court
Northampton
Massachusetts 01060
USA

A catalogue record for this book
is available from the British Library

Library of Congress Control Number: 2010926008

Mixed Sources
Product group from well-managed
forests and other controlled sources
www.fsc.org Cert no. SA-COC-1565
© 1996 Forest Stewardship Council
FSC

ISBN 978 1 84980 395 3

Printed and bound by MPG Books Group, UK

Contents

List of figures, tables and boxes	vi
List of contributors	viii
Foreword	x
Acknowledgments	xii

1. Introducing risk management   1
   Marijn van Daelen and Arco van de Ven
2. Risk management from an accounting perspective   7
   Arco van de Ven
3. Risk management from a business law perspective   56
   Marijn van Daelen
4. Risk management in financial law   109
   Christoph Van der Elst and Filip Bogaert
5. Risk management in taxation   163
   Ronald Russo
6. Risk management interconnections in law, accounting and tax   191
   Marijn van Daelen, Christoph Van der Elst and Arco van de Ven

Index   233

Figures, tables and boxes

FIGURES

2.1	The COSO I cube	23
2.2	The COSO ERM cube	31
4.1	The financial system	115
4.2	Risks in the financial system	117
4.3	Financial law and risk assessment	133
4.4	Overview of the true sale securitization	137
4.5	The balance sheet of the bank and the SPE before securitization	140
4.6	The balance sheet of the bank and the SPE after true sale securitization	140
4.7	The balance sheet of the bank and the SPE after secured lending	140
4.8	The segmented liability side of the SPE's balance sheet	142
4.9	The credit default swap	151
4.10	The total return swap	152
6.1	Interconnections: the risk management landscape	209

TABLES

3.1	Overview of the main pre-21st century internal control and risk management provisions	72
3.2	US internal control and risk management framework	79
3.3	US and EU internal control and risk management frameworks	82
3.4	US and EU internal control and risk management frameworks including Dutch provisions	89
3.5	US and EU internal control and risk management frameworks including Dutch and UK provisions	93
3.6	Overview of the main 21st century internal control and risk management provisions	95
4.1	Overview of financial crises between the 15th and 20th centuries	111
4.2	Worldwide systemic risk banks	120
4.3	Credit assessment for capital requirements	124

5.1 The relationship between tax accounts and commercial
    accounts   169
5.2 Audit of tax model   175
6.1 Developments in stage 2: reporting to stakeholders   196
6.2 Developments in stage 3: codification of reporting
    requirements   198
6.3 Developments in stage 4: corporate governance movement   201
6.4 Developments in stage 5: codification of internal control
    and risk management   205
6.5 Developments in stage 6: maturity or reinvention of risk
    management   207

BOXES

2.1 Internal control over financial reporting – Ericsson annual
    statement 2008   24
2.2 Internal control over financial reporting of Lehman Brothers   43
2.3 Internal control of the Royal Bank of Scotland   44

Contributors

Filip Bogaert
Filip Bogaert was admitted to the Bar of Ghent in 2002. In 2006 he also became a member of the Financial Law Institute of the Ghent University (Belgium). His research focuses on credit risk, credit risk transfer, credit derivatives and securitization. At present he's preparing a Ph.D. in law about credit risk and credit risk transfer.

Marijn van Daelen
Marijn van Daelen has been a research fellow and lecturer at Tilburg University Faculty of Law (Netherlands) since 2006. Her research focuses on business-law-related topics, such as corporate law, corporate governance, disclosure, risk management, internal control and compliance. Currently she is preparing a Ph.D., which analyses risk management and internal control from a legal perspective. Moreover, she works on several research projects related to the above subjects.

Christoph Van der Elst
Christoph Van der Elst is Professor of Business Law and Economics at the Law School of the University of Tilburg (The Netherlands). He combines this position with a professorship at the Law School of the Ghent University (Belgium). He is also a member of the disciplinary court for the Belgian registered auditors. He holds a Master degree in Law, a Master degree in Economics and a Ph.D. in economics. His research interests primarily concern different issues of corporate governance, corporate risk management and company law and, in particular, the position of shareholders in the law and finance theory.

Ronald Russo
Ronald Russo has been a researcher and lecturer at the Fiscal Institute of Tilburg University (Netherlands) since 2006. Prior to this he worked for the universities of Utrecht and Leiden, combining this with his work as a tax inspector and tax consultant. His holds a Ph.D. in (tax) law (1992). His current research includes the concept of profit for taxation purposes and the interactions with profit for commercial purposes, nationally but also in a European perspective.

Arco van de Ven

Arco van de Ven is Professor of Accounting Information Systems at TiasNimbas, the business school of Tilburg University and Eindhoven University of Technology. He is a registered auditor (Register Accountant), the Dutch equivalent of a Certified Public Auditor (CPA) and received his Ph.D. at Erasmus University Rotterdam, where he has also been programme director of the following courses: the postgraduate Executive Master of Finance and Control (Dutch: register controller RC); and the postgraduate Master Certified Public Controlling (CPC). He has also taught various post-experience programmes at Vlerick Leuven Gent Management School. Professor Van de Ven is also a partner at ACN Management Consultants and has performed many (interim) functions as CFO, controller and consultant.

Foreword

How much risk is a company involved in and how does it manage these risks? These questions have probably been raised more often over the last couple of years than any other business-related question. Risk management is high on the agenda of legislators, governments, supervisors, consultants and, not least of all, companies, not only in the financial sector, but also in many other businesses as well. The stakeholders and shareholders also have huge expectations regarding the proper disclosure of risk management. It poses other risks of which the appropriate balance between (1) the necessary disclosure of risks and (2) the appropriate confidentiality of some business activities is the most important one. It raises important questions such as which types of transparency, standardization and attestation rules can reduce the risk of misappropriation of corporate funds, misstatement of financial reports and can also mitigate the engagement in too-risky strategies. The processes and procedures that are developed both at the regulatory level as well as at the corporate level should take into account standardization of the internal control and risk management systems. Moreover the disclosure of these elements could overemphasize the actual risk and crowd out the agility of organizations and the entrepreneurial spirit needed for the continuity of the organizations and companies. Procedures to standardize the disclosure of internal control and risk management systems are in place. A recent interesting example of this development is the 'High Level Principles for Risk Management' of the Committee of European Banking Supervisors of February 2010. Further, transparency, standardization and attestation rules need to be approached in an integrated way: disclosure of information has not always led to increased transparency and requires content standardization for which appropriated control mechanisms, that is, attestation rules are necessary.

In different disciplines risks and risk management systems are approached in a uni-dimensional way. However, companies are confronted with risks at many different levels and in many layers inside and outside the business: strategic or generic risks, operational risks, financial risks and legal risks and risk management systems that must be able to cope with all these different kinds of threats. It requires a more holistic approach. This book provides the initial impetus for a more interdisciplinary approach. The authors give a comprehensive overview of historical and current provisions relating to internal control and risk management in Europe and the US. Next, the interconnected consequences of the necessity of risk management (the risk management landscape) are addressed. It shows that a comprehensive approach (accounting, business law, financial law and tax law) needs to be further improved. In different fields of practice and in particular, in accounting, an expectation gap is visible: users of services expect that the services are always reliable and cannot contain any errors, while information systems and control frameworks increase the reliability and reduce the probability of fraud and failure, but it remains impossible to provide 'hard' control guarantees. The answer to the gap lies, *inter alia*, in the requirement to deliver the best audit quality possible. The public expects auditors to detect all fraudulent behavior and auditors do not accept responsibility for this level of fraud detection. Risk management is an integrative part of the general framework to increase the likelihood of reliable procedures, operations and (financial) information, including tax management. The latter requires the fulfillment of all formal tax duties and the appropriate record of the amounts of taxes payable in commercial accounts.

Many of the aforementioned topics are addressed in this book. It will serve the discussion to further develop the integrative academic analysis of risks and risk management systems. The last chapter provides the authors' valuable insights about how to proceed. Reading between the lines, it is clear that they support a more principle-based approach of both accounting standards and the accompanying risk-management approach. Based on an analysis of the pros and cons of both the rule-based and the principle-based approach, the book shows that the latter makes it more feasible that sound business practices can be combined with the strategic goals of the company and the relationship between entrepreneurial risk taking and sound risk governance management is in equilibrium. It will also necessitate a balanced supervision framework that both prevents excessive risk taking *ex ante* and addresses risk failures *ex post*. Enjoy reading!

André Kilesse
Vice President
Federation of European Accountants

Acknowledgments

This book arose out of the idea that academics in different fields were addressing the developments and state-of-the-art of the risk management environment in which corporations operate. All authors responded enthusiastically to the request to cooperate and provided insights in their different contributions. We would like to thank these authors for sharing their views and providing us with their latest work in this field.

We also want to thank Arco for his professionalism and support of this project. We owe a large debt of gratitude to Kim Raaijmakers for her excellent editing assistance. We are also grateful to COSO, managed by AICPA as well as Ericsson for providing the right to publish the 'cubes' and an excerpt from the annual report.

We have benefitted from the valuable insights that practitioners provide to our students in the law and management master programme. We would like to thank them for their inspiring lectures. Finally, we would like to thank the University of Tilburg and, in particular, the department of business law for its stimulating research environment.

Tilburg, February 2010.

Marijn van Daelen
Christoph Van der Elst

1. Introducing risk management

Marijn van Daelen and Arco van de Ven

1.1 INTRODUCTION

In reaction to the recent financial crisis and the corporate failures and frauds at the beginning of the millennium, the emphasis of the business community in corporate governance has shifted towards internal control and risk management issues. This shift has not only been fuelled by fraud but also by excessive directors' remunerations, growing internationalisation, inadequate reporting, failing auditors and – especially in recent years – the development of complex financial instruments and their associated risks. Although risk management is not a new feature of businesses and corporate governance, it is currently high on the corporate agenda. Risk management discussions were never of this magnitude before, either among academics, policymakers, lawmakers or practitioners.

This book provides a comprehensive approach in accounting, and business, financial and tax law to risk management. These fields are all interrelated and describe and require particular behaviour within organizations. Chapters 2 to 5 provide an elaborate account of the development of risk management at EU level, within some EU member states and in the USA. These chapters explore relevant current risk management discussions and reforms in order to address possible future directions. Chapter 2 deals with risk management from an accounting perspective and Chapter 3 addresses risk management from a business law perspective. Chapter 4 analyses risk management in financial law and Chapter 5 describes risk management in taxation. Finally, Chapter 6 paints the overall risk management landscape in order to show the interconnections between the developments in law, accounting and tax. Some of the developments in these areas do not stand on their own but are (knowingly or unknowingly) influenced by developments in the other disciplines. Other developments are a reaction to irregularities on markets or in companies and do not take account of the developments in other disciplines. Chapter 6 concludes with some challenges and problem areas that risk management faces. The international and multidisciplinary approach of this final chapter gives an insight into the overall influence of risk management on companies and on society as a whole, taking the corporate governance discussion to a higher level. In general, all chapters focus on listed companies because internal control and risk management reforms specifically address publicly held companies, although the reforms also affect non-listed companies and government governance. To start off, this chapter will briefly discuss the concept of risk management, as well as some leading definitions.

1.2   THE CONCEPT OF RISK MANAGEMENT

According to Beck today's society is a risk society.[1] Modernity is characterized as and influenced by a *risk management discourse*. Decisions can apparently only be taken after a thorough risk analysis. Companies need a business control, an accounting control and a tax control framework to survive and risk management has become an important corporate governance issue. To many people risk has become ubiquitous[2] and it seems as if a risk-based description of everything is pivotal.[3] Risk is not to be seen as an act of providence, but as a potential event that can be measured and managed.

The struggle to master risks is one of all times. The ancient Greeks prayed to their gods to protect them on their journeys and in their wars. Peter Bernstein[4] wrote a book on the story of risk: *Against the Gods*. In it, he describes the development of risk management as a process of man being liberated from oracles and soothsayers and taking the management of risk into his own hands. The law of probabilities defined by Fermat and Pascal in 1654 was a first important step in this process. The outcome of a game of chance was no longer just a belief. Risks could be seen as probabilities and could even be calculated. The transition from a game of chance to natural events was soon made. In a book published in 1662 the probability of being struck by lightning was compared with the intensity of people's fear of thunder. The author concluded that given the slight possibility of such an event occurring, people's fear was too strong and that fear ought to be proportional to the gravity of the harm and the probability of the event.[5] Today, risk management systems are still based on these two pillars: probability and gravity.

---

[1]   Beck 1992.
[2]   Hood, Jones, Pidgeon, Turner, Gibson et al. 1992, p. 135.
[3]   Power 2004, p. 2.
[4]   Bernstein 1996.
[5]   Bernstein 1996, p. 71.

The possibility of predicting probabilities increased when in 1733 the French mathematician Abraham de Moivre revealed his normal-distribution formula, also known as the bell curve. Observations far from the mean are less frequent than observations close to the mean and when plotted are bell-shaped. With this formula it could be determined whether a set of observations represented the universe of which they are a part, making statistical predictions possible without measuring all possible events. Forecasting probabilities has since moved on from natural events such as lightning to virtually all elements of life. For instance, life insurance premiums can be calculated on the basis of mortality statistics.

A model presented by Black and Scholes[6] made it possible to calculate the value of options. The ramifications of this technique were mind-boggling. Valuation of all kinds of complex financial products was now attainable. For example, only a few people expected that it would be possible to sell football tickets for future matches of Arsenal Football Club, but this is exactly what Arsenal did in 2006: it sold the future revenue of tickets for £260 million.[7] Ticket sales and ticket value no longer depend on uncertain events such as coach tactics, player transfers, injuries or missed penalties. To a large extent they can be predicted, calculated and valued up front.

The journey from being passive prisoners of providence, who felt they could not but resign themselves to submitting to all risks that life threw at them, to independent actors, who think that all possible events can be measured (and sold) in advance, has been a long one. With the increased possibilities to manage risks has come the unprecedented rise in hazards and potential threats. Welcome to the risk society![8] This is the society where most are stakeholders who depend on how organizations manage their risks. For example, consumers rely on the quality of the food they buy, shareholders face the risks of losing their investments, and employees depend on pension funds for their retirement benefits. Moreover, society as a whole is exposed to a broad range of hazards that may cause irreversible harm, ranging from radioactivity and global warming to pollution. History shows that these risks unfortunately are very real. Next to bad management caused by incompetence, economic theory predicts opportunistic behaviour or self-interest-seeking with guile, which refers to 'incomplete or distorted disclosure of information, especially to calculated

---

6   Black & Scholes 1973.
7   Euromoney 2006.
8   Beck 1992.

efforts to mislead, distort, disguise, obfuscate, or otherwise confuse'.[9] History abounds with examples of poor governance.[10] Different types of standards and codes have been developed over the years to describe, measure and report on varied risk-related items. Different accounting and auditing standards as well as business, financial and tax laws and corporate governance codes describe and sometimes prescribe behaviour within organizations. There is an evolving trust in numbers and standards as a basis for rational decision making.[11]

1.3   LEADING DEFINITIONS

Before describing the development of risk management in the following chapters, this chapter will first give some of the leading definitions of risk and risk management. To begin with, risk from an organizational perspective is often seen as 'a threat to an organization that reduces the likelihood that the organization will achieve one or more of its objectives'.[12] This definition limits risk to the negative aspects of possible events. The International Standards Organization (ISO) also includes the positive impacts of events in its definition: 'risk is the effect of uncertainty on objectives'.[13]

Risk is often distinguished from uncertainty,[14] because of the difference between the incalculability of uncertainties and the calculable nature of risks based on the availability of probabilistic knowledge. Power declines this view,[15] arguing that practitioners of risk management do not differentiate between risk and uncertainty on these grounds. Risks and uncertainties are not two different classes of *objects*. Uncertainties become risks as soon as they enter the management domain. He draws on the notions of Luhmann that the concept of risk itself implies these dangers have entered the domain for decision making, where responsibilities for these dangers are allocated. Positioning risk in the management domain means that risks are perceived as being open not only to analysis, but also to systematic management. The practice of risk management is thus transformed from risk analysis into an organizational process with a standard set of perform-

---

9   Williamson 1985, p. 47.
10   See e.g. Skeel 2005.
11   Power 2007, p. 13.
12   Knechel 2001, p. 26.
13   ISO 2009, p. V.
14   Knight 2006, p. 20.
15   Power 2007, p. 5.

ance activities for risk management, the business control frameworks. The leading framework of enterprise risk management is given in the COSO II Report, which defines Enterprise Risk Management as [16]

[. . .] a process, effected by an entity's board of directors, management and other personnel, applied in strategy setting and across the enterprise, designed to identify potential events that may affect the entity, and manage risk to be within its risk appetite, to provide reasonable assurance regarding the achievement of entity objectives.[17]

Risk management cannot deliver absolute certainty. *Reasonable assurance* reflects the notion that uncertainty and risk relate to the future, which no one can predict with precision.[18] Yet *reasonable* does not imply that enterprise risk management will frequently fail.[19] *Risk appetite* is defined as 'the amount of risk, on a broad level, an entity is willing to accept in pursuit of value'.[20]

Enterprise risk management as defined by COSO II is a broad and all-encompassing concept. The objective of risk management includes the objectives of internal control, which is the process within an organization to achieve reasonable assurance of effectiveness and efficiency of operations, reliable reports, compliance with applicable laws and regulations and of safeguarding the organization's assets against misappropriation (fraud). In addition to internal control, enterprise risk management is aimed at the strategic control of an organization. From a corporate governance perspective the purpose of effective risk management could be aimed at different types of risks, ranging from fraud and embezzlement to financial shenanigans,[21] mismanagement or a perilous strategy.

REFERENCES

Beck, Ulrich (1992), *Risk Society – Towards a New Modernity*, London: Sage Publications.
Bernstein, Peter L. (1996), *Against The Gods*, New York: John Wiley & Sons.
Black, F. and M. Scholes (1973), 'The Pricing of Options and Corporate Liabilities', *Journal of Political Economy*, **81**, pp. 637–54.

---

[16] COSO 2004, p. 2.
[17] © COSO.
[18] COSO 2004, p. 20.
[19] COSO 2004, p. 20.
[20] COSO 2004, p. 19.
[21] Financial shenanigans are actions that intentionally distort a company's reported financial performance and financial condition. Schilit 2002, p. 24.

Euromoney (2006), 'Football Securitization: Arsenal kicks off public ticket receivables deals', available at http://www.euromoney.com/Article/105 0208/BackIssue/50151/Football-Securitization-Arsenal-kicks-off-public-ticket-receivables-deals.html?Type=BackIssueArticle&ArticleId=1050208&ID=501 51 (accessed 10 February 2010).

Hood, Christopher, David Jones, Nick Pidgeon, Barry Turner, Rose Gibson, et al. (1992), *Risk Management* in The Royal Society *Risk: Analysis, Perception and Management,* London: The Royal Society.

Knechel, Robert, (2001), *Auditing, Assurance & Risk*, Cincinnati, Ohio: South-Western College Publishing.

Knight, Frank H. (2006), *Risk, Uncertainty and Profit*, New York: Dover Publications inc.

Power, Michael (2004), *The Audit Explosion,* London: Demos, available at: http://www.demos.co.uk/files/theauditexplosion.pdf?1240939425 (accessed 8 February 2010).

Power, Michael (2007), *Organized Uncertainty – Designing a World of Risk Management*, Oxford: Oxford University Press.

Schilit, Howard M. (2002), *Financial Shenanigans – How to Detect Accounting Gimmicks & Fraud in Financial Reports – 2nd edition*, New York: McGraw Hill.

Skeel, David A. (2005), *Icarus in the Boardroom: The Fundamental Flaws in Corporate America and Where They Came From*, New York: Oxford University Press.

Williamson, Oliver E. (1985), *The Economic Institutions of Capitalism*, New York: The Free Press.

CODES AND GUIDELINES

Committee of Sponsoring Organizations of the Treadway Commission (COSO) (2004), *Enterprise Risk Management – Integrated Framework*, Executive Summary, New York: AICPA Inc., (COSO II Report).

International Standard Organization (ISO) (2009), *31000: 2009 Risk management – Principles and guidelines*, Geneva: ISO.

2. Risk management from an accounting perspective

Arco van de Ven

2.1 DEVELOPMENT OF RISK MANAGEMENT AND ACCOUNTING

2.1.1 Introduction

The history of risk management and accounting is a story of transparency, standardization and attestation. The risks to which these requirements are applied and their form have changed over the years. Transparency, standardization and attestation have been recurring topics, which have been put forward as means to reduce the risk of misappropriation of corporate funds, misstatement of financial reports or the risk of ineffective and inefficient controls or too-risky strategies.

Transparency, in the form of disclosing accounting information, has given shareholders insight into the financial affairs of the company. Accounting regulation has been made over time to force management to disclose financial information. In the 17th century the Dutch East India Company (VOC) was forced by shareholders to publish balance sheet statements and profit and loss statements. Over the years, the call for transparency of financial figures has evolved into a demand for disclosure of company specific information. Companies nowadays not only have to give an insight into their financial affairs, they also have to be transparent about the effectiveness of their internal control systems, their risk appetite and which risks their organization faces.

The call for transparency implies independent audits. How do stakeholders know that the companies information can be relied upon? Reports alone are not enough; they have to be attested. The need for independent attestation to assure the reliability of information has led to an increasing reliance on audits. Next to the auditing of financial statements, different types of audits have arisen, such as tax audits, audits of internal control over financial reports and operational audits on the effectiveness and efficiency of business processes. Nowadays, there is an increasing call for independent auditing of risk-management practices.

Disclosure of information has not always led to increased transparency. In order to improve transparency, disclosures have also been accompanied by a standardization of the content that had to be made transparent. Accounting evolved from company specific practices into generally accepted accounting principles of more than 100 000 pages in the USA alone. But it is not only accounting practices that have been standardized: auditing, internal control and risk-management practices are also becoming more and more standardized. Best practices in the form of Business Control Frameworks, rules and regulation have prescribed and standardized internal control and risk-management systems in organizations.

This history of transparency, standardization and attestation in accounting and auditing will be described in the following sections.

2.1.2   Start of the Accounting Profession

The development of the accounting and auditing profession is very much linked to financial shenanigans. The development of accounting and risk management from the start of accounting to accounting in the 21st century has been influenced by numerous examples of accounting fraud.

An early example of misuse of corporate funds and accounting fraud is the *Lodewijk Pincoffs* case.[1] Pincoffs was a very successful late 19th century Dutch businessman. He was actively involved with the start-up of the *Holland-America Lijn*, *Rotterdamse Bank* and the Heineken beer company. He also was a member of the Dutch House of the Representatives. But he will be remembered neither as a successful business man nor as a politician; he has the dubious honour of being held responsible for the first Dutch case of accounting fraud. Pincoffs forced his two accountants to forge the financial statements and to present a profit of 2 million Dutch guilders. In 1879 one of his many companies, AHV (*Afrikaanse Handels Vereeniging*) went bankrupt. A judicial inquiry into the fraudulent activities showed a loss of 9.5 million Dutch guilders. The losses were caused by exuberant management salaries and speculation with Peruvian securities. As a management director of a bank, *Rotterdamse Handelsvereeniging NV,* Pincoffs granted AHV considerable loans, which were used to inflate profits and to pay out dividends, obscuring the true, deteriorating financial situation. Pincoffs did not wait for AHV to collapse and fled to the USA. In his absence he was sentenced to

---

[1]   Van der Hof 2007, pp. 161–164.

eight years' imprisonment. He never returned to the Netherlands and died in New York City in 1911.

At the time of the Pincoffs fraud, the accounting profession had already been established in the United Kingdom for some time. The London city directory mentioned 11 accountants in 1799.[2] The British Companies Act of 1845 required corporations to keep detailed accounting records and undergo an annual audit by a committee of shareholders.[3] By 1881 most English prospectuses for new securities were audited by professional accountants.[4] The Society of Accountants in Edinburgh was founded in 1853. In 1880 different regional accounting institutes were combined into the Institute of Chartered Accountants of England and Wales (ICAEW). At that time there were approximately 1000 accountants in the UK, a number which had grown to approximately 4000 in 1900. And in 1874 the first accounting journal, *The Accountant* was published.[5] In the UK the audit and publication of public companies' balance sheets had been mandatory since the Companies Acts of 1900 and 1907.[6] The 1928 Companies Act extended the requirements by requiring a profit and loss statement to be made available to shareholders.

In the USA the accounting profession also started to develop in the 19th century. In 1850 a few accountants (14) offered accounting services to the public. The regulation of the accounting profession was boosted by the foundation of the American Association of Public Accountants (AAPA) in 1886. The Institute was renamed in 1917 as the American Institute of Accountants (AIA) and in 1957 as the American Institute of Certified Public Accountants (AICPA). The state of New York recognized the accounting association in 1896, and members were allowed to hold the title of Certified Public Accountant (CPA), a title that is still used today. In 1924 the accounting association was recognised in all American states. As in the UK, the development of the accounting profession in the US was supported by a professional accounting journal; the *Journal of Accountancy* was first published in 1905.

2.1.3 Accounting and Auditing in the Early Years

The *Royal Mail* case of 1931 is an interesting case on the standards of accounting and auditing in the UK. The views of the court indicated

---

[2] Clikeman 2009, p. 124.
[3] Clikeman 2009, p. 124.
[4] Clikeman 2009, p. 124.
[5] De Vries 1985, pp. 19–20.
[6] Camfferman 1998, p. 48.

that the accounting profession should devote more effort to the development and application of higher standards of auditing and reporting financial information.[7] The Royal Mail's accounting policies during the 1920s concealed a decline in the company's equity. A provision for wartime taxation was gradually released into income. A loss of £507 104 in 1926 was turned into a profit of £478 563 mainly by an 'adjustment' of the taxation reserves of £750 000. This practice was not evident from the published financial statements. Income was condensed and labelled '[b]alance for the year, including dividends on shares in allied and other companies, adjustments of taxation reserves, less depreciation of the fleet, etc'.[8] The Chairman of the Board, Lord Kylsant, and the auditor, Harold Morland, were tried on charges of publishing false information.[9] Both men were acquitted, largely because of the testimony of Lord Plender, a former president of the ICAEW. The main argument was that the reference to the adjustments of taxation reserves was in accordance with best practice. This case intensified a debate over the responsibility of the auditor. Is the responsibility of the auditor determined by convention, by legal precedent or by economic rationality? Limperg assumed that the long-term future of the auditing profession could only be assured when it was economically beneficial to others.[10] To a rational reader an audit would only be valuable if it assured him that the state of affairs was presented fairly in the financial statements. Next to extending the scope of the audit, Limperg stressed in his 'doctrine of inspired confidence'[11] that the duty of the auditor as an independent appraiser and judge of financial statements was not only to the entity and the shareholder, but also had societal relevance. Criticism in an editorial in the *Journal of Accountancy*[12] provoked a discussion in the UK about expanding the auditor's role from strict adherence to the law towards more moral and ethical responsibilities.[13] The use of auditing as a means of giving assurance to the general public, as Limperg suggested, was limited. In an article published in 1930 Dijker refers to an informal inquiry made by himself into the percentage of audits from seven large audit firms that were attestation engagements. Only between 1% and 30% of the substance of annual audits concerned was aimed at disclosing

---

[7]   Chandler, Edwards et al. 1993, p. 454.
[8]   Camfferman 1998, p. 44.
[9]   Camfferman 1998, p. 44.
[10] Camfferman 1998, p. 48.
[11] Limperg Jr 1932.
[12] Camfferman 1998, p. 45.
[13] Camfferman 1998, p. 45.

an audit opinion for assuring the public of the fair presentation of the financial statements.[14]

Ivar Kreuger was what would nowadays be called the CEO of the Swedish Match Company. Kreuger's 250 companies produced 80% of the 40 million boxes that were consumed worldwide per year. Like Pincoffs he was held in high regard. He earned the epithet of 'Saviour of Europe' by lending European countries nearly $400 million after World War I to rebuild their economies. Kreuger had attracted investors by paying dividends as high as 20% per year. He raised more than $250 million from American investors for his US subsidiary International Match Corporation (IHC). He used the money to secure match monopolies in Europe by lending governments huge sums. The money often passed through several of his subsidiaries before reaching its destination. The transfers concealed the company's true financial condition. The audit procedure of the auditor of IHC, Ernst & Ernst, consisted primarily of confirming transactions with employees at Swedish Match headquarters via transatlantic cable. No contracts, statements or vouchers had to be produced. Ernst & Ernst partner A.D. Berning started to ask questions about an initial loan of $50 million to Germany. The German bonds were not deposited in the US. He informed Kreuger that he would come to Europe to examine the bonds. In reality, the bonds were no longer in the possession of Swedish Match but had been pledged as collateral for yet another loan. On 12 March 1932 Ivar Kreuger shot himself, choosing death over public disgrace. Price Waterhouse, engaged by the Swedish government, reported a 'gross misrepresentation' of assets. And the true earnings for 1918 through to 1932 were approximately $40 million rather than the reported $316 million.[15]

The Kreuger fraud received a great deal of public attention. The *New York Times*, for instance, published more than 300 articles on it in 1932 and 1933.[16] US Congress called for legislation to protect investors against such frauds, which resulted in the Security Act of 1933 and Security and Exchange Act of 1934. The 1934 Act prescribed that the financial company statements had to be audited by an independent auditor, who had to report whether the financial statements 'present fairly' a company's state of financial affairs.

As the *Kreuger* case influenced regulation to increase transparency of prospectuses and mandatory auditing, so did the McKesson & Robbins

---

[14]　Dijker 1930.
[15]　Based on a description of the Kreuger case in Clikeman 2009, Chapter 2.
[16]　Based on a description of the Kreuger case in Clikeman 2009, Chapter 2.

fraud have a significant impact on the standardization of auditing. F. Donald Coster was the president and the largest shareholder of McKesson & Robbins, a pharmaceutical company with annual revenues exceeding $170 million. But nothing was what it seemed. Coster was in fact a man called Philip Musica, a twice-convicted fraudster, and a profitable Canadian subsidiary was actually no more than an office 'creating' customers and producing forged documents. Approximately $20 million of the $87 million in assets on the company's balance sheet were made up. Throughout Coster's presidency the annual financial statements had been audited by Price Waterhouse.[17]

The SEC started an investigation to determine whether Price Waterhouse performed the audit using generally accepted audit standards and whether those standards were adequate to ensure the reliability and accuracy of financial statements.[18] The auditor association IPA also started an investigation to see if auditing standards should be amended due to what happened at McKesson & Robbins. A committee chaired by Patrick Glover, recommended that auditors should spend more time verifying assets through inventory count and confirmation of receivables via direct communications with debtors.[19] The recommendations were approved and published in the first auditing standard: Statements on Auditing Procedure No. 1, Extensions of Auditing Practice. The final report of the SEC in 1940 pleaded for more than only testing the accuracy of the client's accounting records. The SEC also recommended a more thorough assessment of the internal controls of the client. The auditor had to assess how the company itself had put checks and balances in place to assure the reliability of its financial statements. This was a first step to include a form of assessment of the internal control/risk management system in the audit.

A joint study of the New York Stock Exchange and the AIA conducted in 1934 and named 'Audit of Corporate Accounts' initiated the practice of formulating accounting standards. These standards were principles that had 'substantial authoritative support'.[20] The study signalled the start of a process of standardization of accounting principles and rules. The wording of the typical attestation statement would come to include not only that financial statements presented fairly the company's financial position, but also that they were in conformity with generally accepted accounting principles.[21]

---

17   Based on a description of the case in Clikeman 2009, Chapter 4.
18   Based on a description of the case in Clikeman 2009, Chapter 4.
19   Based on a description of the case in Clikeman 2009, Chapter 4.
20   Burgert & Timmermans 1987, pp. 10–11.
21   Benston, Bromwich et al. 2006, p. 165.

2.1.4 Accounting Measures and Risk

The changing business environment influenced the types of risks organizations faced. Companies could benefit from the revolution in information and communication technologies. Unlike in the old economy, risk and return increasingly reflected a probabilistic judgement of future events. This was accompanied by the development of financial engineering. Complex financial instruments were developed, extended and traded in increasing volume. The Black and Scholes model made it possible to calculate the value of options, and this in turn created the possibility to separate rights or obligations, to buy or sell shares or bonds, or to receive asset-related payments from the underlying assets or liabilities. Soon this opportunity was used to create all kinds of new financial products. For example, mortgages were packaged into Mortgage-Backed Securities (MBS) and were traded from the 1980s in the USA and the mid-1980s in the UK.[22] This market in the USA grew from $100 billion in 1980 to $3 trillion in 2000[23] and $6.3 trillion in the second quarter of 2007.[24] The phenomenon of MBS is an example of securitization, 'the creation and issuance of securities backed by a pool of loans, bonds or notes issued by a special purpose entity that purchases the underlying assets, which are used as collateral to back the notes.'[25] Not only mortgages but all kinds of assets, such as credit card debts, car loans and commercial loans, have been securitized. The determination of profit and loss of financial products of this kind differs immensely from profit and loss of the sale of goods and services.

Accounting numbers, such as profit and loss, do not reflect the amount of risk a company faces. Over the years different approaches have been developed to forecast and quantify risk. Different types of risks are distinguished, such as market risk, credit risk, liquidity risk and operational risk, and models are made of probabilities and effects. An explicit assumption of most risk models is 'that market data follows a stochastic process which depends on past observations of the data itself and on other market variables.'[26] One of the most used techniques is risk modelling through Value at Risk (VAR),[27] a statistical measure of unanticipated loss, derived from loss distributions of the different risk types.[28] The unanticipated loss

---

[22]   Hayre, ed. 2001, p. 65.
[23]   Hayre, ed. 2001, p. 10.
[24]   Goodman, Li et al. (eds) 2008, p. 4.
[25]   Tavakoli 2003, p. 15.
[26]   Daníelsson 2002, p. 1274.
[27]   Jorion as cited by Mikes 2009, p. 23.
[28]   Jorion as cited by Mikes 2009, p. 23.

is calculated at a certain risk level; for example, market risk disclosure for a one-day holding period and a 99% confidence level, which works out to a probability of occurrence of 2.5 times a year.[29]

Aggregation of the different kinds of risk into one accounting measure has been a challenge to risk practitioners.[30] Risk has to be taken into account when calculating the value of the firm. Economic capital is the emerging common denominator of the aggregation of risk, to calculate capital adequacy. Economic capital is defined as 'a statistically estimated amount of capital that could be used to cover all liabilities in a severe loss event given a specific confidence level'.[31] An institutional force behind the economical capital framework as a best practice is the rating agency community. Banks tailor economic capital to the adequacy expectations from rating agencies.[32] If a financial institution aims for an AAA rating, then the confidence level is determined by the default probability of the AAA rating of that rating agency.

To manage the amount of risk that financial institutions take, risk-adjusted performance measures are introduced. Risk-based management offers two theoretical approaches, the ratio approach and the shareholder value approach.[33] Risk Adjusted Return On Capital (RAROC) is an example of the ratio approach. The risk-adjusted profit is divided by the economic capital that is required to support the transaction.[34] Economic Value Added (EVA) is an example of shareholders value. EVA is defined as the operating profit less the cost of all capital employed to produce those earnings.[35] The cost of equity is the risk-free rate plus a risk premium. An important element of assessing the risk premium is the volatility of the individual stock.[36]

2.1.5   Auditing, Risk and Internal Control

One of the first descriptions of how an audit should be performed appeared in a book by Pixley in 1881 and it implied 100% vouching of transactions:

---

[29]   The regulators apply a time horizon of historical data of one year (250 working days). A one percent chance thus means an occurrence of 2.5 times a year.

[30]   Mikes 2009, p. 24.

[31]   Mikes 2009, p. 24.

[32]   Mikes 2009, p. 24.

[33]   Mikes 2009, p. 25.

[34]   Marrisson 2002, p. 21.

[35]   Stewart 1991, p. 2.

[36]   Rappaport 1986, p. 58.

'A thorough and efficient audit should embrace an examination of all the transactions of a Company, and an auditor acting on this principle would ascertain that all had been duly entered and discharged.'[37] Practical difficulties of a 100% check implied introducing risk and uncertainty into the auditing process. Auditing without a 100% check meant reliance on a company's internal controls and a limited testing of transactions to check these controls. Was it possible to ascertain financial reports with only a partial check of transactions? The application potential of the probability theory of Fermat, Pascal and De Moivre to auditing was not that evident. Even the great Dutch accounting scholar Limperg in 1905 regarded partial checking as a kind of lottery which could be seen as a bad audit practice.[38] However, the 'system audit' approach, 'in which the auditor would attest the quality of the company internal controls by conducting test of control compliance, became conventional practitioner wisdom'[39] in the 1920s.[40] The practice of sampling to support the decision about which controls the auditor could rely on (and how many transactions should be checked) was not formalized until the 1930s.[41]

Historically, much more attention was paid to internal control in the Netherlands than in the USA. This attention was not only related to the possibility of partial testing, but was also aimed at the possibility and necessity of having an adequate system of internal control to prevent material misstatements of financial statements. Dutch publications in this area go back as far as 1909, the year in which Hierneiss published a paper in *De Accountant*.[42] The subject of internal control, under such diverse Dutch names as *inrichtingsleer, administrative organisatie* and *bestuurlijke informatieverzorging*, was and still is one of the two cornerstones of the post-graduate course to qualify as a *registeraccountant* (registered accountant), the Dutch equivalent of the CPA. The important role of internal control for the assessment of the reliability of financial statements

---

[37]   Chandler, Edwards et al. 1993, p. 450.
[38]   'Weder aannemende, dat de opdracht geene beperking inhoudt, zal men in het algemeen verplicht zijn, om *alle* boeken *in hun geheel*, te controleren. Ik weet dat vele accountants dit ' reuzenwerk' niet willen verrichten, doch zich vergenoegen met enige steekproeven; maar ik weet ook , dat het resultaat van hun onderzoek op die wijze wordt gebaseerd op een kansberekening, dat de controle wordt gemaakt tot een *loterij*! Een steekproef is een greep in den blinde: slechts een *systematisch volledig* onderzoek, waarbij elk onderdeel aansluit aan het andere, kan leiden tot een doeltreffende controle.' Hen, Berendsen et al. 1995, p. 270.
[39]   Power 1997, p. 20.
[40]   Chandler, Edwards et al. 1993, p. 451.
[41]   Power 1997, p. 19.
[42]   Hartman 1993, p. 32.

was emphasized. Attention was also given to the existence of irreplaceable controls, such as separation of duties. Such controls could not be reperformed by an auditor. In the early 1960s Starreveld developed a theory on how to design internal controls for different types of organizations that would give reasonable assurance regarding the completeness of revenues.[43] A separation of duties within a company combined with comprehensive coherence testing formed the basis of this theory. Known relationships between types of transactions, based on the flows of goods and money within an organization, were used to determine the theoretical value of the revenues.[44]

A more formal risk audit model was developed in the United States, based on probability theory. The quantification of audit risk started with a paper by Elliot and Roger in 1972, in which they distinguished the risk of rejecting perfectly correct financial statements (alpha risk) and the beta risk of accepting incorrect financial statements given a material amount of acceptable errors.[45] This led to a significant movement in the early 1980s towards a risk-based approach. This movement is reflected in auditing standards (SAS 39 and SAS 47)[46] and in auditing practices of the big audit firms.[47] The risk-based approach to auditing was adopted in the Netherlands in the late 1980s.[48] This quantification was included in the risk audit model. Audit risk (AR) is defined as 'the risk that the auditor may unknowingly fail to appropriately modify his opinion on financial statements that are materially misstated.'[49] Audit risk can be decomposed into three types of risk:

1. Inherent risk (IR): 'The susceptibility of an assertion to a material misstatement, assuming that there are no related internal controls.'[50]
2. Control risk (CR): 'The risk that a material misstatement that could occur in an assertion will not be prevented or detected on a timely basis by the entity's internal control.'[51]

---

[43] Starreveld 1962, p. 843.
[44] English language deliberations on this Dutch approach can be found in Blokdijk, Drieënhuizen et al. 1995, Chapter 3 and in Vaassen 2002.
[45] Cushing & Loebbecke 1983, p. 24.
[46] Kinney 2005, p. 96.
[47] Cushing & Loebbecke 1983, p. 23.
[48] Blokdijk, Drieënhuizen et al. 1995, p. 27.
[49] Knechel 2001, p. 325.
[50] Knechel 2001, p. 326.
[51] Knechel 2001, p. 326.

3. Detection risk (DR): 'The risk that the auditor will not detect a material misstatement that exists in an assertion.'[52]

Mathematically these three risk types relate to each other as follows:

$$AR = IR \times CR \times DR$$

The audit risk model enables the auditor to determine the level of detection risk of a specific audit client. It starts with assessing the maximum audit risk that is acceptable. How reliable should a financial statement be? Given the purpose of financial reporting, a material misstatement is linked to the judgement of a reasonable person. If that person's judgement is affected by the misstatement then the misstatement is material. How does this translate to the amount of audit risk an audit firm wants to take? There is no clear and shared acceptable audit risk percentage. This makes audit risk a matter of policy. Given the acceptable audit risk for the audit firm, the audit model is used to assess the amount of checking the auditor has to perform and it determines, to a large extent, the cost of the audit. The audit formula shows that the amount of testing depends on the level of risk the auditor is prepared to take (AR), the inherent risk of the organisation (IR) and the extent to which the risk is lowered by the client's internal control system (CR).

Due to the auditor's lack of expertise and his inability to be continuously present, absolute certainty is an impossibility.[53] Only reasonable certainty can be achieved. Audit firms may decide which audit-risk level is acceptable or not. The acceptable amount of risks for all engagements normally lies between 1% and 5%.[54] The inherent risk is affected by a number of factors, such as the nature of the client's business and industry, integrity of management, client motivations, tenure of auditor, and the existence of related parties.[55]

2.1.6 Risk, Accounting Standards and Regulation

The changing environment also had its impact on accounting standards. The first accounting standards in the USA, Accounting Research Bulletins (ARB), were released by the AIA Committee on Accounting Procedure.

---

[52] Knechel 2001, p. 326.
[53] Blokdijk, Drieënhuizen et al. 1995, p. 61.
[54] Knechel 2001, p. 325.
[55] Knechel 2001, p. 334.

In 1950 a new standard-setting body was founded, the Accounting Principle Board (APB), which released APB Opinions. The ARBs and APB Opinions did not have the substantial authoritative support that was needed, and compliance was voluntary.

From 1965 onwards all deviations from generally accepted accounting principles (GAAP) had to be disclosed in the annual financial statements, and auditors have to include non-compliance in their audit opinion.[56] In 1973 the ARB was replaced by the Financial and Accounting Standards Board (FASB). The FASB and its predecessors developed many rule-based standards. Benston et al. argue that the large number of accounting rules is influenced by the litigious situation in the US, and increasingly in other countries. The litigation risk gives accountants a strong incentive to ask for rules, which they hope will protect them from criticism and lawsuits.[57]

Next to accounting, auditing standards were developed, to guide the execution of audits. The International Foundation of Accountants (IFA) issues International Statements on Auditing (ISA) and the AICPA issues Statements on Auditing Standards (SAS). In the USA the principle of fair presentation was essentially converted into a rule-based approach by SAS 69, which states that 'present fairly' implies that the application of officially established accounting principles almost always results in a fair presentation.[58]

The expansion of auditing and accounting standards could not guarantee the fair presentation of financial affairs of companies. In the savings and loan crisis of 1986–95 more than 1000 banks and thrifts failed. At the end of 1999 the total loss was $153 billion, of which the taxpayers paid approximately $124 billion.[59] The savings and loan crisis revealed several accounting oddities. Loans were valued at the original loan amount. Although recommendations were made for current market accounting, historical cost accounting (HCA) was the generally accepted practice. Much of the criticism of HCA focused on hiding the real financial position and income of companies. The book value of HCA is the historical amount not the market value of that asset. For example, the value of a loan varies inversely with the prevailing interest rates. If a $100 000 loan at a fixed interest rate of 6% is sold at a time when the interest rate is 15%, the market value of the loan is much lower. When in 1980 the interest

---

[56] Burgert & Timmermans 1987, p. 13.
[57] Benston, Bromwich et al. 2006, p. 168.
[58] Benston, Bromwich et al. 2006, p. 166.
[59] Shapiro & Matson 2008, p. 220.

rates soared to 15.6% no losses had to be reported, because the loans were reported at historical costs. HCA was gradually replaced by fair value accounting (FVA). In 1990 Douglas Breeden, the SEC chairman, declared that FVA was the only relevant measure and that all financial investments made by financial institutions should be reported at market value. This statement was referred to as the 'most significant initiative in accounting principles development in over 50 years'.[60] In 1991 the FASB issued a statement of financial accounting standard (SFAS) 107 stating that the fair value of all financial instruments, both assets and liabilities recognized and not recognized in the financial statements, should be disclosed. The determination of fair value extended from situations where quoted market prices are available to situations where quoted market prices are not available. SFAS 125t (1996) considers the use of valuation techniques such as option-pricing models to calculate the fair value of assets and liabilities.

The savings and loan crisis also led to the tightening of other accounting issues. For example, in December 1986 the FASB issued guidance on accounting for loan origination and commitment fees. Fees were customarily recognized at the moment of origination. SFAS 91 required recognizing them as income over the life of the loan.[61] The impairment of loan losses was also tightened. In May 1993 the FASB issued SFAS 114, which stated that loans had to be classified as impaired if it was likely that a loss would occur.[62] In 2006 the FASB issued SFAS 157 on fair value measurements. Prior to the statement, there were different definitions of fair value, which created inconsistencies and guidance for application had been limited. SFAS 157 became effective on 15 November 2007.

In 1988 guiding principles for capital adequacy were proposed. The Basel Capital Accord was gradually adopted by the central banks. To ensure adequate resources to absorb unexpected losses caused by credit risk, minimal capital requirements were introduced. The minimum capital was 8% of the total of risk-weighted assets.[63] In 1996 the Basel committee introduced a Market Risk Amendment to include market risk and offered the possibility to measure market risk on an internal VAR model. And in 1997 the SEC published Financial Reporting Release 48, which required disclosing the market risk of all public filers that made material use of derivatives.[64]

The increased complexity of financial instruments also opened the way

---

[60]   Barlev & Haddad 2003, p. 390.
[61]   Clikeman 2009, p. 118.
[62]   Clikeman 2009, p. 118.
[63]   Different risk weights were recognized for different categories of obligors.
[64]   Perignon & Smith 2009, p. 1.

to new financial rackets. The cases of Joseph Jett at Kidder Peabody and Nick Leeson at Barings Bank have demonstrated the importance of having effective internal controls.

Joseph Jett, a trader, created bogus profits by buying a STRIP[65] and booking a sale that would occur at a future date at a much higher price.[66] Jett's $9 million bonus for 1993 became world news.[67] In 1994 it appeared that a loss of $350 million on Jett's transactions was hidden from the financial statements of Kidder Peabody. In addition to Jett's accounting fraud, Kidder Peabody had an enormous exposure (24% market share) to mortgage backed securities (MBS).[68] This led to huge losses when the bond prices collapsed in March 1994. It has been estimated that Kidder Peabody cost General Electric, its parent company, more than $1.5 billion.

Even more infamous is Nick Leeson, the man responsible for the downfall of one of the most prestigious banks of the UK, Barings. Nick Leeson was asked in 1992 to set up and manage the Singapore office.[69] He accounted trading losses on error account 88888 (the five eight account).[70] The losses increased from the first loss of £20 000 to £827 million in February 1995, more than twice the total value of the Barings bank. In 1994 Leeson was regarded as a very successful trader, but his reputation later turned out to have been primarily based on false profits of £28.5 million. Being responsible for both the front and back office, Leeson could easily influence the journal entries and hide the losses on the error account, fooling the internal auditors of Barings by forging documents. He was sentenced to six and a half years' imprisonment and was released early in 1999.

Over the years the emphasis on the important role of risk management within organizations and the internal control systems has grown. From 1976 onwards there have been calls in the US to regulate, assess, report on and attest by independent auditors the internal control of organizations.[71] In 1976 the SEC and subsequently the Senate Foreign Relations Subcommittee documented that more than 200 large US corporations

---

[65] The right to the repayment of the loan amount, in this case US government bonds is separated from the annual interest payments. The right to an interest payment is called a STRIP and is valued and traded separately.

[66] Chorafas 2001, p. 68.

[67] Chorafas 2001, p. 78.

[68] Chorafas 2001, p. 71.

[69] Leeson 1996, p. 39.

[70] In China the number eight is considered to bring luck.

[71] Shapiro & Matson 2008, p. 206.

had secret funds to pay foreign bribes. For example, over a 12-year period Lockheed paid more than $25 million and Exxon more than $56 million.[72] Amendments made by California Representative Moss to the draft of the Foreign Corrupt Practice Act to strengthen the requirements for internal control were rejected. Moss proposed a mandatory review and approval by the board of directors of the corporation's internal accounting controls and code of conduct, as well as a public attestation by an independent auditor on the quality of the controls to safeguard the assets of the organization.[73] The final Foreign Corrupt Practice Act of 1977 prohibited bribery and imposed modest accounting and internal control requirements:[74]

(A)   make and keep books, records, and accounts, which, in reasonable detail, accurately and fairly reflect the transactions and dispositions of the assets of the issuer; and

(B)   devise and maintain a system of internal accounting controls sufficient to provide reasonable assurances that –

   (i)   transactions are executed in accordance with management's general or specific authorization;

   (ii)   transactions are recorded as necessary (I) to permit preparation of financial statements in conformity with generally accepted accounting principles or any other criteria applicable to such statements, and (II) to maintain accountability for assets;

   (iii)   access to assets is permitted only in accordance with management's general or specific authorization; and

   (iv)   the recorded accountability for assets is compared with the existing assets at reasonable intervals and appropriate action is taken with respect to any differences.

The US General Accounting Office (GAO) documented that internal control weaknesses contributed to the savings and loan crisis. Of 184 bank failures, federal regulators signalled the most significant internal control deficiencies: inadequate or imprudent loan policies (79%); inadequate supervision by the board of directors (49%); weak loan administration (42%); poor loan documentation and inadequate credit analysis (41%); over reliance on volatile funding sources (32%); the presence of a dominant figure (31%) and a failure to establish adequate loss allowances (29%).[75]

The importance of internal control was clear, but a common framework was lacking. This changed in 1992 when the Committee of Sponsoring

---

[72]   Shapiro & Matson 2008, p. 206.
[73]   Shapiro & Matson 2008, p. 214.
[74]   Shapiro & Matson 2008, p. 210.
[75]   US General Accounting Office (1989), p. 13.

Organizations (COSO) published the COSO I report. This report defined and described internal control to establish a common definition and provided a standard against which businesses could assess their control system and determine how to improve it. The COSO I definition of the objective of internal control was much broader than preventing fraud or improving the reliability of financial reporting; the objective of internal control was to help ensure an entity's success, and internal control was defined as:[76]

> [. . .] a process, effected by an entity's board of directors, management and other personnel, designed to provide reasonable assurance regarding the achievement of objectives in the following categories:
> 1. Effectiveness and efficiency of operations.
> 2. Reliability of financial reporting.
> 3. Compliance with applicable laws and regulations.
> 4. [Safeguarding of the assets against unauthorized acquisition, use or disposition.][77]

The COSO report warned against unrealistic expectations: internal control 'will not ensure achievement of basic business objectives or, ensure survival. It can only help an entity to achieve its objectives, it is not a panacea'.[78]

The components of the COSO I framework are often represented in a cube (Figure 2.1). The objectives are shown on the top surface. The different organizational layers are depicted on the right-hand side and five components that are important to internal control on the front side.

Effective internal control is based on the *Control Environment*. The effectiveness of internal controls, such as separation of duties and detailed reconciliations, depends on the company's culture. The tone at the top influences the control consciousness of the employees and is regarded as the foundation for all components of the COSO framework. Important elements of the control environment include integrity, ethical behaviour, competences, management philosophy and operating style.

The COSO framework is a risk-based approach. To achieve reasonable assurance of reaching the different objectives (operations, financial reporting and compliance) a *Risk Assessment* has to be performed. The identification and analysis of relevant risks to the achievement of these objectives form the basis for further mitigation of risks.

Within the organization *Control Activities* mitigate the relevant risks.

---

[76] COSO I Report 1992. The original COSO report only states three objectives. In May 1994 'safeguarding of assets' was included after a GAO consultation.
[77] © COSO.
[78] COSO I Report 1992, p. 6.

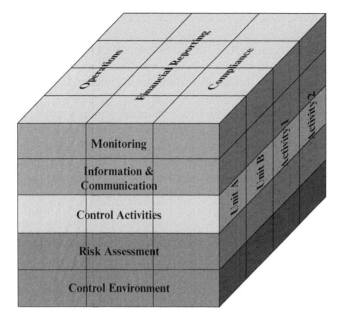

Monitoring

Information & Communication

Control Activities

Risk Assessment

Control Environment

Source: © COSO.

Figure 2.1 The COSO I Cube

They include a wide range of activities varying from segregation of duties, approvals, reconciliations and reviews of document to physical security of assets.[79]

Information and Communication plays an important role within the internal control of organizations. It enables employees to carry out their responsibilities. High quality of information helps management to make appropriate decisions in managing and controlling the activities of the entity. To assure high-quality information, internal control includes ascertaining if the content is appropriate and the information timely, current, accurate and accessible.[80] 'Effective communication must occur in a broader sense, flowing down, across and up the organization.'[81]

The last component of the COSO framework is *Monitoring*. Current effectiveness of internal control does not guarantee effectiveness in future years. The other four components need to be monitored over time.

---

[79] COSO I Report 1992, p. 49.
[80] COSO I Report 1992, p. 62.
[81] COSO I Report 1992, p. 59.

Internal control deficiencies should be detected and reported upstream, with serious matters reported to top management and the board.

The COSO framework became best practice on how to evaluate internal control systems. Box 2.1 includes an example of reporting on internal control over financial statements shown in Ericsson's annual statement.

The resistance to internal control regulation was broken by debates on the effects of the savings and loan crisis. US Congress recognized the need for early identification of weak internal controls over financial reporting and the importance of adequate assets safeguards. In 1991 the CEO and CAO[82] or CFO of federally insured depository institutions were required to:[83]

(1)   sign a report stating management's responsibilities on internal control over financial reporting and compliance with applicable laws and regulations.
(2)   assess and report annually on the effectiveness of such controls and the compliance with the laws and regulations.
(3)   have an independent auditor attest these reports and
(4)   install an independent audit committee.

However the scope of the mandatory internal control report and attestation were limited to the federally insured depository institutions (savings and loan banks). It would take another crisis to broaden this scope.

BOX 2.1   INTERNAL CONTROL OVER FINANCIAL REPORTING – ERICSSON ANNUAL STATEMENT 2008

Internal control over financial reporting for the year 2008

This section has been prepared in accordance with the Sweden Code of Corporate Governance, section 10.6, and is thereby limited to internal control over financial reporting.

Since the Company is listed in the United States, the requirements for establishing and maintaining internal controls over

---

82   Chief Accounting Officer.
83   Shapiro & Matson 2008, p. 221.

financial reporting and for management to report on its assessment of the effectiveness of internal controls over financial reporting, outlined in the Sarbanes Oxley Act (SOX) apply. The Company has implemented detailed controls, documentation and testing procedures in accordance with the COSO framework for internal control, issued by the Committee of Sponsoring Organizational of the Treadway Commission to ensure compliance with SOX. Management's internal control report according to SOX will be included in Ericsson's Annual Report on Form 20-F which will be filed with the SEC in the United States. During 2008, the Company has continued to work with the improvement in design and execution of its financial reporting controls.

Internal control over financial reporting

Ericsson has integrated risk management and internal control into its business processes. As defined in the COSO framework components of internal control are a control environment, risk assessment, control activities, information and communication and monitoring.

Control environment

The Company's internal control structure is based on the division of labor between the Board of Directors and its Committees and the Presidents and CEO and the Company has implemented a management system that is based on:

- The Company's organization and mode of operations, with well-defined roles and responsibilities and delegations of authority.
- Steering documents such as policies and directives, and a Code of Business Ethics.
- Several well-defined processes for planning, operations and support.

The most essential parts of the control environment relative to financial reporting are included in steering documents and processes for accounting and financial reporting. These steering documents are updated regularly to include, among other things, changes to laws, financial reporting standards and listing requirements, such as IFRS and SOX. The processes include specific controls to be performed to ensure high quality reports.

Risk assessment

Risks related to financial reporting include fraud and loss of embezzlement of assets, undue favorable treatment of counter parties at the expense of the company. Other risks of material misstatements in the financial statements can occur in relation to recognition and measurement of assets, liabilities, revenue and cost or insufficient disclosure, identified types of risks are mitigated through segregation of duties in the Company's business processes and through appropriate delegation of authority, requiring specific approval of material transactions. Accounting and financial reporting policies and directives cover areas of particular significance to support correct accounting, reporting and disclosure.

Control activities

The Company's business processes include financial controls regarding the approval and accounting of business transactions. The financial closing and reporting process has controls for recognition, measurement and disclosure, including the application of critical accounting policies and estimates for individual subsidiaries and in the consolidated accounts. All legal entities, business units and market units in Ericsson have their own dedicated controller functions which participate in the planning and evaluation of each unit's performance. Regular analysis of the financial results for their respective units cover the significant elements of assets, liabilities revenues, costs and cash flow. Together with analysis of the consolidated financial statements performed at Group level, this important element of internal control ensures that the financial reports do not contain material errors.

For external financial reporting purposes, additional controls performed by a Disclosure Committee established by Company management ensures that all disclosure requirements are fulfilled.

The Company has implemented controls to ensure that the financial reports are prepared in accordance with its internal accounting and reporting policies and IFRS as well as with relevant listing regulations. To ensure that the company's CEO and CFO can assess the effectiveness of the controls in a way that is compliant with SOX. The Company also maintains detailed documentation on internal controls related to accounting and financial reporting, as well as records on the monitoring of the execution and results of such controls. A review of materiality levels related to the financial reports has resulted in the implementation of detailed process controls and documentation in almost all subsidiaries. Ericsson has also implemented overall entity wide controls in all subsidiaries related to the control environment and compliance with the policies and directives related to financial reporting. To ensure efficient and standardized accounting and reporting processes, the Company has established several shared services centres, performing accounting and financial reporting services for subsidiaries based on a common IT platform with a common chart of account and common master data.

Information and communication

The Company's information and communication channels support completeness and correctness of financial reporting, by making internal process instructions and policies regarding accounting and financial reporting accessible to all employees concerned and through regular updates and briefing documents regarding changes in accounting policies and reporting and disclosure requirements.

Subsidence and operating units make regular financial and management reports to internal steering groups and company management, including analysis and comments on financial performance and risks. The Board of Directors receives financial reports monthly. The Audit Committee of the Board has established a "whistle blower" procedure for reporting violations in accounting, internal controls and auditing matters.

Monitoring

The Company's financial performance is reviewed at each Board meeting. The committees of the Board fulfill important monitoring functions regarding remuneration, borrowing, investments, customer finance, cash management, financial reporting and internal control. The Audit Committee and the Board of Directors review all interim and annual financial reports before they are released to the market. The Audit Committee also receives regular reports from the external auditors. The Audit Committee follows up on any actions taken to improve or modify controls.

The Company's process for financial reporting is reviewed

annually by management and forms a basis for evaluating the internal management system and internal steering documents to ensure that they cover all significant areas related to financial reporting. The shared service center management continuously monitors the accounting quality through a set of performance indicators. Compliance with policies and directives is monitored through annual sell assessments and representation letters from heads and controllers in all subsidiaries as well as from business units and market units. The Company's internal audit function, which reports to the Audit Committee performs independent audits.

2.1.7   Enron and Internal Control Regulation

Hopes were high when the new millennium started. Prices of Internet companies' stock grew rapidly from 1997 onwards. On 14 January 2000 the Dow-Jones reached an all-time high of 11 723, but the Internet bubble, the Enron and WorldCom failures and 316 earnings restatements in 2000 and 2001 shattered the trust of investors.

Fortune magazine named Enron America's most innovative company for six years in a row.[84] Revenues increased from $13.3 billion in 1996 to $100.8 billion in 2000. On 2 December 2001 Enron declared bankruptcy. Under the leadership of CEO Jeff Skilling and Chairman of the Board Kenneth Lay, the company pioneered risk management products and long-term contracting structures in the natural gas business.[85] From 1997 onwards off-balance sheet financing and related-party transactions became increasingly important elements of the firm's strategy.[86] Several large special purpose vehicles (SPVs) were run by employees of Enron who reported to Enron CFO Andrew Fastow. There is evidence that the SPVs were used to 'manipulate earnings and extract rents for Fastow rather than to enhance corporate value'.[87] The Enron case also shows the problems and pitfalls of using fair value in financial reporting. Enron was able to 'monetize' physical assets by bringing them into the realm of mark-to-market accounting. On 30 January 1992 Enron received a letter stating that the SEC would not object to Enron's use of mark-to-market accounting for its natural gas trades. Without any further consultation Enron extended its use to other

---

[84]   Clikeman 2009, p. 245.
[85]   Gillan & Martin 2007, p. 3.
[86]   Gillan & Martin 2007, p. 15.
[87]   Gillan & Martin 2007, p. 15.

energy and non-energy commodities and merchant investments. Enron also applied fair value to assets for which there was no readily available market price.[88] To quote the bankruptcy examiner,[89]

> it would then determine the present value of these contacts over their lifetime, making assumptions as to future energy prices (including forecasts of timing and likely effect of future price deregulations in the states in which the energy was provided) and as to likely energy savings consequent to the installation of energy saving devices at the customer.

Next to the problem of fair value in incomplete markets, the unreliability of valuation estimates of independent third parties and the avoidance of recognizing mark-to-market losses are apparent in the Enron case.[90]

Enron was not the only corporation whose accounting irregularities were revealed in the wake of the Internet bubble of 2001. WorldCom overstated its profits by billions of dollars just by capitalizing expenditures. Enron and the accounting fraud at WorldCom triggered new accounting regulation in the form of the 2002 Sarbanes-Oxley Act (SOX). SOX is aimed at enhancing the quality of financial reporting, promoting audit effectiveness, regulating the auditing profession and increasing criminal and civil liability for violations of securities laws. It effectively enforces the 1976 Moss amendment proposals, demanding a mandatory review and approval of the internal accounting controls and an independent audit. SOX also introduced the Public Company Accounting Oversight Board (PCAOB) to oversee the auditors of public companies in order to protect the interests of investors and further the public interest in the preparation of informative, fair and independent audit reports. Other countries also introduced oversight boards to 'audit' the auditors.[91] The PCAOB issued standards AS2 (2004) and AS5 (2007) to establish requirements and provide direction for auditors on how to assess the effectiveness of internal control over financial reporting. An unqualified (or clean) opinion can only be given if no material weaknesses exist. A material weakness is defined as 'a significant deficiency or combination of significant deficiencies, which results in more than a reasonable possibility that a material misstatement of the annual or interim financial statements will not be prevented or detected on a timely basis'.[92]

---

[88]   Gwilliam & Jackson 2008, p. 251.
[89]   Gwilliam & Jackson 2008, p. 251.
[90]   Gwilliam & Jackson 2008, p. 240.
[91]   E.g., the *Professional Oversight Board* in the UK and the *Autoriteit Financiële Markten* (Authority for the Financial Markets) in the Netherlands.
[92]   AS5, 2007, p. A7.

One of the consequences of the financial reporting frauds is the convergence project of the International Accounting Standards Board (IASB) and the FASB. By the end of 2002 the two boards issued a memorandum of understanding, pledging their best efforts to make their existing accounting standards compatible as soon as possible and to coordinate future programmes.[93] They hope to complete the convergence in 2011.[94] In a testimony before a subcommittee of the House of Representatives, Robert Herdman, SEC Chief Accountant, addressed the concerns of the SEC on three points: first, that the current standard-setting process was too cumbersome and slow; second, too many guidelines were rule-based and focused on a check-the-box mentality that inhibits transparency; and third, that many of the FASB guidelines were too complex.[95]

The then FASB chairman, Edmund Jenkins, responded by commenting that the board had active projects underway in over half a dozen areas that would propose significant improvements, including issues related to SPVs. The possibility of hiding debt off-balance with SPVs was restricted in 2003 by FIN46 (R).

2.1.8 Enterprise Risk Management

The Enron case also showed the need to regard risk management as an important element of corporate governance and one which has to include a strategic component. Gillian and Martin conclude that:[96] 'although many aspects of corporate governance failed at Enron, the firm's viability ultimately rested on an inherently risky business strategy, a strategy that the board and others apparently failed to understand.' A standard framework of enterprise risk management was needed that would be readily usable by management to evaluate and improve their organization's enterprise risk management. In 2004 COSO published the Enterprise Risk Management (ERM) framework.[97] The new COSO ERM framework encompasses the old COSO I framework.

Within COSO ERM, much more attention is directed at the strategy process within organizations. Opportunities should be seized and possible risks should be identified. Based on COSO ERM, management should consider the amount of risk they are willing to take, their risk appetite, in a process of determining strategy and risk management. The risk manage-

---

93 Epstein, Nach et al. 2005, p. 1133.
94 Macpa 2008.
95 Herdman 2002.
96 Gillan & Martin 2007, p. 1.
97 COSO II Report 2004.

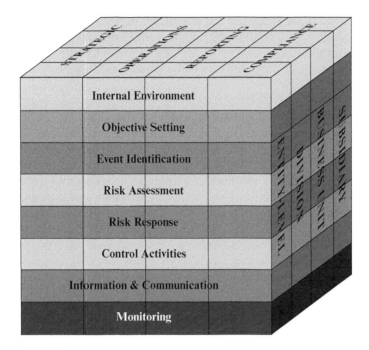

Source: © COSO.

Figure 2.2   The COSO ERM cube

ment system must not only address individual risks but also help to understand and address interrelated impacts.

The major difference between COSO I and COSO ERM is the more elaborate assessment of risks. The risk assessment component is replaced by four components: 1) objective setting; (2) event identification; (3) risk assessment; and (4) risk response. The new COSO ERM framework now consists of eight components as represented in the COSO ERM cube.

The *Internal Environment* includes the control environment of COSO I. In addition to highlighting the importance of integrity, ethical behaviour and competences, COSO ERM pays attention to risk appetite and risk consciousness.

Objective Setting is an important element of ERM. A process should be in place to set objectives. ERM should ensure that the mission and objectives are aligned and are consistent with the risk appetite of the organization.

Event Identification, Risk Assessment and Risk Response are distinguished as important steps in the risk analysis of companies. The events that can endanger or further the realization of the objectives have to be identified. Risks can be derived from the identified events. The likelihood and impact of these risks have to be assessed and a suitable risk response has to be made to align risks with the entity's risk tolerances and risk appetite.

Control Activities, Information & Communication and *Monitoring* are similar to the same components in COSO I.

The shift from internal control towards risk management is not only perceptible from the COSO framework. Annual statements increasingly disclose information on risks and risk management. To make risks transparent in annual statements, companies make use of accounting techniques that have been developed over the years. For example, ING Bank mentions the change in RAROC and economic capital in its annual statement over the year 2008:[98] 'The underlying risk-adjusted return on capital (RAROC) after tax declined to 4.9% from 19.8% in 2007. Average Economic Capital increased 34.1% to €9.3 billion mainly because of the implementation of Basel II and increased market volatility.'

ING also discloses its risk appetite: [99]

> The Group's risk appetite is captured in three different metrics which are disclosed below:
> - Earnings at Risk; the potential reduction in IFRS earnings over the next year relative to expected IFRS earnings during a moderate (i.e. '1 in 10') stress scenario. Maintaining a high quality of earnings helps ING to safeguard against being downgraded by the rating agencies;
> - Capital at Risk; the potential reduction of the current net asset value (based on fair values) over the next year relative to the expected value during a moderate (i.e. '1 in 10') stress scenario;
> - Economic Capital; the amount of capital that is required to absorb unexpected losses in times of severe stress given ING Group's 'AA' target rating.

2.1.9   Accounting and Risk Today

The description in this section of the development of the accounting and auditing profession will unfortunately conclude with yet another crisis and two more accounting frauds.

In June 2007 two hedge funds run by the Bear Stern investment bank ran into trouble because of derivatives backed by subprime mortgages.[100]

---

[98]   ING Group 2008, p. 34.
[99]   ING Group 2008, p. 128.
[100]   Sommer 2007.

The subprime-mortgage crisis spilled over into all financial institutions and in September 2008 led to the downfall of Lehman Brothers, the fourth largest investment bank in the US, with more than 24000 employees worldwide. Richard Fuld Jr received a bonus over the year 2007 of more than $40 million, partly because of the effectiveness of risk management at Lehman Brothers.[101] Yet its risk-management system and internal control statement could not prevent bankruptcy. The financial system nearly collapsed and the public sector had to come to the rescue. In the US the original $700 billion of the Troubled Asset Relief Plan was not enough and in the UK and the Netherlands renowned banks such as Royal Bank of Scotland, ING and Fortis/ABN Amro could not survive without governmental support, and just as in 1929 and 1987, this crisis also revealed accounting frauds.

Jérôme Kerviel's accounting fraud at Société Générale came to light in January 2008. As Joseph Jett had done at Kidder Peabody, so did Kerviel enter and cancel fictitious transactions to conceal market risk caused by fraudulent transactions. His trading accumulated into a long position of €46 billion in index futures. Clearing this position resulted in a global loss of €4.9 billion for Société Générale. It was the biggest corporate fraud ever until the Ponzi scheme of Madoff was discovered. Madoff was accused of paying out high returns to investors using new investors' money. The 71-year old Bernard Madoff was sentenced to 150 years' imprisonment in 2009 after pleading guilty to an 11-count criminal complaint. Federal prosecutors estimated the fraud at nearly $65 billion. His annual statements were audited by the small (three persons) auditing firm of Friehling & Horowitz. The auditing firm told the AICPA that it did not conduct audits. Unfortunately, in the state of New York auditors do not have to undergo an AICPA peer review. In 44 other states this is a requirement of being licenced to work as an auditor.[102]

2.2 CURRENT MAIN RISK MANAGEMENT TOPICS

2.2.1 Accounting: Principles-Based Versus Rules-Based Standards

The history of risk and accounting told so far shows an increasing amount of standardization of generally accepted accounting principles. An important question to ask is to what extent should these standards be high-level

---

[101] Van Hamme 2008.
[102] Wyckoff 2009.

principles or specified into precise bright-line thresholds and a large number of rules?

According to Schipper, the positive effects of such detailed accounting guidance[103] are: (1) increased comparability; (2) increased verifiability; (3) decreased earnings management through a restriction of management judgements; and (4) reduced difficulties with enforcement and litigation in after-the-fact disputes and over allegedly defective accounting. The Enron scandal revived the discussion on the negative side-effects of such detailed rules and resulted in a call for a more principles-based system. The negative effects according to Benston and Hartgraves are caused by the fact that the rules-based model allows and even encourages corporate officers to view accounting requirements as a tax code. 'For taxes, avoidance of a tax liability by any legal permissible means not only is acceptable, but is an obligation of corporations acting in the interests of their shareholders.' [104] An analysis of these negative aspects at Enron made Benston and Hartgraves conclude that the US model of specifying rules 'appeared to have allowed or required Andersen to accept procedures that accord with the letter of the rules, even though they violated the basic objectives of GAAP accounting.'[105] Two other negative aspects of rules-based standards are that they contain numerous exceptions to the principles, resulting in inconsistencies and create a need for voluminously detailed guidance, creating complexity and uncertainty.[106]

SOX prompted the SEC to conduct a study of the adoption of a principles-based accounting system. This SEC study recommends that standard setters more consistently develop standards on a principles-based basis, which: [107]

- Are based on an improved and consistently applied conceptual framework;
- Clearly state the accounting objective of the standard;
- Provide sufficient detail and structure so that the standard can be operationalized and applied on a consistent basis;
- Minimize exceptions from the standard;
- Avoid the usage of percentage tests ('bright-lines') that allow financial engineers to achieve technical compliance with the standards while evading the intent of the standard.

According to a widely held view, US GAAP are still more rules-based[108] than the International Accounting Standards and UK and Dutch GAAP.

---

103   Schipper 2003, pp. 67–68.
104   Benston & Hartgraves 2002, p. 126.
105   Benston & Hartgraves 2002, p. 124.
106   SEC (2003), p. 11.
107   SEC (2003), p. 5.
108   Benston, Bromwich et al. 2006, p. 165.

The latter standards allow an override of the standards if these do not lead to a fair presentation. US SAS 69 states that the term 'presented fairly' implies that the application of the accounting standards *almost always* results in a fair presentation. This qualifier theoretically offers an override, but it has not been interpreted as such.[109] And the SEC study explicitly mentions that a true and fair override is not a necessary component of a principles-based standard and that its recommendations should reduce concerns that the standards would not lead to a true and fair view.[110] It remains to be seen if the recommendations made by the SEC for a more principles-based approach will reduce the negative aspects of the rules-based system and if they will lead to fewer inconsistencies in the accounting standards and to less detailed prescriptions. A proper balance between overarching principles and sufficient details is hard to strike and depends on the accounting topic of the standard.[111] Contrary to the results of the SEC study, academics have argued to include overrides[112] with a mandatory factual disclosure to sustain the objectives of the financial statements.

An important future development is the convergence of the more principles-based IFRS and the rules-based FASB. Since 2002 the FASB and the IASB have been working on a project to align US GAAP and IFRS. The two boards have issued several statements in close cooperation and are working on a joint conceptual framework. Since November 2007, the SEC has allowed foreign companies to file their financial statements prepared on the basis of IFRS. No reconciliation with US GAAP is required. And more recently, on 27 August 2008, the SEC released a proposal that requires mandatory adoption of IFRS in the United States beginning in 2014.[113]

2.2.2 Fair Value Accounting

In 1990 Douglas Breeden referred to FVA as the 'most significant initiative in accounting principles development in over 50 years'.[114] Critics argue that FVA has 'significantly contributed to the financial crisis and exacerbated its severity for financial institutions in the US and around the world'.[115] Perhaps most critical of FVA has been the former chairman of

---

[109] Benston, Bromwich et al. 2006, p. 166.
[110] SEC 2003, p. 32.
[111] Ter Hoeven 2005, p. 483.
[112] Ter Hoeven 2005, p. 483; Benston, Bromwich et al. 2006, p. 180.
[113] Tribunella 2009, p. 32.
[114] Barlev & Haddad 2003, p. 390.
[115] Laux &Leuz 2009, p. 826.

the US Federal Deposit Insurance Corporation (FDIC) William Isaac, who has said that 'hundreds of billions of dollars have been lost because of these rules'[116] and that FVA has limited the lending capacity of banks by some 5 trillion dollars.[117] Proponents argue that FVA has played the role of the proverbial messenger that is now being shot.[118] What role does FVA play and should FVA be abandoned? Answering this question requires looking at how fair value is established and at the key arguments of critics and opponents. FAS 157 defines fair value as 'the price that would be received to sell an asset or paid to transfer a liability in an orderly transaction between market participants at the measurement date.' When quoted market prices for identical assets or liabilities are available, they have to be used as the measurement for fair value. If not, observable comparable input should be used, which includes similar assets or liabilities in active markets or information on identical assets or liabilities in inactive markets, and other relevant market data. If these inputs are also not available, the fair value should be based on a financial model.

Critics argue that in times of crisis or bubbles the market is not efficient and market values do not represent the underlying fundamental value of the asset or liability. The consequences in a period of crisis are that although the assets or liabilities have not been transferred, fair value accounting obliges the company to record a loss, which reduces its equity. To maintain solvency ratios, for example demanded by the Basel agreements, the company is forced to raise new capital under depressed valuation conditions. The same reasoning applies to a bubble, when profits and solvency levels are fundamentally overstated. This line of reasoning brings critics to state that FVA enforces procyclicality of the economy.[119] Critics typically advocate abandoning FVA and returning to a form of HCA or, less extreme, to altering FVA to reduce the amount of reported losses.[120]

Accounting researchers recognize some of the concerns about FVA but they insist that their impact is overstated and that critics do not acknowledge the far more severe limitations of the advocated alternatives.[121] The concern that observed prices may not always reflect fundamental values is not solved by HCA. The important question is how to deal with this problem. HCA offers no solution, because it does not reflect the fundamental value either. Viable solutions include giving additional guidance

---

[116] Dzinkowski 2009, p. 48.
[117] Dzinkowski 2009, p. 50.
[118] Laux & Leuz 2009, p. 826.
[119] Véron 2008, p. 2.
[120] Ryan 2009, p. 163.
[121] Ryan 2008; Ryan 2009; Laux & Leuz 2009.

on how to determine fair value when market illiquidity is high, combining FVA with mandatory disclosures, and encouraging additional voluntary disclosures about fair value gains and losses and about how these losses have resulted from market illiquidity.[122]

The argument of procyclicality is reinforced by tight coupling between accounting standards and regulatory requirements, which results in contagious consequences of FVA in combination with capital requirements imposed by bank regulators or by bond covenants based on accounting numbers. Models show that FVA in pure form can create such contagion effects.[123] A way to tackle this problem is to deviate from GAAP in situations where contagion is likely to occur. Both US GAAP and IFRS allow such deviations in certain situations.[124] Another way to address contagion and procyclicality is not to have direct regulatory and contractual ties to FVA. It would be possible to loosely couple accounting numbers based on GAAP for the calculation of regulatory capital.[125]

Although the FVA concerns are legitimate, giving management more possibilities to deal with potential FVA-induced problems, by reducing the amount of reported losses in times of crisis, opens the door to manipulation.[126] Laux and Leuz argue that in view of the evidence in other accounting areas and the savings and loans crisis, this concern about manipulation should not be underestimated.[127] FVA seems preferable to HCA, but standard-setters face a delicate trade-off between contagion effects and timely impairments.

2.2.3 Scope and Limitation of Audits

The restoration of public trust depends on the extent to which the public expectations of the auditor can be met. The major accounting and auditing reforms were triggered by fraudulent behaviour. The general public expects auditors to be public watchdogs detecting all fraudulent behaviour. Auditors do not accept responsibility for this level of fraud detection for two reasons. First of all, from the beginning the objective of a financial audit has been to assure the reliability of a company's financial statements. This objective has come to include conformity with generally accepted accounting principles. However, assessing the reliability of

---

[122] Ryan 2009, p. 164.
[123] Laux & Leuz 2009, p. 829.
[124] Laux & Leuz 2009, p. 830.
[125] Laux & Leuz 2009, p. 839.
[126] Laux & Leuz 2009, p. 866.
[127] Laux & Leuz 2009, p. 827.

financial statements differs from detecting fraud. Fraudulent activities do not need to have a material impact on financial statements. In the early stages of fraud especially, the financial impact may be limited. Second, the audit process has inherent limitations. Members of a fraudulent organization may conspire and do anything in their power to leave no traces for auditors. This discrepancy between the expectations of the general public and the responsibility which auditors can prove to hold is called the expectation gap. Flint summarized the problem in 1988 as follows:[128] 'Investors and depositors are losing faith in the ability of the accounting profession to perform the job which has historically been its unique function in our society – assuring the integrity of the financial information upon which our capitalistic society necessarily depends.'

The auditing profession has wrestled with this expectation gap for years. The first attempts aimed to convince the general public of the limitations of financial audits. The first publication of auditing procedures in the US (in 1929) warned that audits would not necessarily disclose falsifications.[129] SAS 16, issued in 1977, required auditors to plan and search for errors and irregularities that would have a material impact on the financial statements. It also stipulated that the examination of the auditor is subject to the inherent limitations of the auditing process. In 1988 triggered by the savings and loan crisis, SAS 58 was issued. The expectation of the public was taken more seriously and the new standard required auditors to treat management representations with professional scepticism. In 1997 (SAS 82) and 2002 (SAS 99) the Auditing Standard Board provided more detailed guidance to assess the risk of fraud. Auditors have to assess different risk factors caused by incentives/pressures, opportunities and attitudes/rationalizations.[130] And they have to vary their audit procedures on a yearly basis to make it more difficult for clients to anticipate and evade the audit tests.

Will the revised standards close the expectation gap? Probably not. The SAS 99 definition of fraud is limited to material misstatements of the financial reports. Frauds that do not lead to material misstatements may therefore not be discovered. And although there is more professional scepticism and more attention paid to the possibility of fraud, auditors are not trained to discover conspiracies. Three solutions to bridge the expectation

---

[128]   Flint in Hassink 2002, p. 316.

[129]   Clikeman 2009, p. 824.

[130]   The grouping of the risk factors is based on the fraud triangle developed by Donald R. Cressey in 1973. A fraud only occurs when 1) there are incentives/pressures; 2) there is an opportunity; and 3) the employee's can rationalize their behaviour.

gap can be presented.[131] The first is to extend the objective of the audit. In addition to the financial audit, consideration could be given to more in-depth assignments to discover fraudulent behaviour, for example, by basing the scope and fraud-objectives of the additional audits on problems in socially relevant areas. Second, the competences of the audit team performing these fraud-related audits should include fraud detection skills, for example by having such specialists as forensic auditors or detectives on the audit team. Third, it is probable that a risk-based audit approach is not always the most suitable one to take in order to detect fraud. Analyzing data to discover irregularities could be a promising approach.

2.2.4 Auditing Quality

Auditing has become an important instrument to protect stakeholders against the risk of financial fraud, unreliable financial reports, internal control weaknesses or irresponsible risks. The frauds and cases of accounting misconduct described in this chapter have increased the pressure for more transparency, standardization and attestation of the audit itself. GAAP have developed over the years and oversight bodies have been extended such as the PCAOB (US), the AFM (the Netherlands) and the Professional Oversight Board (UK).[132] An important element of the audit quality is the independence, objectivity and integrity of the auditor. Independence, both in fact and in appearance, is stressed especially to be a pivotal aspect. After Enron, different measures have been taken to increase formal independence requirements. For listed companies, responsibility for the external auditors has shifted from the Executive Board to the Supervisory Board/Audit-Committee. In addition, mandatory audit partner rotation has been introduced in the US, the UK and the European Union (EU). Every five years in the EU and after no more than seven years, the lead and reviewing engagement partners have to be replaced in order to prevent a close relationship from developing between the audit partners and the listed company.[133] In Italy and Brazil, mandatory rotation goes even further: a mandatory audit firm rotation has to take place

---

[131] Arguments are based on Bindenga 2003.

[132] The Professional Oversight Board is a part of the Financial Reporting Council.

[133] In the Netherlands the Executive Board and the Audit Committee will report on the desirability of rotating the responsible audit partners. The Supervisory Board will take this into account when deciding on its nomination for the appointment of an external auditor to the general meeting.

every nine and five years respectively.[134] The provision of additional non-audit services is restricted and has to be made transparent. SOX prohibits explicit categories of non-audit services that were deemed to impair independence. Bookkeeping, design and implementation of financial information systems, and internal auditing outsourcing services are among those categories and services of external auditors that have to be approved by the audit committee. The PCAOB offers further guidance and restriction of non-audit services. For example, new PCAOB rules focus on the restriction of certain tax services that independent auditors may provide for their clients.[135] Furthermore SOX Section 206 establishes a one-year cooling-off period before a member of an engagement team can accept employment in key client positions.

The question that arises is to what extent do these measures increase audit quality? Empirical studies show unexpected consequences. A study carried out by Ruiz-Barbadillo et al. in Spain looked at the difference in independence between a period in Spain when there was mandatory audit firm rotation (1988–95) and the following period without audit firm rotation. Their study found no evidence that mandatory rotation mitigates the effects of economic dependence.[136] Rather to the contrary, their results are consistent with the notion that mandatory audit firm rotation may harm audit quality. Reputation concerns appear to have a greater impact on auditors' reporting behaviour. In that respect, increased reputational and economic concerns after the downfall of Arthur Andersen may be a more important mechanism for audit quality than detailed imposed restrictions. Geiger et al. found that auditors became more conservative in their judgments in order to enhance their reputation, reduce litigation risk and to reduce government intervention. They suggest that standard-setters should evaluate the extent of the changed behaviour of the audit profession before promulgating further detailed, prescriptive regulation.[137] A study by Robinson draws different conclusions on imposed restrictions of non-audit tax services.[138] She examined whether auditor independence is impaired through the provision of tax services by focusing on auditors' issuance of going-concern opinions among a sample of bankruptcy-filling firms. Her results are inconsistent with diminished auditor independence, but rather suggest an enhanced audit quality.[139]

---

[134]   Jackson, Moldrich et al. 2008, p. 421.
[135]   PCAOB release no. 2008–03.
[136]   Ruiz-Barbadillo, Gómez-Aguilar et al. 2009, p. 132.
[137]   Geiger, Raghunandan et al. 2005, p. 33.
[138]   Robinson 2008.
[139]   Robinson 2008, p. 52.

Auditor independence remains a concern. In 2009, Rentokil, a UK-based firm, announced a saving of £1 million on its annual payments, which amounted to 30% of its total annual fees, by outsourcing its internal audits. Rentokil decided to outsource a large part of its internal audit to its new external auditor KPMG.[140] In the US, internal auditing is one of the prohibited non-audit services and may not be outsourced to the firm conducting the financial audit. The deal has prompted concern and protest in auditing circles. Pheijffer, a Dutch professor in forensic auditing, regards the deal as a form of creative compliance,[141] following the letter and not the spirit of the law. Especially when independence, which is closely related to integrity, is at stake applying creative compliance seems to undermine the essence of the societal role of auditors, so beautifully put forward by Limperg in the doctrine of inspired confidence. John Grant, director of the standard-setting body APB, part of the Financial Reporting Council (FRC) in the UK, says that the rules on this point are to be reviewed.[142]

2.2.5 Internal Control: Costs of and Effectiveness of SOX

SOX is the result of a very political process. A study into its genesis and substance made Romano conclude that 'Sarbanes-Oxley may have satisfied a political need, but it will do little to protect investors or strengthen the market'.[143] Implementing and auditing compliance with SOX is a costly business. The out-of-pocket expenses incurred to implement SOX were estimated in 2005 to average $1.7 million per company.[144] And additional out-of-pocket expenses for auditing SOX in the 2003–2005 period amounted to $850 000.[145] The benefits of SOX are much harder to determine. Empirical research suggests that the costs may be higher than the benefits. Zhang found a statistically significant negative cumulative abnormal stock return around key SOX events.[146] This can be translated into an economic negative effect of SOX between $428 billion and $936 billion.[147] He also found that the market reaction to the announcement of postponing compliance with SOX 404 was particularly beneficial for

[140] Hughes 2009.
[141] Pheijffer 2009.
[142] Baker 2009.
[143] Romano 2005, p. 36.
[144] Engel, Hayes et al. 2007, p. 122.
[145] Krishnan, Rama et al. 2008, p. 184.
[146] Zhang 2007, p. 74.
[147] Van de Ven 2008, p. 26.

small firms.[148] Another signal of the possible high costs of SOX is revealed by the study carried out by Engel et al. They found an increasing number of firms leaving the US stock exchange combined with positive abnormal returns for these firms. These findings should be interpreted with caution,[149] but they do seem to suggest that SOX may have unintended negative economic side-effects.

2.2.6   Effectiveness of Internal Control Statements

To make the internal control of organizations transparent to stakeholders, internal control statements are published. These internal control statements come in different forms and with different scopes. The form differs from a statement made by the board on the effectiveness of the internal control system to a narrative description of the system of internal control and the process of reviewing its effectiveness. This can be regarded as the difference between an output statement and a process statement. The scope differs from internal control over financial reporting to the effectiveness of internal control in a broader sense. This includes effectiveness and efficiency of operations, compliance with applicable laws and regulations, and safeguarding of assets.

US SOX Section 404 prescribes a statement on the effectiveness of internal control over financial reporting. See, for example, Lehman Brothers internal control statement, which is shown in Box 2.2.

In the UK the company board acknowledges in a report its responsibility for internal control and for reviewing the effectiveness of internal control. The board summarizes the review process and confirms that where necessary action has been taken to remedy any significant failings or weaknesses.[150] See, for example, the Royal Bank of Scotland's internal control statement, which is shown in Box 2.3.

Although companies benefit from implementing and monitoring internal control systems, the effectiveness of statements on internal control have been questioned. The financial crisis in 2008 led to the collapse of Lehman Brothers and to the UK government rescue of the Royal Bank

---

[148]   Zhang 2007, p. 110.

[149]   Research of Jain and Rezaee only takes into account the final legislative events and arrives at an opposite conclusion. The design and execution of the study of Zhang provides stronger evidence. Jain and Rezaee 2006.

[150]   The Dutch corporate governance code (the Tabaksblat Code) contained a statement on the effectiveness on internal control in a broader sense. The revised code (the Frijns Code) restricts the statement to internal control over financial reporting.

BOX 2.2 INTERNAL CONTROL OVER FINANCIAL REPORTING OF LEHMAN BROTHERS

Management's assessment of internal control over financial reporting

The management of Lehman Brothers Holdings Inc. (the "Company") is responsible for establishing and maintaining adequate internal control over financial reporting. The Company's internal control system is designed to provide reasonable assurance to the Company's management and Board of Directors regarding the reliability of financial reporting and the preparation of published financial statements in accordance with generally accepted accounting principles. All internal control systems, no matter how well designed, have inherent limitations. Therefore, even those systems determined to be effective can provide only reasonable assurance with respect to financial statement preparation and presentation.

The Company's management assessed the effectiveness of the Company's internal control over financial reporting as of November 30, 2006. In making this assessment, it used the criteria set forth by the Committee of Sponsoring Organizations of the Treadway Commission (COSO) in *Internal Control—Integrated Framework*. Based on our assessment we believe that, as of November 30, 2006, the Company's internal control over financial reporting effective based on those criteria.

The Company's independent registered public accounting firm that audited the accompanying Consolidated Financial Statements has issued an attestation report on our assessment of the Company's internal control over financial reporting. Their report appears on the following page.

---

of Scotland. These events beg the question how much certainty do these institutions' statements on internal control give to the stakeholders?

The reliability of the Lehman financial report is not the main topic of the debate. It was probably excessive risk taking and subsequent liquidity problems that caused the downfall of Lehman Brothers, not unreliable financial reports. Lehman's internal control statement on financial reporting does not have this broader take on internal control. Even a correct internal control statement and application of

BOX 2.3   INTERNAL CONTROL OF THE ROYAL
          BANK OF SCOTLAND

Internal Control

The Board of Directors is responsible for the Group's system of internal control that is designed to facilitate effective and efficient operations and to ensure the quality of internal and external reporting and compliance with applicable laws and regulations. In devising internal controls, the Group has regard to the nature and extent of the risk, the likelihood of it crystallising and the cost of controls. A system of internal control is designed to manage, but not eliminate, the risk of failure to achieve business objectives and can only provide reasonable, and not absolute, assurance against the risk of material misstatement, fraud or losses.

The Board has establishment a process for the identification, evaluation and management of the significant risks faced by the Group, which operated throughout the year ended 31 December 2007 and to 27 February 2008, the date the directors approved the Report and Accounts. This process is regularly reviewed by the Board and meets the requirements of the guidance 'Internal Control: Revised Guidance for Directors on the Combined Code' issued by the Financial Reporting Council in October 2005.

The effectiveness of the Group's Internal control system is reviewed regularly by the Board and the Audit Committee. Executive management committees or boards of directors in each of the Group's businesses receive regular reports on significant risks facing their business and how they are being controlled. In addition, the Group Board receives monthly risk management reporting. Additional details of the Group's approach to risk management are given in the 'Risk management' section of the 'Business review' on pages 70 to 90. The Audit Committee also receives regular reports from RBS Risk Management and Group Internal Audit. In addition, the Group's independent auditors present to the Audit Committee reports that include details of any significant internal control matters which they have identified. The system of internal controls of the authorised institutions and other regulated entities in the Group is also subject to regulatory oversight in the UK and overseas. Additional details of the Group's regulatory oversight are given in the 'Supervision and regulation' section on pages 231 to 233.

SOX could not prevent Lehman's collapse. Kirkpatrick concludes that attention in recent years focused too much on internal controls related to financial reporting and not enough on the broader context of risk management.[151]

The board of the Royal Bank of Scotland has reviewed the effectiveness of internal control to manage material misstatements, fraud and losses. The statement warns that internal control only provides reasonable and not absolute assurance. With hindsight it is hard to maintain that the Royal Bank of Scotland and numerous other financial institutions were in control. A legitimate question arises: what is the value of the internal control sections in annual statements? Paape refers to internal control statements as purely 'hot air'. There is no objective knowledge on which to design and evaluate systems of effective internal control. And stating that organizations are 'in control', without giving a reference, provides no certainty for stakeholders.[152] Van de Ven[153] even warns against the negative effects of internal control statements. He fears a downward spiral where trust in humans is replaced by trust in formal systems. If internal control statements suggest levels of certainty and expectations that cannot be attained, they will undermine the confidence of stakeholders in management and auditors. If expectations are not met, trust in management and auditors will decline and more detailed regulation will be put in place to ensure effective control of organizations. This downward spiral of trust and increasing standards and audit will have a negative influence on important elements of the control environment and will ultimately erode risk management within organizations.

2.2.7 Limits of Quantitative Risk Management

Financial models play an important role in risk assessment. But how much guidance and certainty do these quantitative risk models give? There is an increasing body of evidence on the inherent limitations of risk management techniques.[154] Rebonato claims that top financial professionals rely on ever-more sophisticated models for controlling financial risks and that this excessive reliance on quantitative precision is misleading.[155] Research carried out by Makridakis and Hibon shows that more complex models do

---

[151] Kirkpatrick 2009, p. 6.
[152] Paape 2008.
[153] Van de Ven 2008, p. 57.
[154] Danielsson 2002, p. 1274.
[155] Rebonato 2007.

not lead to better predictions.[156] Moreover, according to Daníelsson, most existing risk models break down in times of crisis.[157]

As described earlier, financial institutions often use VAR to quantify potential losses under the assumption of a confidence level of 99%. In the ING's 2008 annual statement, limitations of VAR are described as follows: [158]

> VaR as a risk measure has some limitations. VaR quantifies the potential loss under the assumption of normal market conditions. This assumption may not always hold true in reality, especially when market events occur, and therefore could lead to an underestimation of the potential loss. VaR also uses historical data to forecast future price behaviour. Future price behaviour could differ substantially from past behaviour. Moreover, the use of a one-day holding period (or ten days for regulatory calculations) assumes that all positions in the portfolio can be liquidated or hedged in one day. In periods of illiquidity or market events, this assumption may not hold true. Also, the use of 99% confidence level means that VaR does not take into account any losses that occur beyond this confidence level.

What do these limitations mean? A one-day VAR with a 99% confidence level means that it is possible a violation will occur 2.5 times a year on average.[159] The usage of historical data poses the question about the robustness of the forecasts. Does the historical data set contain a period of crisis? And what are the consequences in an economic downturn?

Is it possible to comprehend and assess the impact of the limitations referred to? And how should these limitations influence the use of quantitative models within organizations? Rebonato highlights that quantitative models are important, but that 'no single risk metric will be able *by itself* to tell the whole story.'[160] Balanced decisions require understanding the limitations of the models and calculating the effects of different scenarios.[161]

2.2.8   Limitations of Risk Assessment

Risk management as discussed here is based on assessing the probability and impact of future events. Is it possible to make accurate predictions? Beck, a sociologist, emphasizes the difference between catastrophe as an actual event and risk as an anticipated event that may occur and threat-

---

[156]   Makridakis & Hibon 2000, p. 460.
[157]   Daníelsson 2002, p. 1293.
[158]   ING Group 2008, p. 196.
[159]   Daníelsson 2002, p. 1291.
[160]   Rebonato 2007, p. 225.
[161]   Rebonato 2007, p. 227.

ens us.[162] The fact that risks are not the actual events means that there is an 'imaging and staging process' in which risks are being created. This staging process shapes our expectations of possible future events and guides our actions. Future events that are uncertain and hard to predict are transformed into risks which are being presented as calculable and controllable.

Next to this social construction of risks, event probabilities are not always bell-shaped. Taleb refers to events which he labels 'black swans'. These are highly improbable events with three principal characteristics: they are unpredictable; they carry a massive impact; and after the fact, an explanation is concocted that makes the events appear less random, and more predictable than they were.[163] Risk assessment is not as unproblematic as the risk frameworks seem to suggest. The distinction between uncertainty, which cannot be predicted, and risk is blurred. Van Asselt discusses 'triple question mark' risks, where probability, impact and total risk are all question marks. Examples can be found in risk controversies between promising technological innovations and negative consequences that are hard to assess. This makes risk management a policy issue and not a mere technical exercise.[164]

2.2.9 Effectiveness of Controls

One of the steps to mitigate risks entails the design and implementation of controls. Well-known formal controls include separation of duties, procedures, instructions and audits. The effectiveness and impact of these controls is not as straightforward as it seems. A theoretical example of the ultimate system of formal control is the Panopticon, a type of prison suggested by Jeremy Bentham in 1785; this was designed in such a way that a guard could watch all prisoners all the time without the prisoners being able to tell whether they were being watched. Bentham decreed that power should be visible yet unverifiable. For Foucault, the Panopticon resembles how discipline and punishment work in modern society: formal control by omniscience, a way to monitor all human activities and thereby prevent and mitigate risks. The Panopticon was never built and the possibility and advisability of such total formal control systems are questionable. Even in prisons, formal systems cannot and indeed do not prevent outbreaks. And formal systems can negatively impact on the motivation of employees in organizations. In the crowding-out theory, intrinsic motivation is crowded out by

---

[162]   Beck 2009, p. 9.
[163]   Taleb 2007, p. XVIII.
[164]   Van Asselt 2008, p. 18.

extrinsic rewards and regulation.[165] In explaining this theory, Bruno Frey uses a case study of university professors. Some teach more and some teach less than the required number of hours a week. There is substantial evidence that tightly controlling the number of teaching hours also leads the engaged professors to reduce their hours to the minimum.[166] Self-determination is an important aspect of intrinsic motivation and can be undermined by detailed prescription of activities.[167] Next to formal controls soft controls are distinguished. The COSO frameworks highlight the importance of soft, or behavioural, controls such as trust, ethics, integrity, building relationships, and effective leadership.[168] Empirical research studies offer, each of course in its specific empirical settings, preliminary support for the importance of these softer controls. Ethical leadership has a positive impact on reporting problems to management.[169] The level of trust employees have in management is positively correlated to value-added activities and organizational citizenship behaviour.[170] Furthermore, fairness perceptions are related to the degree of opportunistic behaviour.[171] Experiments show an interrelationship between penalties and moral group values. An experiment by Mulder, van Dijk and Cremer[172] shows identical levels of opportunistic behaviour in groups based on interpersonal trust and in groups based on formal punishment. However, in the latter groups abolishing penalties led to a significant increase in their members' opportunistic behaviour. The consequences of the outcome of this study are that the introduction of formal systems could negatively influence the shared values of the group and constrain the possibility of effectively implementing soft controls in the future. Crowding-out effects and the importance of soft controls suggest that the effectiveness of the controls ultimately depends on a context-specific mix of formal and soft controls.

2.3   CONCLUSIONS

Where do the history of risk management and reflection on risk-management practices from an accounting perspective lead to? The following tentative conclusions can be drawn.

---

[165]   Frey 1997.
[166]   Frey 1997, p. 8.
[167]   Gagné & Deci 2005.
[168]   Buhariwalla 2006, p. 81.
[169]   Brown, Treviño et al. 2005.
[170]   Mayer & Gavin 2005.
[171]   Cohen, Holder-Webb et al. 2007.
[172]   Mulder, Van Dijk et al. 2006.

2.3.1 Need for Risk Management

The examples used in this chapter show that opportunistic behaviour is not imaginary and that its fallout can be immense. Risks are of all times and the damage caused by Société Générale, Madoff and the Lehman bankruptcy is enormous. The assets of Lehman Brothers alone were estimated to exceed $600 billion, more than the Gross National Product (GNP) of most countries.[173] The need for risk management in organizations is real and risk management practices play an important role in organizations.

2.3.2 Developments of Accounting and Auditing

Over the years financial risks and ways to mitigate them have shifted. The *Royal Mail* case is an example of information asymmetry. Information is either not supplied or supplied in such a condensed way that it is useless for investors. Standards have been developed over the years to make the financial results, cash flows and financial position of organizations transparent to different stakeholders. Disclosure of information, however, could not and does not guarantee the reliability of the statements presented. The cases of *Ivan Kreuger's Swedish Match Corporation* and *McKesson & Robbins* show the importance of safeguarding assets and of reliability of financial information. Mandatory auditing and attestation of financial reports, together with an increasing number of auditing standards have been introduced to mitigate risks. Auditing evolved into risk-based auditing, in which more and more attention was paid to the internal control system of organizations to minimize audit risks for auditing firms. The savings and loans crisis and financial shenanigans at the beginning of this century showed that existing auditing and accounting standards were not sufficient to guarantee the reliability of financial reporting. Accounting standards were adapted towards a more principles-based system and fair value and the importance of internal control systems was highlighted. SOX also introduced a mandatory audit of internal control over financial reporting. The 2008 financial crisis following the subprime crisis of 2007 highlighted the importance of how companies manage their business risks. A shift has been observed from the reliability of information towards the reasonable assurance that companies, in reaching their objectives, would at least survive in times of crisis. Additional disclosures and auditing of enterprise risk management within organizations are being considered and implemented. New standards and governance codes are being developed

---

[173] According to the IMF, only 17 counties had a higher GNP in 2007.

to make risk information and the risk management process transparent, and there is much discussion about the possibilities of additional audits.

2.3.3   Limitations

Over the years organizations have become more transparent, disclosures and activities have been standardized and auditing has become an important part of corporate life.[174] Yet the high level of attention for risk management and increased transparency could not prevent financial misconduct and poor corporate governance. Higher levels of transparency, more standards and increased auditing have been inadequate to enforce effective risk management. Adopting and using risk management to legitimize behaviour, creative compliance and following the letter (and not the spirit) of rules are hard to prevent with formal risk management systems. In addition to the potential misuse of risk management systems, risk management has inherent limitations. To what extent can future events and impacts be foreseen? The potential of quantitative risk management models are overestimated and formal controls disregard the effects of the complex interaction of these controls with the level of trust, integrity and fairness in organizations. What are the consequences of these limitations? The negative side effects of a purely technical and instrumental approach to risk management could increase rather than decrease risk. Effective risk management has to take these limitations into account and must be based on a solid foundation of soft controls.

2.3.4   Further Development of Standards

Today's risk society is characterized by high levels of uncertainty. These imply that it is harder to prescribe and standardize behaviour. However, to restore public trust after financial crises regulators are inclined to produce more standards and prescribe audits. The advantages of detailed rules (comparability, verifiability, restriction of management judgements and reduced difficulties with enforcement and litigation) have to be weighed against advantages using higher level-principles. Apart from the disadvantages of detailed rules, such as complexity, inconsistency of rules and creative compliance, applying principles offers greater opportunities in a rapidly changing environment. But there is no win-win situation. A more principles-based approach means that advantages of the detailed rules are lost and vice versa. The challenge for the different regulators is to create a

---

[174]   Power 1997.

new balance between high-level principles and detailed rules. A complex task for regulators in an institutional environment where political pressure for concrete measures and bright-line thresholds is high. The negative side effects of the current rules suggest a shift towards more principles, but the pressure to add more rules remains high.

REFERENCES

Asselt, Marjolein van (2008), 'Risk governance: Over omgaan met onzekerheid en mogelijke toekomsten', inaugural reading of 26 October 2007 at Maastricht University, available at: http://arno.unimaas.nl/show.cgi?fid=13167 (accessed 14 December 2009).
Baker, Neil (2009), 'U.K. to review ethics rule', *Compliance Week*, available at http://www.complianceweek.com/blog/glimpses/2009/09/16/uk-to-review-ethics-rule/ (accessed 14 December 2009).
Barlev, Benzion and Joshua R. Haddad (2003), 'Fair value accounting and the management of the firm', *Critical Perspectives on Accounting*, **14** (4), 383–415.
Beck, Ulrich (2009), *World at Risk*, Cambridge: Polity Press.
Benston, George J. and Al L. Hartgraves (2002), 'Enron: what happened and what we can learn from it', *Journal of Accounting and Public Policy*, **21** (2), 105–127.
Benston, George J., Michael Bromwich and Alfred Wagenhofer (2006), 'Principles-versus rules-based accounting standards: the FASB's standard setting strategy', *Abacus*, **42**(2), 165–188.
Bindenga, André (2003), 'Fraude en accountant in het huidige tijdsbeeld', *Maandblad Accountancy en Bedrijfseconomie*, **7/8**, 12–14.
Blokdijk, Hans, Frank Drieënhuizen and Philip Wallage (1995), *Reflections on Auditing Theory – A Contribution from the Netherlands*, Amsterdam: Kluwer.
Brown, Michael E., Linda K. Treviño and David A. Harrison (2005), 'Ethical leadership: A social learning perspective for construct development and testing', *Organizational Behavior and Human Decision Processes*, **97** (2), 117–134.
Buhariwalla, Adil (2006), 'The softer side of controls', *Internal Auditor*, **63** (5), 81–87.
Burgert, R. and C.W.A. Timmermans (1987), *De jaarrekening nieuwe stijl – deel 1*, Alphen aan den Rijn,: Samsom H.D. Tjeenk Willink.
Camfferman, Kees (1998), 'Perceptions of the Royal Mail case in the Netherlands', *Accounting & Business Research*, **29**, 43–55.
Chandler, Roy A., John R. Edwards and Malcolm Anderson (1993), 'Changing perceptions of the role of the company auditor, 1840–1940', *Accounting & Business Research*, **23** (92), 443–459.
Chorafas, Dimitris N. (2001), *Managing Risk in the New Economy*, New York: New York Institute of Finance
Clikeman, Paul M. (2009), *Called to Account*, New York: Routledge.
Cohen, Jeffrey R., Lori Holder-Webb, David J. Sharp and Laurie W. Pant (2007), 'The effects of perceived fairness on opportunistic behavior', *Contemporary Accounting Research*, **24** (4), 1119–1138.
Cushing, Barry E. and James K. Loebbecke (1983), 'Analytical approaches to

audit risk: A survey and analysis', *Auditing: Journal of Practice and Theory*, **3**, 23–41.

Daníelsson, Jon (2002), 'The emperor has no clothes: Limits to risk modelling', *Journal of Banking & Finance*, **26** (7), 1273–1296.

Dijker, R.A. (1930), 'De "publieke" en "private" taak van de accountant', in: *Vijftig jaar Maandblad Accountancy en Bedrijfseconomie deel 2*, Purmerend: Muusses.

Dzinkowski, Ramona (2009), 'Whodunnit?', *Intheblack*, **79** (1), 48–51.

Engel, Ellen, Rachel M. Hayes and Xue Wang (2007), 'The Sarbanes-Oxley Act and firms' going-private decisions', *Journal of Accounting and Economics*, **44**(1–2), 116–145.

Epstein, Barry J., Ralph Nach and Steven M. Bragg (2005), *Wiley GAAP 2006*, New York: John Wiley & Sons.

Frey, Bruno S. (1997), *Not Just For The Money – An Economic Theory of Personal Motivation*, Cheltenham: Edward Elgar.

Gagné, Marylène and Edward L. Deci (2005), 'Self-determination theory and work motivation', *Journal of Organizational Behavior*, **26**, 331–362.

Geiger, Marshall A., Kamineni Raghunandan and Dasaratha V. Rama (2005), 'Recent changes in the association between bankruptcies and prior audit opinions', *Auditing: Journal of Practice and Theory*, **24** (1), 21–35.

Gillan, Stuart L. and John D. Martin (2007), 'Corporate governance post-Enron: Effective reforms, or closing the stable door?', *Journal of Corporate Finance*. **13**, 929–958.

Goodman, Laurie S., Shumin Li, Douglas J. Luca, Thomas A. Zimmerman and Frank J. Fabozzi, Eds (2008), 'Subprime Mortgage Credit Derivatives', in *The Frank J. Fabozzi Series*, New York: John Wiley & Sons.

Gwilliam, David and Richard H.G. Jackson (2008), 'Fair value in financial reporting: Problems and pitfalls in practice: A case study analysis of the use of fair valuation at Enron', *Accounting Forum (Elsevier)*, **32**, 240–259.

Hamme, Kris van (2008), 'Bankiers furieus op Lehman', *Financieel Dagblad*, 15 September 2008.

Hartman, Wim (1993), *Organisatie van de Informatieverzorging*, Rotterdam: CODIS.

Hassink, Harold (2002), 'Accountants en verwachtingskloof – een onderzoek onder vakbonden', *Maandblad Accountancy en Bedrijfseconomie*, **7/8**, 316–323.

Hayre, Lakhbir, Ed. (2001), *Salomon Smith Barney guide to Mortgage-Backed and Asset-Backed securities*, New York: John Wiley & Sons.

Hen, Paul E., Jacobus G. Berendsen and Jan W. Schoonderbeek (1995), *Hoofdstukken uit de geschiedenis van het Nederlandse accountantsberoep na 1935*, Assen: Van Gorcum & Comp.

Herdman, Robert K. (2002), 'Testimony: are Current Financial Accounting Standards Protecting Investors?', available at http://www.sec.gov/news/testimony/021402tsrkh.htm (accessed 14 December 2009).

Hoeven, Ralph ter (2005), 'Principle-based versus rule-based accounting standards', *Maandblad Accountancy en Bedrijfseconomie*, **21** (October), 475–485.

Hof, Kees van der (2007), *Boekhoudschandalen – De grabbelton van bestuurders en raiders*. Rijswijk: Elmar.

Hughes, Jennifer (2009), 'Rentokil's KPMG deal raises eyebrows', *Financial Times*, available at http://www.ft.com/cms/s/0/bee07652-7fc9-11de-85dc-00144feabdc0.html (accessed 14 December 2009).

Jackson, Andrew B., Michael Moldrich and Peter Roebuck (2008), 'Mandatory audit firm rotation and audit quality', *Managerial Auditing Journal,* **23**(5), 420–437.

Jain, Pankaj K. and Zebihollah Rezaee (2006), 'The Sarbanes-Oxley Act of 2002 and capital-market behavior: early evidence', *Contemporary Accounting Research,* **23**(3), 629–654.

Kinney, William R. (2005), 'Twenty-five years of audit deregulation and re-regulation: What does it mean for 2005 and beyond?', *Auditing: Journal of Practice and Theory,* **24**, 89–109.

Kirkpatrick, Grant (2009), 'The Corporate Governance Lessons from the Financial Crisis', *OECD Steering group on corporate governance,* 2009 (1).

Knechel, W.R. (2001), *Auditing, Assurance & Risk,* Cincinnati, Ohio: South-Western College Publishing.

Krishnan, Jagan, Dasaratha Rama and Yinghong Zhang (2008), 'Costs to comply with SOX Section 404', *Auditing: Journal of Practice and Theory,* **27** (1), 169–186.

Laux, Christian and Cristian Leuz (2009), 'The crisis of fair-value accounting: Making sense of the recent debate', *Accounting, Organizations and Society,* **34** (6–7), 826–834.

Leeson, Nick (1996), *Rogue Trader,* London: Sphere.

Limperg Jr, Théodore (1932), 'De functie van de accountant en de leer van het gewekte vertrouwen', in: *Vijftig jaar MAB inhoudende een aantal bijdragen gedurende deze jaren verschenen in het Maandblad voor accountancy en bedrijfshuishoudkunde,* Purmerend: Muusses, 222–251.

Macpa (2008), 'FASB, IASB hope to complete convergence by 2011', *CPA Resources,* available at http://www.macpa.org/Content/24446.aspx (accessed 14 December 2009).

Makridakis, Spyros and Michele Hibon (2000), 'The M3-Competition: results, conclusions and implications', *International Journal of Forecasting,* **16** (4), 451–476.

Marrisson, Christopher I. (2002), *The Fundamentals of Risk Measurement,* New York: McGraw-Hill.

Mayer, Roger C. and Mark B. Gavin (2005), 'Trust in management and perform-ance: Who minds the shop while the employees watch the boss?', *Academy of Management Journal,* **48** (5), 874–888.

Mikes, Anette (2009), 'Risk management and calculative cultures', *Management Accounting Research,* **20** (1), 18–40.

Mulder, Leatitia B., Eic van Dijk, David de Cremer and Henk A.M. Wilke (2006), 'Undermining trust and cooperation: The paradox of sanctioning systems in social dilemmas', *Journal of Experimental Social Psychology,* **42** (2), 147–162.

Paape, Leen (2008), 'In Control' verklaringen: gebakken lucht of een te koesteren fenomeen?', inaugural reading of 25 June 2008 at Nyenrode University, availa-ble at: http://www.nyenrode.nl/facultyandresearch/Documents/Lectures/paape. pdf (accessed 14 December 2009).

Perignon, Christophe and Daniël R. Smith (2009), 'The Level and Quality of Value-at-Risk Disclosure by Commercial Banks', available at http://papers.ssrn. com/sol3/papers.cfm?abstract_id=952595 (accessed 14 December 2009).

Pheijffer, Marcel (2009), 'Creative compliance: een voorbeeld', available at http://www.accountant.nl/Accountant/Weblogs/Marcel+Pheijffer/Creative +compliance+een+voorbeeld (accessed 14 December 2009).

Power, Michael (1997), *The Audit Society – Rituals of Verification*, Oxford: Oxford University Press.

Rappaport, Alfred (1986), *Creating Shareholder Value the New Standard for Business Performance,* New York: The Free Press.

Rebonato, Ricardo (2007), *Plight of the Fortune Tellers*, Princeton: Princeton University Press.

Robinson, Dahlia (2008), 'Auditor independence and auditor-provided tax service: Evidence from going-concern audit opinions prior to bankruptcy filings', *Auditing: Journal of Practice and Theory,* **27** (2), 31–4.

Romano, Roberta (2005), 'Quack corporate governance', *Regulation,* **28** (4), 36–44.

Ruiz-Barbadillo, Emilliano, Nieves Gómez-Aguilar and Nieves Carrera (2009), 'Does mandatory audit firm rotation enhance auditor independence? Evidence from Spain', *Auditing: Journal of Practice and Theory*, **28** (1), 113–135.

Ryan, Stephen G. (2008), 'Accounting in and for the Subprime Crisis', *Accounting Review,* **83**, 1605–1638,

Ryan, Stephen G. (2009), 'Fair value accounting: policy issues raised by the credit crunch', *Financial Markets, Institutions & Instruments,* **18** (2), 163–164.

Schipper, Katherine (2003), 'Principles-based accounting standards', *Accounting Horizons,* **17** (1), 61–72.

Shapiro, Brian and Diane Matson (2008), 'Strategies of resistance to internal control regulation', *Accounting, Organizations and Society,* **33** (2–3), 199–228.

Sommer, Jeff (2007), 'Mortgage Crisis Drives Stocks Down Sharply', *New York Times,* available at http://www.nytimes.com/2007/06/24/busin ess/yourmoney/24data.html?_r=2&scp=1&sq=suprime%20mortgages&st=cse (accessed 14 December 2009).

Starreveld, R.W. (1962), *Leer van de administratieve organisatie – deel 1 algemene grondslagen,* Alphen aan den Rijn: N. Samsom.

Stewart, G.B. (1991), *The Quest for Value,* New York: Harper Business.

Taleb, Nassim N. (2007), *The Black Swan*, New York: Random House.

Tavakoli, Janet M. (2003), *Collaterized Debt Obligations & Structured Finance – New Developments in Cash & Synthetic Securitization*, New York: John Wiley & Sons.

Tribunella, Heidi (2009), 'Twenty questions on international financial reporting standards', *CPA Journal,* **79** (3), 32–37.

United States General Accounting Office (1989), *Bank failures: independent audits needed to strengthen internal control and bank management: report to the Congress,* Washington D.C.: The Office.

Vaassen, Eddy H.J. (2002), *Accounting Information Systems: A Managerial Approach,* Chichester: John Wiley & Sons.

Ven, Arco C.N. van de (2008), 'Administratieve Organisatie; praktisch relevant maar ook wetenschappelijk interessant?' inaugural reading of 5 November 2008 at Tilburg University, available at: http://www.accountant.nl/Sites/ Files/0000026600_Oratie_Arco_van_de_Ven.pdf (accessed 14 December 2009).

Véron, Nicolas (2008), 'Fair value accounting is the wrong scapegoat for the crisis', *Accounting in Europe,* **5** (2), 63–69.

Vries, Johan de (1985), *Geschiedenis der Accountancy in Nederland. Aanvang en Ontplooing, 1895–1935,* Assen: Van Gorcum.

Wyckoff, John (2009), 'Commentary: Madoff scandal teaches valuable lesson', *Daily Journal of Commerce,* available at http://www.allbusiness.com/banking-finance/financial-markets-investing-investment/11807197-1.html (accessed 14 December 2009).

Zhang, Ivy X. (2007), 'Economic consequences of the Sarbanes-Oxley Act of 2002', *Journal of Accounting and Economics*, **44** (1–2), 74–115.

CODES AND GUIDELINES

Committee of Sponsoring Organizations of the Treadway Commission (COSO) (1992), *Internal Control – Integrated Framework,* New York: AICPA Inc., (COSO I Report).

Committee of Sponsoring Organizations of the Treadway Commission (COSO) (2004), *Enterprise Risk Management – Integrated Framework,* Executive Summary, New York: AICPA Inc., (COSO II Report).

ING Group (2008), 'Annual report 2008', available at: http://annualreports.ing.com/2008/downloads/372261_EN_ING_2008AnnualReport.pdf (accessed 14 December 2009).

Public Company Accounting Oversight Board (2007), 'An Audit of Internal Control over Financial Reporting that is Integrated with an Audit of Financial Statements', Washington D.C.: PCAOB (AS5).

Public Company Accounting Oversight Board release no. 2008–03 (2008), SEC Filing Form 19b-4, concerning Rulemaking Docket 017: Ethics and Independence Rules Concerning Independence, Tax Services and Contingent Fees, Washington D.C.: PCAOB (PCAOB release no. 2008–03).

United States Securities and Exchange Commission (2003), 'Study Pursuant to Section 108(d) of the Sarbanes-Oxley Act of 2002 on the Adoption by the United States Financial Reporting System of a Principles-Based Accounting System', SEC, available at http://www.sec.gov/news/studies/principlesbased-stand.htm (accessed 14 December 2009) (SEC 2003).

3. Risk management from a business law perspective

Marijn van Daelen

3.1 INTRODUCTION

In recent years lawmakers have emphasized the importance of risk management in restoring public confidence following the corporate collapses and frauds at the beginning of this millennium and the more recent financial scandals (see Section 3.3). A short historical overview may deepen understanding of the current corporate legal framework of risk management. Section 3.2 will pave the way by describing the development of risk management over time from a business law perspective, as managing risks is part of the wider task of governing the corporation. The current legal risk management framework is still developing. Some issues that may prove significant for future revision of the legal framework are discussed in Section 3.4.

3.2 HISTORICAL DEVELOPMENT OF INTERNAL CONTROL AND RISK MANAGEMENT PROVISIONS

This section provides a brief historical overview of the development of internal control and risk management provisions from a corporate governance perspective. It starts with the development of the company as a separate legal person and reduced risks for shareholders who are protected by limited liability. It then describes the separation of ownership and control and the legal responses to reduce information asymmetry and mitigate poor governance. It also looks at how the responsibility and liability of company directors for the proper performance of the duties assigned to them came to more clearly include (in the course of the 20th century) maintaining a system of internal controls and disclosing the company's risks.

3.2.1 Pre-20th Century Developments: Starting at 1600

Corporate governance as a controversy has a long history; it already faced what is arguably the precursor of the Dutch publicly held company (*Naamloze Vennootschap*, NV), the Dutch East India Company (*Vereenigde Oost-Indische Compagnie*, VOC).[1] Established in 1602, this trading company was the first multinational corporation in the world.[2] The licence granted by the States General gave the VOC a monopoly over the Asian trade and quasi-governmental powers. The company had participants (*participanten*), the non-managing partners, and directors (*bewindhebbers*), the managing partners. The non-managing partners raised the start-up capital of the VOC.[3] Traditionally, non-managing partners provided the capital required for one voyage only and the enterprise was liquidated after its conclusion. Innovatively, the VOC was set up to secure a long-term involvement of ten years, which was extended several times later on, turning the capital into fixed capital. From a company law perspective, the main feature of the VOC was that risk capital was raised among unknown investors by the non-managing partners. These investors were not linked to the company as *persons* but only with their *capital*, which is why it has been said that the VOC is the forerunner of the public company. Again, traditionally all partners were subject to unlimited liability for the company's obligations. At the VOC, however, the company itself, instead of its partners, was liable for the obligations. The liability of the participants was limited to the amount they agreed to pay in buying shares. In this way, the VOC participants became what would nowadays be called investors. The shift from unlimited to limited liability reduced the risks of the non-managing partners. The issued shares became tradable at the Amsterdam stock market, which has been claimed to be the first stock exchange in the world.[4] With hundreds of ships and over 20000 employees in the Netherlands and Asia, the directors' refusal to account for themselves and

---

[1]   See for a discussion of this topic Den Heijer 2005, pp. 216ff.

[2]   Although the English East India Company was also a joint stock company (which received its charter in 1600), the VOC was most likely to have been the first company in the world that issued shares.

[3]   The non-managing partners came from six VOC Chambers in port cities: Amsterdam, Delft, Enkhuizen, Hoorn, Middelburg and Rotterdam. These cities were represented in a board of directors, known as the Gentlemen Seventeen (*De Heeren XVII*). See with regard to the raised capital Ricklefs 1991, p. 27; Den Heijer 2005, p. 61.

[4]   See, e.g., Raaijmakers 2006, pp. 306–307. Shares were initially traded on the Damrak, but in 1607 the city council had a building designed that eventually opened in 1611.

the company's lack of an integrated bookkeeping system[5] clearly show that *management* and corporate governance, especially internal control and risk management, had some way to go yet.[6]

Nonetheless, in Europe, the next years were characterized by colonial expansion and the surge of international trade and stock exchanges. In England, for example, the transferability of shares was commonplace by the end of the 17th century and over 150 companies had their shares publicly traded at London's *Exchange Alley*.[7] The fall of the securities market in 1720 and the corporate failures of the South Sea Company and the Mississippi Company drew public attention to the market. In 1721 the British Parliament responded by enacting the Bubble Act in order to suppress fraud. This Act prohibited the sale of stock in unchartered companies or companies that exceeded the scope of their charters. This Act was repealed in 1825 during the next major stock market decline.[8] The UK Companies Act of 1844[9] established a register which enabled joint stock companies to incorporate by registration instead of by royal charter. This Act was amended in 1847 and replaced by the Joint Stock Companies Act of 1856,[10] which revised the old system of registration into the system which, despite several revisions, remains the foundation of the current known UK company law. The 1856 Act together with the Limited Liability Act of 1855[11] enables the incorporation of the company as a separate legal person with shareholders protected by limited liability.[12] To increase public confidence, the 1856 Act included Table B, the first prescribed format of Articles of Association.[13] Table B contained regulations for managing the company, such as the powers of directors, accounts and audit. Although directors were responsible for keeping true

---

[5]   See De Vries & Van der Woude 2005, pp. 450ff; Gaastra 2002, pp. 29ff.

[6]   See Frentrop 2002; Den Heijer 2005, p. 70.

[7]   Years later, in 1801, the London Stock Exchange (LSE) was founded.

[8]   Banner 2002, pp. 20–80; See clause 18 of the Bubble Act (6 Geo. I, c. 18). For more on this subject, see Harris 1994, pp. 610–627.

[9]   7 & 8 Vict. c.110.

[10]   19 & 20 Vict. c.47.

[11]   18 & 19 Vict. c.133.

[12]   See the UK company law landmark case *Salomon v. Salomon & Co Ltd* (1897) AC 22, in which the House of Lords confirmed the separate legal personality of companies. The House noted that '[t]he company is at law a different person altogether from the [shareholders]' and 'after incorporation [. . .] the company is not in law the agent of the [shareholders] or trustee for them. Nor are the [shareholders], as members, liable in any shape or form [. . .].'

[13]   In 1862, the Memorandum was moved into the body of the Act and the Articles of Association became Table A.

accounts and although disclosure of certain information was required, no provisions that dealt with internal control or risk management were included.[14]

In the US too, companies and stock markets started to develop. For example, in 1792, the Buttonwood Agreement effectively created the New York Stock Exchange (NYSE); twenty-four stockbrokers and merchants agreed to trade securities on a commission basis. In the US, incorporation had originally only been possible through a charter granted by the State and the state legislatures had done so by huge numbers. Even incorporation with limited liability had occasionally been granted.[15] New York passed both the first Incorporation Act in 1811 and the first Limited Partnership Act in 1822. The New Jersey Incorporation Act of 1875 was amended in 1889 and followed by the New Jersey Holding Company Act 1891. This Holding Company Act was revised in 1896 by removing most restrictions and limitations, which made New Jersey the first state to adopt more flexible and permissive statutory provisions for the purpose of attracting corporations. Delaware followed in 1899 with the Delaware Corporation Act – largely a copy of the liberal New Jersey laws – and soon became the most preferred state of incorporation.[16]

3.2.2 Industrial Growth and the Need for Transparency in the 20th Century

The European and American creation in the 17th and 18th centuries of financial markets generated a new legal and financial environment, which set the scene for industrial growth. During the Industrial Revolution of the late 19th and early 20th centuries, risk management theories received

---

[14] See, e.g., Section 46: 'The business of the company shall be managed by the directors [. . .]'; Section 57: 'The directors may delegate any of their powers to committees [. . .]'; Section 69: 'The directors shall cause true accounts to be kept [. . .]'; Section 70: Once at the least in every year the directors shall lay before the company in general meeting a statement of the income and expenditure for the past year [. . .]'; Section 74: 'The accounts of the company shall be examined and the correctness of the balance sheet ascertained by one or more auditor or auditors [. . .]'; Section 84: 'The auditors shall make a report to the shareholders upon the balance sheet and accounts, and in every such report they shall state whether, in their opinion, the balance sheet is a full and fair balance sheet [. . .] and properly drawn up so as to exhibit a true and correct view of the state of the company's affairs [. . .]'.

[15] Talbot 2007, pp. 5ff.

[16] Moye 2004, p. 159; Talbot 2007, pp. 14ff. New Jersey lost its attraction due to a series of anti-trust laws.

more attention in literature. In 1911, Taylor, an American mechanical engineer, advocated a new system of scientific management and introduced the concept of breaking a complex task down into a sequence of simple and small subtasks the performance of which could be optimized. His approach to improving industrial efficiency included enforced standardization of methods and triggered quality control.[17] In 1916, Fayol described five functions of management: planning, organizing, commanding, coordinating and controlling.[18] Control meant that a manager had to verify whether all activities happened in accordance with the established plans, orders, principles, rules and procedures. A few years later, in 1921, Knight pointed out the distinction between risk and uncertainty. He argued that a risk can be measured and is therefore not an uncertainty, while an uncertainty can be characterized as being non-quantifiable.[19]

3.2.3   The US in the 20th Century

The steep industrial growth of the late 19th and early 20th centuries ended with the American stock market crash of October 1929 and the worldwide Great Depression. Around that time, Berle and Means described the problem of separated ownership and control: the managers decide how a corporation's capital or resources are to be spent although it is not they but the shareholders who own that capital. They argued that the structure of American corporate law enforced the separation of ownership and control, and that[20]

> ... where the bulk of the profits of enterprise are scheduled to go to owners who are individuals other than those in control, the interests of the latter are as likely as not to be at variance with those of ownership and that the controlling group is in a position to serve its own interests.

According to Berle and Means, the separation implies shortfalls of competence and responsibility. Problems that are still shaping company law today.

Meanwhile, in response to the Great Depression and in order to reduce the information asymmetry – shareholders having less up-to-date company information than managers – Congress enacted two securities Acts: the

---

[17]   See Taylor 1911, Chapter II.
[18]   See Fayol [1916] 1949.
[19]   Knight 1921, I.I.26. See also Keynes 1921. Others followed: Ramsey 1931; Savage 1954. See for an analysis of the distinction between risk, uncertainty and ignorance Zeckhauser 1991, pp. 16ff.
[20]   Berle & Means 1932, p. 116.

Securities Act of 1933,[21] the first major federal legislation to regulate the offer and sale of securities, and the Securities Exchange Act of 1934,[22] which imposes regulation upon the financial markets and its participants. The main market regulatory approaches of the 1933 Act are to: (1) require issuers making a public offer to file disclosure documents providing material information to investors; (2) provide a public offering procedure; and (3) impose heightened antifraud liability. The main objectives of the 1934 Act are to ensure the maintenance of fair and honest markets in securities transactions by regulating these transactions, requiring appropriate reports and removing impediments to and perfecting the mechanisms of a national market system for securities.[23] The Securities and Exchange Commission (SEC) was established pursuant to the 1934 Act.[24] The 1933 Act regulates the primary market – and thus the original issues – and requires such one-time disclosure documents as the registration statement and the prospectus.[25] The 1934 Act regulates the secondary trading of securities and aims at the continuous disclosure of information. These security laws therefore protect investors primarily through disclosure. Together, the 1933 Act, requiring issuers to publicly disclose significant information about the company and about the securities, and the 1934 Act, requiring mandatory corporate reporting and independent audits, laid the foundations of American federal securities law.

For the historical development of internal control and risk management in law it is important that, as the effects of the Great Depression were felt, the early Regulation S-X Rule 2–02(b) of the 1933 Act required that – as was the generally recognized practice of independent accountants – '[i]n determining the scope of the audit necessary, appropriate consideration shall be given to the adequacy of the system of internal check and internal control. Due weight may be given to an internal system of audit regularly maintained by means of auditors employed on the registrant's own staff'.[26] Although this was the first regulatory recognition of the importance of internal control, external auditors were allowed to rely on the system of internal control implemented by the corporation if they considered that

---

[21]   48 Stat. 74, enacted 27 May 1933, codified at 15 U.S.C. § 77a et seq.

[22]   48 Stat. 881, enacted 6 June 1934, codified at 15 U.S.C. § 78a et seq.

[23]   Section 2 of the Securities Exchange Act of 1934.

[24]   Section 4 of the Securities Exchange Act of 1934. Prior to the establishment of the SEC, securities were registered with the Federal Trade Commission.

[25]   For these two mandatory disclosure documents see Section 7 which requires issuers to file the registration statement with the SEC and Section 10 which requires issuers to draw up a prospectus in order to inform investors.

[26]   Fernald 1943, p. 228.

system to be appropriate. The system only served the audit and had a limited scope.[27] In its final report of 1940, the SEC recommended a more thorough assessment of the internal control system.[28]

Around that time, Coase suggested that transactions between market participants are associated with substantial costs, which deviated from the then common economic assumption that informed markets bring together buyers and sellers at an equilibrium price without additional costs. According to Coase, more complex transactions could be accomplished more efficiently and thus more cheaply within firms than on markets.[29] The internal organization and functioning of firms has received more attention from the 1970s onwards.[30] Jensen and Meckling describe the firm as a complex of contracts between the owners of the firm. In the relationship between the agent and the principal the agent has controlling power over some aspects of the principal's investment. An agency problem arises from the different incentives of the agent and the principal.[31] As a result of this conflict of interests, companies can incur costs, such as monitoring costs, bonding costs and residual costs.[32] So, while a corporation reduces the transactions costs of complex economic contracts, it can create agency problems and agency costs. Corporate law aims to reduce these problems and costs.[33]

As mentioned above, from the 1970s onwards, the internal organization and functioning of firms received growing attention from lawmakers. This is also reflected in the development of internal control. Internal control only served the audit and had a limited scope under the 1933 Act. However, as Chapter 2 of this book (Section 2.1.6) shows, in the 1970s the focus shifted to the assessment and attestation of the internal control system by an independent auditor. The American regulatory approach to internal control also changed in 1977 after a number of corporate scandals related to the bribery of foreign officials in the mid-1970s. In accordance with the 1977 Foreign Corrupt Practices Act (FCPA), the SEC requires reporting companies to keep books, records and accounts and to maintain a system of internal accounting controls in order to control management

---

[27] Van Daelen & Van der Elst 2009, p. 84.
[28] See for more information Chapter 2 of this book (Section 2.1.3).
[29] Coase 1937, pp. 386–405.
[30] Allen, Kraakman & Subramanian 2007, p. 9.
[31] See for the conflicting interests of managers and shareholders Kraakman et al. 2004, p. 22.
[32] Jensen & Meckling 1976, pp. 305–360. See p. 5 for a definition of the agency relationship.
[33] Allen, Kraakman & Subramanian 2007, p. 13.

activities.[34] Although companies are allowed to choose the framework they consider suitable to comply with the FCPA requirements, corporate violators may face criminal and civil liability claims for non-compliance. Penalties are subject to the Sentencing Commission's guidelines that became effective in 1991.[35]

The importance of internal control – especially the role of the auditor, management and the board for internal control – was highlighted by the reports of the Cohen Commission and the Minahan Committee. Both were established by the American Institute of Certified Public Accountants (AICPA) that originated from 1887 and issued several Statements on Auditing Standards (SAS), which formed the basis of the external auditor's review and evaluation of financial statements.[36] The Cohen Commission on Auditor's Responsibilities was established in 1974 to study the external auditor's responsibility for reporting on internal controls. Its 1978 report recommended that corporate management should be required to present a statement on the condition of its company's internal controls to accompany the financial statements, and concluded that it was the responsibility of auditors to audit this information and express an opinion about it. On the basis of, among other things, this recommendation the SEC proposed, but later withdrew, rules for mandatory management reports on an entity's internal accounting control system.[37] The Minahan Committee was formed in 1977 to provide guidance on internal control for, among others, management and boards of directors. In its 1979 report the committee writes that internal accounting control involves 'the reliability of financial statements and [. . .] the broad internal control objectives of authorization, accounting, and asset safeguarding and, further, that accounting controls should extend to all external reports of historical financial information.'[38]

---

[34] 15 U.S.C. Section 78m (b) (2) (B).

[35] Van Daelen & Van der Elst 2009, pp. 84ff for the 1996 Caremark decision, which provides insight into the management of appropriate internal control systems.

[36] See, e.g., SAS No. 30 of 1980 (Reporting on Internal Accounting Control), SAS No. 55 of 1988 (Consideration of Internal Control in a Financial Statement Audit) and SAS No. 78 of 1995 (Consideration of Internal Control Structure in a Financial Statement Audit: An Amendment to SAS No. 55).

[37] Moeller 2005, p. 80.

[38] Minahan Report 1979, p. 11. See Heier, Dugan & Sayers 2004, p. 7, where they report that one of the members argued that the scope of internal control in the report was too heavily influenced by the existing auditing literature and that the scope and objectives of internal accounting control should have been significantly expanded. For a further discussion of the 1978 Cohen Report and the 1979 Minahan Report, see Moeller 2005, pp. 79ff.

In addition to focusing increasingly on internal controls and controlling management activities, lawmakers started to emphasize the importance of adequate disclosure of management's risk assessment. In 1982, Item 303 on Management's Discussion and Analysis of Financial Condition and Results of Operations (MD&A) was added to Regulation S-K. It requires that '[t]he discussion and analysis shall focus specifically on material events and uncertainties known to management that would cause reported financial information not to be necessarily indicative of future operating results or of future financial condition'.[39] In other words, this reporting requirement compels management to assess all risks and threats companies may encounter and to address the issues in a reliable management discussion and analysis statement.[40] This shift to management's risk assessment and disclosure also shows in the 1987 report of the Treadway Commission. This commission was formed in 1985 in response to the above-mentioned 1977 FCPA. Its report recommended as follows:[41]

> To set the right tone, top management must identify and assess the factors that could lead to fraudulent financial reporting; all public companies should maintain internal controls that provide reasonable assurance that fraudulent financial reporting will be prevented or subject to early detection – this is a broader concept than internal accounting controls – and all public companies should develop and enforce effective, written codes of corporate conduct. As a part of its ongoing assessment of the effectiveness of internal controls, a company's audit committee should annually review the program that management establishes to monitor compliance with the code. The Commission also recommends that its sponsoring organizations cooperate in developing additional, integrated guidance on internal controls.

Furthermore, the commission recommended that audit committees of the board of directors should exercise vigilant and informed oversight of the financial reporting process, including the company's internal controls. It also recommended a management report in which management acknowledges that it takes responsibility for the company's financial reporting process and in which management's opinion on the effectiveness of the company's internal controls is included.[42] As a result of this 1987 report, the Committee of Sponsoring Organizations of the Treadway Commission (COSO) was formed. In 1992, this Committee issued its report 'Internal

---

[39]   See 17 CFR 229.303.a-3-ii and 'Instructions to paragraph 303(a)', under no. 3.

[40]   Van Daelen & Van der Elst 2009, p. 85.

[41]   Treadway Report 1987, p. 11.

[42]   Treadway Report 1987, p. 12. In addition, see the COSO report on fraud of 1999.

Control – Integrated Framework, the COSO I report'. This report was the basis for SAS No. 78, which revised the definition and description of internal control of SAS No. 55 in order to recognize the definition and description of the COSO I report. The COSO I report (and thus also SAS No. 78) defines internal control as a process consisting of five components – control environment, risk assessment, control activities, information and communication, and monitoring – designed to provide reasonable assurance regarding the achievement of objectives in three categories: (1) the effectiveness and efficiency of operations; (2) the reliability of financial reporting; and (3) compliance with applicable laws and regulations.[43] A more thorough discussion of the COSO I report can be found in Chapter 2 of this book (Section 2.1.6).

The upshot is that by the end of the 20th century internal control and risk management had entered American business law. However, these requirements covered only a few aspects of the internal control and risk management framework. The above-mentioned FCPA and Regulations S-X and S-K requirements focus on financial reporting. The difference is that the FCPA requires companies to maintain a system, while Regulation S-X requires external auditors to monitor the system. In addition, Regulation S-K requires management to report on material events and uncertainties – not to report on the system. Contrary to these requirements, the 20th century recommendations and guidelines started to point out the broader and more coherent scope of the internal control and risk management framework. For example, the 1978 Cohen Commission's report mentioned the responsibility of management and of the external auditor to report on the company's internal control system. The 1987 Treadway Commission's report focuses on a more coherent financial reporting system by recommending identifying and assessing relevant information and maintaining internal controls, as well as assessing the effectiveness of internal controls, monitoring the reporting process, and reporting on the internal controls. The 1992 COSO I report focuses on a broader scope of the system by pointing out that an integrated internal control framework includes not only financial reporting, but also the company's objectives relating to operations and compliance.

3.2.4   The EU in the 20th Century

The development of corporate law in the European Union (EU) starts with the establishment of a European common market. The 1957 Treaty

---

[43]   COSO I Report 1992; Heier, Dugan & Sayers 2004, p. 10. In addition, see the COSO report on internal controls of 1996.

of Rome was designed to encourage the creation of an integrated market by assuring the free movement of goods, services, people and capital. [44] In order to eliminate disparities among the laws of EU member states, harmonisation of national corporation laws was soon on the EU agenda and resulted in multiple EU corporate law directives. EU lawmakers started with fairly strict corporate law directives – including minimum capital requirements and disclosure rules – but later shifted towards more flexible corporate law directives granting states options with respect to compliance.[45] In the 20th century, EU legislators mainly focused on appropriate corporate disclosure rules, while requirements for management systems to endorse the reliability of reporting and internal control remained outside their scope.

3.2.5   The Netherlands in the 20th Century

The reaction to the Great Depression in the Netherlands was quite different from that in the USA in that, contrary to the USA, no noteworthy new company legislation was introduced.[46] The main revision of Dutch law did not occur until 1970 and 1971 and only as of 1976 did it include a major expansion of accounting law.[47] Previously there had only been one provision on the obligation of accounting.[48] This changed with the enactment of the 1971 Annual Accounts of Companies Act.[49] In general, Dutch corporate law was characterized by directors disclosing accounts and having to account for fulfilling their task as corporate directors. They were, and are, responsible for the proper performance of the duties assigned to

---

[44]   The signing countries were Belgium, France, Italy, Luxemburg, the Netherlands, and West Germany. See also the following EU documents: Treaty of Paris of 18 April 1951, Treaty of Rome of 25 March 1957, Treaty of Maastricht of 1 November 1993, Treaty of Amsterdam of 2 October 1997, Treaty of Nice of 26 February 2003 and the Treaty of Lisbon of 1 December 2009.

[45]   See for more information McCahery & Vermeulen 2008, pp. 56ff.

[46]   Raaijmakers 2006, p. 309.

[47]   As of 1976 the Dutch Civil Code (*Burgerlijk Wetboek*, BW) included Book 2, which regulates legal persons. See Act of 12 May 1960, *Staatsblad* (Bulletin of Acts and Decrees) 1960, 205 and Act of 2 June 1976, *Staatsblad* 1976, 395, entry into force 26 July 1976.

[48]   Former Section 42c *Wetboek van Koophandel* (Commercial Code, WvK). For the enactment of the Commercial Code, see Act of 23 March 1826, *Staatsblad* 1826, 18, entry into force 1 October 1838. Also in 1838, the civil law was first codified in the Dutch Civil Code (BW).

[49]   *Wet op de Jaarrekeningen van Ondernemingen*; see current Title 2.9 of the Civil Code, Section 360ff. See on this issue Raaijmakers 2006, pp. 314ff.

them.[50] Further developments of the mandatory corporate law framework were initiated by the implementation of EU directives in the 21st century, which shifted the focus to monitoring and reporting. In the 20th century the corporate governance debate gained attention with the Peters Committee issuing its Forty Recommendations in 1997. According to these recommendations, the board of directors must report the company's objectives, strategy, associated risks, and mechanisms used to control risks of a financial nature. Further, the report recommended that the board of directors should report to the supervisory board on the risks entailed in the policy and strategy and on the results of its assessment of the structure and functioning of the internal control systems. The committee acknowledged that internal control systems aim for reliable financial information, effective and efficient corporate processes and compliance with relevant laws and regulations. Even so, the committee stressed the board's responsibility to assess the systems intended to provide reasonable assurance of the reliability of the financial information. It also recommended that the annual report should contain the main items of the board of directors' report. The committee provided guidance as to the risks that could be referred to, such as the risks associated with currency developments, interest rates, economic growth, political risks, raw materials and the environment. The main point of the Peters Committee was that it considered the board of directors to be primarily responsible for effective systems of internal control.[51] It also recommended that the supervisory board annually review the company's risks and the board's assessment of the internal control system.[52] Unfortunately, the committee's report was not adequately received by most companies.

3.2.6 The UK in the 20th Century

In general, the main UK rules on mandatory disclosure are given by the Companies Act of 1985 and the Listing Rules. Section 221 of the 1985 Companies Act[53] stipulates the duty to keep accounting records: '[e]very

---

[50] Article 2:9 BW. This rule originates from Article 47c WvK, which in turn originates from Article 31 of the *Wet op de Coöperatieve Verenigingen* (Cooperative Associations Act) of 1925.

[51] Peters Report 1997, Recommendation 21, paragraph 4.2 (Objectives and Strategy) and paragraph 4.3 (Risk Control).

[52] Peters Report 1997, Recommendation 17.

[53] See for the amended Companies Act 1985 Regulations 2004: 2004 (S.I. 2004/2947), reg. 3. From 1856 until 1985 many UK Companies Acts were published, such as the Companies Acts of 1862, 1908, 1929, 1948 – amended in 1967, 1976, 1980 and 1981 – and 1985.

company shall keep accounting records which are sufficient to show and explain the company's transactions and are such as to disclose with reasonable accuracy, at any time, the financial position of the company at that time.'

Following the governance failures in the late 1980s and early 1990s,[54] the Cadbury Committee was set up in 1991 by the Financial Reporting Council, the London Stock Exchange, and the accountancy profession. Unlike the Dutch Peters report, the 1992 Cadbury report was widely accepted. It provides that the board of directors needs to maintain a system of internal control over the financial management of the company, including procedures to mitigate corporate governance risks and failures.[55] To ensure an effective system of internal control, directors should make a statement in the annual report and accounts on the effectiveness of their internal control system and the auditors should report on the directors' statement.[56] One of the main recommendations was that an audit committee should be established, comprising at least three non-executives. The commission further recommended establishing criteria for assessing the effectiveness and guidance of companies and auditors, with the accountancy profession taking the lead.[57] The basic role of corporate governance was first given by this report, which focused on the aspects of corporate governance specifically related to financial reporting, controls and accountability. The Cadbury committee asserted that companies with high corporate governance standards were more likely to gain the confidence of investors and that this would support the development of the businesses.[58] The London Stock Exchange acted on this report by introducing a requirement into the Listing Rules that demanded companies to include a statement of (non-)compliance with the provisions of the report in their annual report and accounts.[59]

The 1994 Rutteman report subsequently introduced disclosures in financial statements regarding systems of internal financial control. The report proposed guidelines that were eventually superseded by the 1999 Turnbull report. These guidelines were developed from the above-mentioned COSO

---

[54]   Due to a series of corporate collapses and scandals, e.g., Polly Peck, the 1991 collapse of the BCCI bank and the 1991 Robert Maxwell pension fund scandal.

[55]   Cadbury Report 1992, Recommendation 4.31. The report applied to listed companies reporting their accounts after 30 June 1993. See Arcot and Bruno 2006.

[56]   Cadbury Report 1992, Recommendation 4.32.

[57]   Cadbury Report 1992, Section 5.16.

[58]   Cadbury Report 1992, Section 1.6.

[59]   See also Cadbury Report 1992, Section 1.3.

I report. According to the Rutteman report, the internal control statement must be embedded in the corporate governance statement and should contain:[60]

(1) A declaration from the directors of a listed company that they are responsible for the company's system of internal control;
(2) A description of the internal control procedures that have been established by the directors, as well as an assessment of their effectiveness;
(3) A statement that such a system can provide only reasonable and not absolute assurance against material misstatement or loss; and
(4) Confirmation that the directors have reviewed the effectiveness of the internal control system.

Next, the Hampel Committee issued its final report in January 1998.[61] The Hampel report emphasized that the board should maintain a sound system of internal control to safeguard shareholders' investment and the company's assets. The Hampel report furthered internal control by arguing that this system not only covers financial controls but also operational and compliance controls, as well as risk management.[62] The Hampel Committee suggested combining its report with the Cadbury and Greenbury reports in a combined code to supplement the Listing Rules.[63]

Following the recommendations of the Hampel Committee, the London Stock Exchange issued the Combined Code on Corporate Governance in June 1998. The Turnbull Committee was set up in September 1998 to provide guidance on how to apply this 1998 Combined Code, especially the internal control provision. In 1999, the Turnbull Committee published its report, which sets out best practices on internal control and assists listed companies in applying principle D.2 and its associated provisions of the Combined Code. The board of directors is responsible for maintaining a sound system of internal control and must ensure that the system is effective in managing risks in a by-the-board-approved manner.[64] The board should therefore consider the following factors:[65]

---

[60] Rayton & Cheng 2004, pp. 29–30.
[61] The Hampel Committee was established in November 1995 on the initiative of the Chairman of the Financial Reporting Council (Sir Sydney Lipworth).
[62] Hampel Report 1998, Section D (Accountability and Audit) under II and subsection 2.20, p. 21.
[63] The 1995 Greenbury Report deals with the disclosure of the remuneration of the board in the annual report.
[64] Turnbull I Report 1999, Section 16.
[65] Turnbull I Report 1999, Section 17.

  – the nature and extent of the risks facing the company;
  – the extent and categories of risk which it regards as acceptable for the
    company to bear;
  – the likelihood of the risks concerned materialising;
  – the company's ability to reduce the incidence and impact on the business
    of risks that do materialise; and
  – the costs of operating particular controls relative to the benefit thereby
    obtained in managing the related risks.

According to the Turnbull report, management is responsible for implementing the board's policies on risk and control. Management should also provide the board with a balanced assessment of the significant risks and the effectiveness of the system of internal control in managing those risks.[66] The board itself should make a public statement on internal control and it should therefore undertake an annual assessment that should consider the changes in the nature and extent of significant risks, as well as the company's ability to respond to changes.

The above demonstrates that at EU level, risk management and internal control systems remained outside the legislative scope in the 20th century. Within EU member states, these issues gained attention but were handled differently. In the Netherlands only self-regulatory recommendations relating to internal control and risk management were issued. In the UK, internal control developed more vigorously. Unlike in the Netherlands, in the UK, corporate governance recommendations already gained more legal gravity in the 20th century due to the Listing Rules requiring a statement of compliance or non-compliance with the provisions of the Cadbury report. In addition, UK reports containing internal control recommendations were issued earlier than in the Netherlands and, in general, more reports and recommendations were issued on this subject. Nonetheless, in both countries the recommendations reflect the broader scope of the COSO I report by acknowledging that internal control not only covers financial controls but also operational and compliance controls. It is noteworthy that, in general, the corporate governance recommendations of the Dutch Peters Committee were not adequately received. The report did not succeed in increasing firm value by influencing governance practices. By contrast, the recommendations of the UK Cadbury Committee brought significant changes in governance practices as well as an increase in the average performance of firms. The different results of self-regulation in the Netherlands and the UK could to some extent result from the market forces that are required for changes to take place and the disparity of

---

[66]   Turnbull I Report 1999, Sections 18 and 30.

shareholder rights in these countries.[67] Strong shareholder rights are an indispensable condition for the proper functioning of the market for corporate control.

3.2.7   Overview of the Main Pre-21st Century Provisions

Table 3.1 summarizes the main 20th century provisions relating to internal control and risk management in the US, the Netherlands and the UK. It shows that internal control originally focused on financial reporting and the risk of fraud. By the end of the 20th century, this focus started to shift towards the broader concept of internal control (which includes financial, operational and compliance controls), largely due to the 1992 COSO I report. It also shows that the internal control provisions often included (or were accompanied by) risk disclosure requirements. At that time, risk management was seen as a component of internal control.

This historical foray provides some insight into the development of risk management. Crucial developments were the emergence of joint stock companies that were considered bodies with legal status and the shift from unlimited to limited liability of the investors for the companies' obligations. The investors were only liable for the amount they agreed to pay in buying shares; their risks were thus reduced to that amount. Directors are responsible for the proper performance of the duties assigned to them and are (only) liable for shortcomings in that respect. During the 20th century the duties of the directors began to include more clearly the maintenance of a system of internal controls. For years the US was the forerunner with requirements and recommendations that were mainly fraud-driven. Those provisions focused on reducing risks by requiring internal accounting controls and on reducing the risk of fraudulent financial reporting.[68] Years later, Europe started to follow with the UK laying down much more detailed and self-regulatory provisions to control the risks that companies face. At first, the UK recommendations were also fraud-driven, but soon the focus of the recommendations started to shift towards the broader internal control concept.[69] Although progress was made in the UK, this was not immediately the case in the rest of Europe. For example, in the Netherlands it took a few more years before a self-regulatory code stated that it is the board of directors that is responsible

---

[67]   De Jong, DeJong, Mertens & Wasley 2001, pp. 1–4.
[68]   See, e.g., the 1977 FCPA and the 1987 Treadway Report.
[69]   See, e.g., the 1992 Cadbury Report and the 1998 Hampel Report.

for effective systems of internal control.[70] The upshot is that – though with major differences in regulations – by the end of the 20th century the USA and most of Europe were aware of the concept of internal control to reduce the risks a company faces.

Table 3.1   Overview of the main pre-21st century internal control and risk management provisions

Date	Document	Requiring or recommending:
United States		
1933	Securities Act of 1933	A system of internal check and internal control for audit purposes.
1977	FCPA	Maintain a system of internal accounting controls in order to control management activities.
1978	Cohen Report	Corporate management should present a statement on the condition of the company's internal controls.
1979	Minahan Report	Internal accounting control involves the reliability of financial statements, and the broad internal control objectives and accounting controls should extend to all external reports of historical financial information.
1982	Item 303 on MD&A	Management's discussion and analysis must focus specifically on material events and uncertainties known to management that would cause reported financial information not to be necessarily indicative of future operating results or of future financial condition.
1987	Treadway Report	Top management must identify and assess the factors that could lead to fraudulent financial reporting, issue a management report in which management acknowledges that it takes responsibility for the company's financial reporting process including management's opinion on the effectiveness of the company's internal controls, and develop and enforce effective, written codes of corporate conduct. The audit committee should assess the effectiveness of internal controls and annually review the programme that management establishes to monitor compliance with the code.
1992	COSO I Report	Internal control is a process consisting of five components – control environment, risk assessment, control activities, information and communication, and monitoring – designed to provide reasonable assurance regarding the achievement of objectives in

---

[70] See the 1997 Peters Report.

Table 3.1 (continued)

Date	Document	Requiring or recommending:
		three categories: (1) the effectiveness and efficiency of operations, (2) the reliability of financial reporting and (3) compliance with applicable laws and regulations.
The Netherlands		
1997	Peters Report	The board of directors must report the risks associated with the company's objectives and strategy, and report the mechanisms used to control risks of a financial nature. The annual report should include the main items of the directors' report. The board should report to the supervisory board on the risks and the results of its assessment of the structure and functioning of the internal control systems. The board is primarily responsible for effective systems of internal control. The supervisory board has to annually review the company's risks and the board's assessment of the internal control system.
United Kingdom		
1992	Cadbury Report	The directors need to maintain a system of internal control over the financial management of the company including procedures designed to minimize the risk of fraud. The directors should make a statement in the annual report and accounts on the effectiveness of their internal control system and the auditors should report on the directors' statement. An audit committee of at least three non-executives should be established. In establishing criteria for assessing the effectiveness and guidance of companies and auditors, the accountancy profession should take the lead.
1994	Rutteman Report	An internal control statement must be embedded in the corporate governance statement, containing a declaration from the directors that they are responsible for the company's internal control system, a description of the internal control procedures and an assessment of their effectiveness, a statement that the system can provide only reasonable and not absolute assurance against material misstatement or loss, and confirmation that the directors have reviewed the effectiveness of the internal control system.
1998	Hampel Report	The board should maintain a sound system of internal control; this system not only covers financial controls but also operational and compliance controls, and risk management.

Table 3.1 (continued)

Date	Document	Requiring or recommending:
1998	Combined Code	The board should maintain a sound system of internal control to safeguard shareholders' investment and the company's assets.
1999	Turnbull Report	The board of directors is responsible for maintaining a sound system of internal control and must ensure that the system is effective in managing risks in a by-the-board-approved manner. The board should consider the nature and extent of the risks facing the company, the extent and categories of risk which it regards as acceptable for the company to bear, the likelihood of the risks concerned materialising, the company's ability to reduce the incidence and impact on the business of risks that do materialize, and the costs of operating particular controls relative to the benefit thereby obtained in managing the related risks. It is the role of management to implement board policies on risk and control and to identify and evaluate the risks. Management should provide the board with a balanced assessment of the significant risks and the effectiveness of the system of internal control in managing those risks. The board should make a public statement on internal control and annually assess changes in the nature and extent of significant risks and the company's ability to respond to changes.

3.3 LEGAL RISK MANAGEMENT ENVIRONMENT OF THE 21ST CENTURY

Regulations on internal control and corporate risk management accumulated after the corporate failures and fraud cases in 2000–2003 and associated stock market problems. The internal control provisions that had been developed in the 20th century were unable to prevent these frauds and failures. In order to restore public confidence, lawmakers turned to firmer internal control provisions and soon shifted their focus from internal control towards internal control and risk management provisions. The more recent financial crisis underpins the crucial role of the risk management profession. In order to provide some insight into the international differences in the legal risk management environment that have arisen, this section will deal with the regulatory risk management framework of the USA and at EU level. The discussion will also include two EU member states, the UK and the Netherlands, in order to address some of the differences within the EU.

3.3.1   The US in the 21st Century

Although each US state has its own system of business law, two documents are considered fundamental. These are the Delaware General Corporation Law (DGCL), because approximately half of US corporations have been incorporated under this law, and the Model Business Corporation Act (MBCA), because it has been adopted by many US states.[71] Besides state corporate law, publicly traded corporations are subjected to federal securities laws, such as the Securities Act of 1933 and Securities Exchange Act of 1934 discussed above and the more recent Sarbanes-Oxley Act of 2002 (SOX).[72]

In response to the failures of Enron, WorldCom and Arthur Andersen, US Congress passed SOX, a major shift in securities and corporate regulation. SOX was intended to restore faith and trust in the reliability of the financial information provided by companies. SOX does not only contain disclosure requirements, but also substantive corporate governance mandates.[73] It requires a number of reforms to enhance internal control and financial disclosures, and to protect against fraud. SOX also created the Public Company Accounting Oversight Board (PCAOB) to monitor the activities of the auditing profession. Ever since the corporate failures manifested themselves, it has been argued that new regulation such as

---

[71]   Twenty-nine states have adopted (most parts of) the Act as their general corporation statute, namely: Alabama, Arizona, Arkansas, Connecticut, Florida, Georgia, Hawaii, Idaho, Indiana, Iowa, Kentucky, Maine, Massachusetts, Mississippi, Montana, Nebraska, New Hampshire, North Carolina, Oregon, Rhode Island, South Carolina, Tennessee, Utah, Vermont, Virginia, Washington, West Virginia, Wisconsin, and Wyoming. Other jurisdictions have statutes based on the 1969 version of the Act, such as Alaska, the District of Columbia, New Mexico, and South Dakota, or have only adopted selected provisions of the Act.

[72]   Officially titled 'An Act to Protect Investors by Improving the Accuracy and Reliability of Corporate Disclosures made Pursuant to the Securities Laws and for other Purposes'. See also the Investment Company Act of 1940. Although they are highly important, this chapter will not discuss the DGCL and MBCA. For information on the risk management and internal control provisions of these and more US documents and case law, as well as a more thorough analysis of the SOX provisions, see Van Daelen & Van der Elst 2009, pp. 86–87.

[73]   Romano 2005, p. 1.

SOX might not succeed in regulating frauds or that its effectiveness would be limited, as the frauds that preceded this legal response occurred despite several levels of monitoring in place at the time.[74]

One of the main SOX sections is Section 404, which compels companies to establish and maintain an adequate internal control structure and procedures for financial reporting, for which management is responsible. It also requires an evaluation of the effectiveness of the internal control structure and procedures for financial reporting. Additionally, the auditor has a duty to check and certify the management effectiveness reports. Section 302 requires the CEO and CFO – thus not management as Section 404 does – to certify the fairness of the financial statements and information as well as their responsibility for establishing and maintaining internal controls in the annual or quarterly report. The CEO and CFO also have to present their conclusions – that is, not the total evaluation of Section 404 – about the effectiveness of their internal controls based on their evaluation. Moreover, the CEO and the CFO must disclose to the auditors and the audit committee significant deficiencies and material weaknesses in the design or operation of internal control over financial reporting and any fraud that involves management or employees who significantly participate in the internal control procedures for financial reporting.[75] Following Section 906, the CEO and CFO must provide the market with a certification that the periodic report fairly presents the issuer's financial condition and results of operations, with non-compliance leading to severe criminal penalties.

According to Section 205 (a), the purpose of the audit committee is to oversee the accounting and financial reporting processes and audits of the financial statements of the company. Section 301 requires that audit committees establish procedures for, among other things, the receipt, retention and treatment of complaints regarding accounting, internal accounting controls or auditing matters. In combination with Section 406, which requires the board to adopt a code of ethical conduct, it obliges companies to develop more formal mechanisms to report on and to handle internal shortcomings in business practice.

While the Securities Act of 1933 originally required the audit to include

---

[74] Ribstein 2002, p. 5. In addition, see Lawrence Cunningham 2002, noting at pp. 16–17 that '[h]istory offers no reason to expect that new rules will prevent a repeat of accounting scandals even of this large size or frequency'. See: Bratton 2002, noting at p. 13 that '[t]he costs of any significant new regulation can outweigh the compliance yield, particularly in a system committed to open a wide field for entrepreneurial risk taking.'

[75] See Sections 404 a (1) and (2) and 302 a (3), (4), and (5) SOX.

an appropriate consideration of the adequacy of the system of internal check and internal control, it now requires that[76]

> [e]very registered public accounting firm that issues or prepares an accountant's report [. . .] must clearly state the opinion of the accountant, either unqualified or adverse, as to whether the registrant maintained, in all material respects, effective internal control over financial reporting [. . .]. The attestation report on internal control over financial reporting shall [. . .] indicate that the accountant has audited the effectiveness of internal control over financial reporting.

SOX may well be the culmination of centuries of internal control evolution.[77] These substantive corporate governance mandates and disclosure requirements forced the SEC and the PCAOB to start a process of promulgating standards and reports to adopt rules in order to implement SOX.[78] Due to criticism – parts of SOX were considered overwhelmingly burdensome – the SEC proposed to soften the procedures of internal control and grant wider management discretion by allowing management to focus on the greatest risks.[79] It is noteworthy that although the SOX requirements stress the importance of internal control for financial reporting, other legislative measures, in particular the sentencing guidelines and the MBCA, have a wider scope. The sentencing guidelines provide relative assurance for investors and companies of what can be considered appropriate behaviour, and the MBCA, *inter alia*, provides the scope of the board's oversight responsibilities relating to the company's major risks and the effectiveness of the company's internal financial, operational and compliance controls.[80]

---

[76] 17 CFR 210.2–02 under (f). See Section 3.1.3 of this chapter for the early Regulation S-X Rule 2–02(b) of the Securities Act of 1933.

[77] Heier, Dugan & Sayers 2004, p. 14.

[78] The most important and influential documents with respect to internal control are: SEC final rule 33–8124 of 29 August 2002 on Certification of Disclosure in Companies' Quarterly and Annual Reports; SEC final rule 33–8238 of 5 June 2003 on Management's Reports on Internal Control Over Financial Reporting and Certification of Disclosure in Exchange Act Periodic Reports; PCAOB 2004 Auditing Standard No. 2 – An Audit of Internal Control Over Financial Reporting Performed in Conjunction with An Audit of Financial Statements (later modified in PCAOB Auditing Standard No. 5).

[79] The SEC adopted the proposed amendments of its December 2006 Proposing Release; see Securities and Exchange Commission, 17 CFR Parts 210, 228, 229 and 240, Amendments to Rules Regarding Management's Report on Internal Control Over Financial Reporting, (Release Nos. 33–8809; 34–55928; FR-76; File No. S7-24-06) RIN 3235-AJ58, 27 June 2007.

[80] Section 8.01(c), subsections (2) and (6) of the Model Business Corporation Act 2005.

The SEC has identified the COSO I report as an example of a suitable framework,[81] and the Treadway Commission has broadened its scope by shifting its focus towards risk management, resulting in its 2004 report entitled 'Enterprise Risk Management – Integrated Framework (COSO II report)'. As described in Section 3.2.7, in the 20th century risk management was seen as a component of internal control. Following this shift in focus, the internal control system is now generally seen as a part of the broader risk management system. The COSO II report defined enterprise risk management as[82]

> [. . .] a process effected by an entity's board of directors, management and other personnel, applied in strategy setting and across the enterprise, designed to identify potential events that may affect the entity, and manage risk to be within its risk appetite, to provide reasonable assurance regarding the achievement of entity objectives.

The COSO I report divided the entity's objectives into three categories: operations, financial reporting and compliance. The COSO II report broadens reporting to encompass non-financial information and internal reporting, and it adds a fourth category: the strategic objectives.[83] Chapter 2 of this book (Section 2.1.8) provides a comprehensive description of the COSO II report.

The requirements described in the current section – especially the SOX requirements – significantly modified the US regulatory internal control and risk management framework. Table 3.2 summarizes the main findings described above by categorizing the rules based on the levels of a coherent internal control and risk management system on the one hand, and the parties involved from a corporate law perspective on the other hand. In general, the US provisions described above cover all levels of the framework, which mainly focuses on an internal control and risk management system for financial reporting.

3.3.2 The EU in the 21st Century

For a long time, EU lawmakers mainly focused on corporate disclosure rules and not so much on requiring management systems to endorse the

---

[81] See Section II. B. 3. a. of Final Rule 33–8238 of 5 June 2003 on Management's Reports on Internal Control Over Financial Reporting and Certification of Disclosure in Exchange Act Periodic Reports.

[82] COSO II Report 2004, p. 2.

[83] COSO II Report 2004, p. 3.

Table 3.2   US internal control and risk management framework

			Board / senior management	Audit committee	External auditor
Level 1: initiate / identify	**Risks / uncertainties**				
	Financial reporting IC/ RM* system		FCPA SOX (302 and 404)		
	Overall IC/RM system**				
Level 2: assess / operate	**Risks / uncertainties**				
	Financial reporting IC/ RM system		FCPA SOX (302 and 404)		
	Overall IC/RM system				
Level 3: monitor	**Risks / uncertainties**		MBCA		
	Financial reporting IC/RM system	**General**	SOX (302)	SOX (205)	Regulation S-X
		Effectiveness	SOX (302 and 404)		SOX (404)
	Overall IC/RM system	**General**			
		Effectiveness	MBCA		
Level 4: report	**Risks / uncertainties**		Regulation S-K		
	Financial reporting IC/RM system	**General**	SOX (302)		
		Effectiveness	SOX (302 and 404)		Regulation S-X SOX (404)
	Overall IC/RM system				

Notes:
* IC/RM system = internal control and/or risk management system.
** Overall IC/RM system = system including most or all of the financial, operational, strategic and compliance controls.

Source: This table is based on Van Daelen and Van der Elst 2009, pp. 91–92.

reliability of the reporting and internal control framework.[84] Responding to the corporate failures and fraud, the EU became more active in areas such as company law, accounting, and auditing law, although large parts

---

[84] Directive 84/253/EEC, the Eighth Company Law Directive, harmonized the approval of persons responsible for carrying out the statutory audits of accounting documents. Articles 3 and 24 demanded such persons to be independent and of good repute.

of these areas remain controlled by the national legislators. The European Commission examined ways to modernize company law and enhance corporate governance.[85] This examination together with the 2002 Final Report of the High Level Group of Company Law Experts[86] resulted in the 2003 Commission's Plan to Move Forward. This action plan refers to enhancing corporate governance disclosure by requiring listed companies to include a corporate governance statement in their annual report and accounts. The statement should cover the key elements of the company's corporate governance structure and practices, including the existence and nature of a risk management system.[87] The European Commission also emphasized the importance of including in the annual corporate governance statement information on how the company has organized itself to establish and maintain an effective internal control system, in view of its essential role in restoring public confidence.[88] Following the action plan, the member states have to draw up a national corporate governance code for listed companies.[89] The Commission's plan also refers to the key role the audit committee plays in supervising the audit function in its external and internal aspects, including the company's risk management system.[90]

The legislative movement was multiple and resulted in, *inter alia*, general directives and recommendations, and several sector-specific measures that refer to risk management. For example, the 2004 Transparency Directive deals with the disclosure of information on risks. It requires a company's annual report to include a description of the principal risks and uncertainties the company faces. It also imposes a company's half-yearly financial report to include an interim management report that contains information on the principal risks and uncertainties for the remaining six months of the financial year.[91] The 2005 Commission Recommendation provides principles to structure the role of the audit committee in monitoring, mainly, the systems. Among other things, the audit committee should assist the board in its task to: (1) annually review the internal control and risk management systems, with a view to ensuring that the main risks are

---

[85]   The Ecofin Council instructed the Commission in 2002 to examine ways of modernizing company law and enhancing corporate governance.

[86]   The High Level Group of Company Law Experts was appointed by Commissioner Bolkestein in September 2001 and chaired by Jaap Winter.

[87]   Commission's Plan to Move Forward 2003, Section 3.1.1, under f, p. 13.

[88]   Commission's Plan to Move Forward 2003, Section 3.1.1, footnote at (b).

[89]   Commission's Plan to Move Forward 2003, Section 3.1.1, under g, p. 13.

[90]   Commission's Plan to Move Forward 2003, Section 3.1.3, p. 15.

[91]   Directive 2004/109/EG (Transparency Directive), Article 4, paragraph 2, under c and Article 5, paragraph 4.

properly identified, managed and disclosed; (2) ensure the effectiveness of the internal audit function, in particular by making recommendations relating to the head of the internal audit department and on the department's budget, and by monitoring the responsiveness of management to its findings and recommendations; and (3) review the effectiveness of the external audit process, and the responsiveness of management to the recommendations made in the external auditor's management letter.[92] The 2006 Audit Directive focuses on the role of the audit committee in monitoring, mainly, the effectiveness of the systems. According to this directive, companies must establish an audit committee or an alternative body to monitor the financial reporting process and to monitor the effectiveness of the company's internal control, internal audit where applicable, and risk management systems. Also, the statutory auditor must report to the audit committee on key matters arising from the statutory audit, in particular on material weaknesses in internal control relating to the financial reporting process.[93] The 2006 amendment to the Accounting Directives – the Fourth and Seventh Company Law Directives – deals with the disclosure of information on risk management systems. It requires an annual corporate governance statement that contains a description of the main features of the company's internal control and risk management systems for the financial reporting process. On the consolidated level, a company must provide a description of the main features of the group's internal control and risk management systems relating to the process of preparing consolidated accounts.[94]

In general, compared to the US the EU provisions deal with a broader concept of internal control and risk management. The EU provisions focus on covering not only the financial reporting systems, but also the strategic, operational and compliance systems. However, the US legislation covers all levels of the internal control and risk management framework for financial reporting, while the EU only mandates monitoring the overall system at level 3 and reporting on the system for financial reporting at level 4. In short, the EU provisions require (1) companies to disclose information on (1a) its overall principal risks and uncertainties, and (1b) its risk management systems for the financial reporting process, as well as (2) the audit committee to monitor (2a) the overall internal

---

[92]   Commission Recommendation 2005/162/EC, Annex I, Committees of the (supervisory) board, p. 61.

[93]   Directive 2006/43/EC (Audit Directive), Article 41, paragraph 2, under a and b, and Article 41, paragraph 4.

[94]   Directive 2006/46/EC (Amendment to Accounting Directives), Article 1, paragraph 7, under c and Article 2, paragraph 2.

control and risk management systems and (2b) the effectiveness of the overall internal control and risk management systems.[95] The fragmented and principle-based EU approach necessitated the EU member states to further complete their internal control and risk management frameworks. This issue will be addressed below. First, Table 3.3 provides insight into the differences between the US and EU internal control and risk management frameworks. It summarizes the main findings described above by categorizing the US and EU rules, based on the levels of a coherent internal control and risk management system on the one hand, and the parties involved from a corporate law perspective on the other hand.

Table 3.3   US and EU internal control and risk management frameworks

		Board / senior management	Audit committee	External auditor
Level 1: initiate / identify	**Risks / uncertainties**			
	Financial reporting IC/ RM* system	FCPA SOX (302 and 404)		
	Overall IC/RM system**			
Level 2: assess / operate	**Risks / uncertainties**			
	Financial reporting IC/ RM system	FCPA SOX (302 and 404)		
	Overall IC/RM system			
Level 3: monitor	**Risks / uncertainties**	MBCA		
	Financial reporting IC/RM system — **General**	SOX (302)	SOX (205)	Regulation S-X
	Effectiveness	SOX (302 and 404)		SOX (404)
	Overall IC/RM system — **General**		Commission Recom- mendation	
	Effectiveness	MBCA	Audit directive	
Level 4: report	**Risks / uncertainties**	Regulation S-K Transparency directive		

---

[95]   For more information on the above-mentioned directives and recommendation as well as a discussion of the risk management and internal control provisions of some industry-specific measures, see Van Daelen & Van der Elst 2009, pp. 88–90.

Table 3.3   (cont.)

		Board / senior management	Audit committee	External auditor
Financial reporting IC/RM system	General	SOX (302) Accounting directives		Audit directive
	Effectiveness	SOX (302 and 404)		Regulation S-X SOX (404)
Overall IC/RM system				

Notes:
  *   IC/RM system = internal control and/or risk management system
 **   Overall IC/RM system = system including most or all of the financial, operational, strategic and compliance controls
  ■ = US
  ■ = EU

Source: This table is based on Van Daelen and Van der Elst 2009, pp. 91–92.

3.3.3   The Netherlands in the 21st Century

As a reaction to the problems that occurred at the turn of the century and as a result of the implementation of EU directives, additional requirements have been laid down in Dutch national laws. Corporate governance codes have further completed this legal internal control and risk management framework. The main legal amendments that are of interest here involve the annual accounts and report.

As of 2005, it is mandatory for both listed and unlisted companies to include in the annual report a description of the main risks and uncertainties they face.[96] The inclusion of this provision results from a legislative movement at EU level. The 2002 IAS Regulation requires listed companies to prepare their consolidated accounts in accordance with the international accounting standards that are adopted by the European Commission for each financial year starting on or after 1 January 2005.[97] According to this

---

[96]   Article 391, paragraph 1 of Book 2 of the Civil Code (2:391 lid 1 BW). This provision was enacted by law of 16 July 2005, *Staatsblad* 2005, 377; entry into force on 27 July 2005. See also paragraph 3 of Article 391 relating to financial instruments.

[97]   Regulation (EC) No. 1606/2002 (IAS Regulation), Article 4. Following Article 2 of this regulation 'international accounting standards' include

Regulation, member states can also require listed or unlisted companies to prepare their annual accounts in conformity with the international accounting standards.[98] The IAS Regulation provides that for the European Commission to adopt an international accounting standard it is necessary that the standard meets the basic requirement of the Fourth and Seventh Company Law Directives on annual accounts and consolidated accounts; the application of such a standard must result in a true and fair view of the financial position and performance of a company.[99] In order to remove inconsistencies between, *inter alia*, the Fourth and Seventh Company Law Directives on the one hand, and the International Accounting Standards (IAS) on the other, Directive 2003/51/EC amends these two company law directives.[100] As a result, the amended Fourth Directive requires the annual report to include a fair review of the development and performance of the company's business and of its position, together with a description of the principal risks and uncertainties it faces.[101] The amended Seventh Directive requires the consolidated annual report to include a fair review of the development and performance of the business and of the position of the undertakings included in the consolidation taken as a whole, together with a description of the principal risks and uncertainties they face.[102] These amendments have been implemented in the Dutch Civil Code, which consequently requires a description of the main risks and uncertainties the company faces in the annual report of both listed and unlisted companies.

For listed companies the Dutch Financial Supervision Act also requires the annual financial reporting to include a statement of the persons responsible that the annual report contains a description of the principal risks and uncertainties the company faces due to the implementation of the Transparency Directive.[103]

International Accounting Standards (IAS) and International Financial Reporting Standards (IFRS).

[98] Regulation (EC) No. 1606/2002, Article 5.

[99] Regulation (EC) No. 1606/2002, Article 3, paragraph 2. See Directive 78/660/EEC of 1978 (Fourth Directive) and Directive 83/349/EEC of 1983 (Seventh Directive). Directives as last amended by Directive 2001/65/EC (IAS 39 Directive).

[100] Directive 2003/51/EC, Consideration (15).

[101] Directive 2003/51/EC, Article 1, paragraph 14, under a, amends Directive 78/660/EEC, Article 46, paragraph 1.

[102] Directive 2003/51/EC, Article 2, paragraph 10, under a amends Directive 83/349/EEC, Article 36, paragraph 1. See also the 2006 amendment to the Fourth and Seventh Company Law Directives described in Section 3.2.2.

[103] Article 5:25c, Section 2, Subsection c, under 2 of the Dutch Financial Supervision Act (*Wet op het financieel toezicht*, Wft); enacted by Act of 25 September 2008 amending the Financial Supervision Law and several other laws in

In 2004, paragraph 4 (now paragraph 5) was added to Article 2:391 of the Civil Code allowing additional provisions regarding the content of the annual report to be set by governmental decree (*Algemene Maatregel van Bestuur*, AMvB). Following the 2003 Commission's Action Plan – recommending that member states draw up a national corporate governance code for listed companies – this Civil Code provision enables requiring compliance with a corporate governance code.[104] By the end of 2004, an AMvB was issued acknowledging the 2003 Tabaksblat Code as the Dutch corporate governance code.[105] All listed companies whose registered offices are in the Netherlands have to apply this code as of the financial year starting on or after 1 January 2004. Applying the code means that a company must either comply with the best practice provisions, or explain in its annual report why and to what extent it does not.[106] The Tabaksblat Code contains principles – reflecting general views on corporate governance – and best practice provisions – creating guidelines for the behaviour of executive and non-executive directors, and shareholders.[107]

The main internal control and risk management provisions are set out in Principle II.1 of the Tabaksblat Code. The principle deals with the responsibility of the management board for complying with laws and regulations, managing the risks associated with the company's activities, and financing the company. Furthermore, it stipulates that the management board has to report related developments to and discuss the internal risk management and control systems with the supervisory board and its audit committee. The best practice provisions require, *inter alia*, that the company must have an internal control and risk management system, including instruments for risk analysis of the company's operational and financial objectives and a monitoring and reporting system. They also introduce an *in control statement*, which requires the management board to declare in the annual report that the systems are adequate and effective.[108]

The Tabaksblat Code has been amended by the 2008 Dutch Corporate

---

order to implement Directive 2004/109/EG, *Staatsblad* 2008, 476; entry into force on 1 January 2009.

[104] Article 391, paragraph 4 (now paragraph 5) of Book 2 of the Civil Code (2:391 lid 5 BW) was enacted by the Act of 9 July 2004, *Staatsblad* 2004, 370; entry into force on 1 October 2004.

[105] Article 2 of the AMvB of 23 December 2004, *Staatsblad* 2004, 747; entry into force on 30 December 2004; Government Gazette (*Staatscourant*) no. 250 of 27 December 2004.

[106] Also known as the 'comply or explain' principle. Articles 3 and 4 of the AMvB of 23 December 2004, *Staatsblad* 2004, 747.

[107] Tabaksblat Code 2003, Preamble.

[108] Tabaksblat Code 2003, Best practice provisions II.1.3 and II.1.4, p. 9.

Governance Code (DCGC 2008), also known as the Frijns Code.[109] Listed companies have to apply this 2008 code as of the financial year starting on or after 1 January 2009. Like the Tabaksblat Code, it requires companies to have an internal risk management and control system suitable for the company with, as instruments of the system, risk analyses of the company's operational and financial objectives and a monitoring and reporting system.[110] Besides being responsible for complying with all relevant primary and secondary legislation and managing the risks associated with the company's activities, the management board is also responsible for the company's risk profile. In line with the Tabaksblat Code, the management board has to report related developments to and discuss the internal risk management and control systems with the supervisory board and the audit committee.[111] The DCGC 2008 has amended the *in control statement* by requiring the management board to declare in the annual report that the systems provide a reasonable assurance that the financial reporting does not contain any errors of material importance and that the systems worked properly.[112] Thus, instead of declaring that the systems are adequate and effective, the management board has to declare that the system provides reasonable assurance, which is a major reduction of the requirement. Another limitation is made relating to the scope, because the declaration only has to address the financial reporting – not other aspects of the system such as strategy, operations and compliance – and only for errors of material importance. The DCGC 2008 does, however, add a provision requiring the management board to give a description in the annual report of: (1) the main risks related to the strategy of the company; (2) the design and effectiveness of the internal risk management and control systems for the main risks during the financial year; and (3) any major failings in the internal risk management and control systems, including significant changes made to the systems and the major improvements planned, and a confirmation that these issues have been discussed with the audit committee and the supervisory board.[113] The system set out by the COSO reports is cited as an example of an internal control and risk management system

---

[109]   AMvB of 10 December 2009 amending the AMvB of 23 December 2004 (see *Staatsblad* 2004, 747), *Staatsblad* 2009, 545; publication date 21 December 2009; entry into force on 1 January 2010; *Staatscourant* no. 18499 of 3 December 2009. In June 2008, the Monitoring Committee proposed amendments to the Tabaksblat Code 2003 (see Corporate Governance Code Monitoring Committee 2008).
[110]   DCGC 2008, Best practice provision II.1.3.
[111]   DCGC 2008, Principle II.1.
[112]   DCGC 2008, Best practice provision II.1.5.
[113]   DCGC 2008, Best practice provision II.1.4.

in the explanatory statement.[114] Also, the DCGC 2008 provides that the supervisory board's oversight of the management board has to include the company's risks inherent to the business activities and the design and effectiveness of the internal risk management and control systems.[115] One of the key committees of the supervisory board, the audit committee, has to monitor the activities of the management board with respect to the operation of the internal risk management and control systems.[116]

Although applying the DCGC 2008 means that a company can also deviate from the provision as long as it explains why it does so in the annual report, parts of the Code correspond with a statutory rule, which means that the company is not allowed to depart from the provision(s) concerned. For example, some best practice provisions regarding the audit committee have become statutory rules, due to the implementation of the 2006 Audit Directive described in Section 3.3.2.[117] In addition, the regulatory requirements relating to the corporate governance statement have been extended, due to the implementation of the 2006 amendment to the Accounting Directives described in Section 3.3.2. By amending Article 2:391, paragraph 5, the Civil Code emphasizes the ability to issue provisions dealing with the disclosure, content and review of the external auditor of a corporate governance statement.[118] By AMvB of 20 March 2009, the AMvB of 23 December 2004 has been amended, making an annual corporate governance statement mandatory for listed companies as of the financial years starting on or after 1 April 2008.[119] The statement must contain, *inter alia*, an announcement about the application of the principles and best practice provisions of the corporate governance code based on the comply or explain principle, and a description of the key

---

[114] See the 'Explanation of and notes to certain terms used in the code' of the DCGC 2008, p. 39 and of the Tabaksblat Code 2003, p. 33.

[115] DCGC 2008, Best practice provision III.1.6.

[116] DCGC 2008, Best practice provision III.5.4.

[117] AMvB of 26 July 2008 implementing Article 41 of Directive 2006/43/EC; *Staatsblad* 2008, 323; publication date 7 August 2008. See, *inter alia*, Section 2, Subsection 2 regarding compliance with Best practice provisions III.5.4, under a, b, c and f and III.5.7, as well as Principles V.2 and V.4 on the external auditor and the supervisory board.

[118] Act of 11 December 2008 to amend Book 2 of the Dutch Civil Code in order to implement Directive 2006/46/EC; *Staatsblad* 2008, 550; publication date 22 December 2008.

[119] AMvB of 20 March 2009 amending the AMvB of 23 December 2004 (see *Staatsblad* 2004, 747), *Staatsblad* 2009, 154; publication date 31 March 2009. See Article 1, Article 2a, paragraph 1 and Article 4, paragraph 2 of the amended AMvB of 23 December 2004.

features of the company's and group's management and control system for the financial reporting process.[120] The statutory auditor has to review whether the annual report is consistent with the annual account.[121] By doing so, according to the 2009 AMvB, the auditor also has to review whether the description of the management and control system as given in the corporate governance statement is consistent with the annual account. Furthermore, the statutory auditor has to verify whether the announcement about applying the code and other mandatory announcements that have to be set forth in the corporate governance statement have indeed been included.[122]

Table 3.4 provides a summary of the Dutch internal control and risk management provisions described above, next to the US and EU requirements. As stated above, the fragmented and principle-based EU approach necessitated the EU member states to further complete their internal control and risk management frameworks. The EU provisions only mandate monitoring the overall system and reporting on the system for financial reporting. Table 3.4 shows that the Dutch code provisions aim to complete the EU framework by mainly focusing on the overall system at all levels of the framework. It points out that the board is responsible for having a suitable system for the company, which means that the board not only has to make sure that there is a system in place, it also has to assess whether the system is suitable for the company. Furthermore, the Dutch code provisions complete the EU reporting provision – which only addresses the financial reporting – by providing that the board has to report on the system's overall design and effectiveness, major failings in it and significant changes made to it.

EU member states have to adopt the requirements of the EU directives. Although member states are granted a measure of flexibility in implementing the requirements in their national laws, most member states will have comparable rules due to this implementation duty. For that reason, only the main additional provisions relating to internal control and risk management in the member states' laws and codes are shown in Table 3.4.

---

[120]   Article 2a, paragraph 2, Article 3, paragraph 1, and Article 3a of the amended AMvB of 23 December 2004.

[121]   Article 393, paragraph 3 of Book 2 of the Civil Code (2:393 under 3 BW).

[122]   Article 3c, paragraphs 1 and 2 of the amended AMvB of 23 December 2004. For the other mandatory announcements, see Article 2a of the amended AMvB of 23 December 2004. See Directive 2006/46/EC, Article 1, paragraph 7, under 2, and Directive 78/660/EEC Article 51, paragraph 1.

Table 3.4 *US and EU internal control and risk management frameworks including Dutch provisions*

			Board / senior management	Audit committee	External auditor
Level 1: initiate / identify	**Risks / uncertainties**				
	Financial reporting IC/RM* **system**		FCPA SOX (302 and 404)		
	Overall IC/RM system**		**2008 DCGC**		
Level 2: assess / operate	**Risks / uncertainties**				
	Financial reporting IC/RM **system**		FCPA SOX (302 and 404)		
	Overall IC/RM system		**2008 DCGC**		
Level 3: monitor	**Risks / uncertainties**		MBCA **2008 DCGC**		
	Financial reporting IC/RM system	**General**	SOX (302)	SOX (205)	Regulation S-X
		Effectiveness	SOX (302 and 404)		SOX (404)
	Overall IC/ RM system	**General**		Commission Recom- mendation **2008 DCGC**	
		Effectiveness	MBCA **2008 DCGC**	Audit directive	
Level 4: report	**Risks / uncertainties**		Regulation S-K Transparency directive **2008 DCGC**		
	Financial reporting IC/RM system	**General**	SOX (302) Accounting directives		Audit directive
		Effectiveness	SOX (302 and 404)		Regulation S-X SOX (404)
	Overall IC/ RM system	**General**	**2008 DCGC**		
		Effectiveness	**2008 DCGC**		

Notes:
  *   IC/RM system = internal control and/or risk management system
 **   Overall IC/RM system = system including most or all of the financial, operational, strategic and compliance controls
■ = US
■ = EU
■ = the Netherlands

Source: This table is based on Van Daelen and Van der Elst 2009, pp. 91–92.

3.3.4   The UK in the 21st Century

Contrary to the US – and much earlier than the Netherlands – the UK responded to the corporate failures in the late 1980s and early 1990s with a new form of regulation, the 'comply or explain' approach.[123] After the frauds and failures at the beginning of this century, the UK has continued this approach.

As mentioned in Section 3.2.6, in 1998 the first Combined Code was based on the Hampel, Cadbury and Greenbury reports. The Combined Code was updated in May 2000 and emphasizes that the board should maintain a sound system of internal control. To do so, the board has to report annually to the shareholders that it has reviewed the effectiveness of the group's internal control system. The Code also stresses that the review has to cover all controls, including financial, operational and compliance controls and risk management.[124]

In 2003, two reports were issued: the Higgs report on the role and effectiveness of non-executive directors and the Smith report on the role of the audit committees. The Higgs report asserts that the role of the board includes providing leadership of the company within a framework of effective controls in order to enable assessing and managing the company's risks. The Higgs report states that one of the key elements of the role of non-executives is risk management and that they must therefore check whether the systems of risk management are robust and defensible.[125] According to the Smith report, the audit committee – unless addressed by a separate risk committee or the board itself – should review the company's internal financial control and risk management systems. The audit committee should also assess the scope and effectiveness of these systems to identify, assess, manage and monitor financial and non-financial risks. Additionally, the audit committee should review and approve the internal financial control and risk management statements that are included in the annual report.[126] As a result, in July 2003 the Combined Code was revised by integrating the above-mentioned recommendations of the Higgs and Smith reports.[127]

---

[123]   See LSE Listing Rule 9.8.6, Sections 5 and 6, and Cadbury Report 1992, Section 1.3.

[124]   Combined Code 2000, Principle D.2 and Provision D.2.1.

[125]   Higgs I Report 2003, Chapters 4 and 6, pp. 21 and 27.

[126]   Smith Report 2003, Chapter 2, Section 2.1 and Chapter 5, Sections 5.6 and 5.8, pp. 6 and 11.

[127]   Combined Code 2003. Principle C.2 relates to internal control (former Principle D.2 of the Combined Code 2000). It only changes 'The review should

Following the frauds and in order to restore public confidence, the Companies Act of 2004 (amending the Companies Act of 1985) grants greater powers to the auditors in order to obtain the information needed.[128] It also requires directors to state that they have not withheld any relevant information from the auditors.[129] Furthermore, the Act prescribes the independent monitoring of audits of listed companies.[130] In 2005, an updated version of the Turnbull report on internal control was released. Retaining the principle-based approach, the report provides that the board should review the information given in the internal control statement of the annual report on a continuing basis. It emphasized the importance of this statement for investors because the board's attitude towards risk management is an important factor when making investment decisions.[131] Next, a revised Higgs report was issued in 2006, which again focused on the role of the board and the non-executive directors.[132] Also, in 2006 and 2008, updated versions of the Combined Code on corporate governance were released, but the changes did not affect Principle C.2 and Provision C.2.1 of the Combined Code 2003. The 2008 Combined Code applies to accounting periods beginning on or after 29 June 2008.

On 8 November 2006, a new Companies Act was enacted to reform company law. According to the Companies Act of 1985, the company's board is responsible for maintaining adequate accounting records. The 2006 Companies Act requires the directors to prepare a directors' report for each financial year of the company. This report must contain a business review that includes a description of the principal risks and uncertainties the company faces to inform the members of the company.[133] In the same month, the Financial Reporting Council issued a report setting out the UK approach to corporate governance.[134] The report stressed that

---

cover all controls' into 'The review should cover all material controls'. See the supporting principles of Principle A.1 on p. 4 and Code provision C.3.2 on p. 16 of the Combined Code 2003 for the added recommendations of the Higgs I Report and Smith Report.

[128]　Section 389A (1) and (2) of the Companies Act 1985.

[129]　Section 234 (2A) of the Companies Act 1985.

[130]　Sections 10A and 12A of the Companies Act 1985.

[131]　See the preface to the Turnbull II Report 2005, pp. 1–2.

[132]　Higgs II Report 2006, see Chapter 2 on the role of the non-executive director (former Chapters 4 and 6), pp. 5–6.

[133]　Rule 415, Section 1 and Rule 417, Sections 1 and 2, and Section 3, subsection b of the Companies Act 2006 (c. 46), Part 15, Chapter 5, pp. 195–196. The directors' report of a company that is subject to small companies' regime does not have to contain a business review.

[134]　This report is a part of the 'City of London – City of Learning' initiative.

studies show that the UK governance standards outperform those of other countries and that the compliance costs of those standards in the UK are considered to be lower than the cost of comparable standards in other countries.[135]

Besides the provisions of the Combined Code and the statement that deals with the comply-or-explain requirement of the Listing Rules, the UK corporate governance disclosure requirements also include the Disclosure and Transparency Rules (DTR) of the Financial Services Authority (FSA). These Listing Authority disclosure rules set forth the minimum functions of and the minimum requirements on the composition of the audit committee or an equivalent body and require its composition and function to be disclosed in the annual report. The audit committee's function includes monitoring the financial reporting process and the effectiveness of the internal control, internal audit where applicable, and risk management systems.[136] Furthermore, the DTR set out which information has to be disclosed in the corporate governance statement. It requires that the corporate governance statement, *inter alia*, contains a description of the main features of the company's internal control and risk management systems relating to the financial reporting process.[137] At the consolidated level, the directors' report has to include a description of the main features of the group's internal control and risk management systems in relation to the process for preparing consolidated accounts.[138]

Table 3.5 summarizes the main UK internal control and risk management provisions, next to the US and EU requirements and the additional code provisions of the Netherlands. It shows that the Dutch and UK requirements aim to complete the EU framework in a comparable manner. The provisions of both countries mainly focus on the overall system at all levels of the framework. In the UK, the board has to maintain – and therefore also has to make sure there is – a sound system of internal control. Monitoring the effectiveness of the overall system is also required. As Table 3.5 shows, these first three levels are also covered by the Dutch code. However, at level 4 there is an interesting difference between the codes of the Netherlands and the UK. The 2008 Combined Code only requires the board to report to the shareholders that it has reviewed the effectiveness of

---

[135]   See the UK Approach to Corporate Governance Report, p. 8. The report also gives examples of studies on performance and costs.

[136]   DTR 7.1.1 R, 7.1.3 R and 7.1.5 R.

[137]   DTR 7.2.5 R; implementing Article 46a, paragraph 1, under c of the Fourth Directive as of 29 June 2008.

[138]   DTR 7.2.10 R; implementing Article 36, paragraph 2, under f of the Seventh Directive as of 29 June 2008.

the overall internal control and risk management system. Thus, the board does not have to give information about the effectiveness of the system. By contrast, the DCGC 2008 requires the board to give a description in the annual report of the design and effectiveness of the systems for the main risks, as well as of major failings in and significant changes made to the system. The latter requirements imply more extended disclosure. In addition, unlike the UK code, the Dutch code requires the board to state in the annual report that the systems for financial reporting provide reasonable assurance that the financial reporting does not contain any errors of material importance and that the systems worked properly in the year under review. The upshot is that although the Dutch and UK approaches seem comparable they contain significant differences.

The EU provisions mandate the member states to issue requirements for monitoring the overall system and reporting on the system for financial reporting. Because most member states will have comparable rules due to the implementation of the EU directives, Table 3.5 only points out the main additional provisions relating to internal control and risk management in the member states' laws and codes.

Table 3.5   US and EU internal control and risk management frameworks including Dutch and UK provisions

		Board / senior management	Audit committee	External auditor
Level 1: initiate / identify	**Risks / uncertainties**			
	Financial reporting IC/ RM* system	FCPA SOX (302 and 404)		
	Overall IC/RM system**	DCGC 2008 **Combined Code**		
Level 2: assess / operate	**Risks / uncertainties**			
	Financial reporting IC/ RM system	FCPA SOX (302 and 404)		
	Overall IC/RM system	DCGC 2008 **Combined Code**		
Level 3: monitor	**Risks / uncertainties**	MBCA DCGC 2008 **Companies Act**		

Table 3.5   (continued)

			Board / senior management	Audit committee	External auditor
	Financial reporting IC/RM system	**General**	SOX (302)	SOX (205)	Regulation S-X
		Effectiveness	SOX (302 and 404)		SOX (404)
	Overall IC/RM system	**General**		Commission Recommendation DCGC 2008 **Combined Code**	
		Effectiveness	MBCA DCGC 2008 **Combined Code**	Audit directive	
Level 4: report	**Risks / uncertainties**		Regulation S-K Transparency directive DCGC 2008		
	Financial reporting IC/RM system	**General**	SOX (302) Accounting directives		Audit directive
		Effectiveness	SOX (302 and 404)		Regulation S-X SOX (404)
	Overall IC/RM system	**General**	DCGC 2008		
		Effectiveness	DCGC 2008 **(Combined Code)**		

Notes:
*   IC/RM system = internal control and/or risk management system
**   Overall IC/RM system = system including most or all of the financial, operational, strategic and compliance controls
▓ = USA
▓ = EU
▓ = the Netherlands
▓ = UK

Source: This table is based on Van Daelen and Van der Elst 2009, pp. 91–92.

3.3.5 Overview of the Main 21st Century Provisions

The overview below summarizes the main provisions relating to internal control and risk management in the US, the Netherlands and the UK at the beginning of the 21st century. As discussed in Section 3.2.7, internal control originally focused on financial reporting and the risk of fraud. By the end of the 20th century, this focus started to shift towards the broader concept of internal control including financial, operational and compliance controls, largely due to the 1992 COSO I report. It was also pointed out that risk management was seen as a component of internal control. Unfortunately, these provisions were unable to prevent the corporate failures and frauds that occurred between 2000 and 2003. This led to additional legislative movements at the beginning of the 21st century and an emphasis on internal control to restore public confidence. Lawmakers and companies turned their focus from the broadened internal control approach towards an even more extended internal control and corporate risk management approach. The COSO II report highlighted this shift by issuing its 2004 report on enterprise risk management.

Table 3.6   Overview of the main 21st century internal control and risk management provisions

Date	Document	Requiring or recommending:
United States*		
2002	SOX	Management is responsible for establishing and maintaining an adequate internal control structure and procedures for financial reporting and the effectiveness of the structure and procedures must be evaluated. The auditor has to control and certify the management effectiveness reports. The CEO and CFO must certify the fairness of the financial statements and information and their responsibility for establishing and maintaining internal controls in the annual or quarterly report. The CEO and CFO have to present their conclusions about the effectiveness of their internal controls based on their evaluation. The CEO and the CFO must disclose to the auditors and the audit committee significant deficiencies and material weaknesses in the design or operation of internal control over financial reporting and any fraud that involves management or employees who significantly participate in the internal control procedures for financial reporting.

Table 3.6   (continued)

Date	Document	Requiring or recommending:
		The CEO and CFO must provide the market with a certification that the periodic report fairly presents the financial condition and results of operations of the issuer. The audit committee must oversee the accounting and financial reporting processes and audits of the financial statements of the company. The audit committee has to establish procedures for the receipt, retention and treatment of complaints regarding accounting, internal accounting controls or auditing matters.
2004	COSO II Report	Enterprise risk management is a process consisting of eight components – internal environment, objective setting, event identification, risk assessment, risk response, control activities, information and communication, and monitoring – and effected by an entity's board of directors, management and other personnel, applied in strategy setting and across the enterprise, designed to identify potential events that may affect the entity, and manage risk to be within its risk appetite, to provide reasonable assurance regarding the achievement of entity's objectives in four categories: (1) strategy, (2) operations, (3) reporting, and (4) compliance.
European Union		
2003	Commission's Plan to Move Forward	Companies have to include in their annual report and accounts a corporate governance statement that covers, *inter alia*, information on the existence and nature of a risk management system, and how the company has organized itself to establish and maintain an effective internal control system. Member states have to draw up a national corporate governance code for listed companies. The audit committee plays a key role in supervising the audit function in its external and internal aspects, including the company's risk management system.
2004	Transparency Directive	The annual report must include a description of the principal risks and uncertainties the company face. The half-yearly financial report must include an interim management report that provides information on the principal risks and uncertainties for the remaining six months of the financial year.

Table 3.6   (continued)

Date	Document	Requiring or recommending:
2005	Commission Recommendation	The audit committee should assist the board in its task to annually review the internal control and risk management systems, ensure the effectiveness of the internal audit function and review the effectiveness of the external audit process, as well as the responsiveness of management to the recommendations made in the external auditor's management letter.
2006	Audit Directive	Companies must establish an audit committee or alternative body to monitor the financial reporting process and to monitor the effectiveness of the company's internal control, internal audit where applicable, and risk management systems. The statutory auditor must report to the audit committee on key matters arising from the statutory audit, in particular on material weaknesses in internal control relating to the financial reporting process.
2006	Amendment to Accounting Directives	An annual corporate governance statement must be issued, containing a description of the main features of the company's (and/or group's) internal control and risk management systems for the financial reporting process (and/or relating to the process for preparing consolidated accounts).
The Netherlands		
2003	Tabaksblat Code	The management board is responsible for complying with laws and regulations and for managing the risks associated with the company's activities. The management board has to report related developments to and discuss the internal risk management and control systems with the supervisory board and its audit committee. The management board has to include an 'in control statement' in the annual report, in which it declares that the systems are adequate and effective. The company must have as instruments for the systems risk analyses of the company's operational and financial objectives, and a monitoring and reporting system.
2005	Civil Code	Listed and unlisted companies have to include in the annual report a description of the main risks and uncertainties the company faces.

Table 3.6   (continued)

Date	Document	Requiring or recommending:
2008	DCGC 2008	The company must have an internal risk management and control system, including risk analyses of the company's operational and financial objectives and a monitoring and reporting system. The management board is responsible for the company's risk profile, complying with all relevant primary and secondary legislation, and managing the risks associated with the company's activities. The management board has to report to and discuss the systems with the supervisory board and the audit committee. The management board must declare in the annual report that the systems provide a reasonable assurance that the financial reporting does not contain any errors of material importance and that the systems worked properly. The management board has to give a description in the annual report of (1) the main risks related to the strategy, (2) the design and effectiveness of the systems for the main risks, and (3) major failings in the systems, significant changes, and major future improvements.
2009	Financial Supervision Law	The annual financial reporting of listed companies has to include a declaration of the persons responsible that the annual report contains a description of the principal risks and uncertainties the company faces.
United Kingdom		
2000	Combined Code	The board should maintain a sound system of internal control. The directors have to conduct an annual review of the effectiveness of the system, covering all controls, including financial, operational and compliance controls and risk management.
2003	Higgs I Report	The board has to provide leadership of the company within a framework of effective controls in order to enable assessing and managing risks. Non-executives must check whether the risk management systems are robust and defensible.
2003	Smith Report	The audit committee should review the company's internal financial control and risk management systems, assess the scope and effectiveness of these systems to identify, assess, manage and monitor financial and non-financial risks and review and

Table 3.6 (continued)

Date	Document	Requiring or recommending:
		approve the internal financial control and risk management statements that are included in the annual report.
2003	Combined Code	The above-mentioned provisions of the 2000 Code and the Higgs and Smith reports.
2005	Turnbull II Report	Adding to the 1999 Turnbull report: The board should review the information given in the internal control statement of the annual report on a continuing basis.
2006	Combined Code	See the 2003 Combined Code.
2006	2006 Companies Act	The directors have to prepare a directors' report for each financial year of the company, which contains a business review, including a description of the principal risks and uncertainties the company faces.
2008	Combined Code	See the 2003 Combined Code.
2008	Disclosure and Transparency Rules	The audit committee has to, *inter alia*, monitor the financial reporting process and the effectiveness of the internal control, internal audit and risk management systems. The corporate governance statement contains a description of the main features of the company's internal control and risk management systems relating to the financial reporting process. At the consolidated level, the directors' report includes a description of the main features of the group's internal control and risk management systems in relation to the process for preparing consolidated accounts.

Note: *This list is incomplete. Among other things, it excludes state corporate law, case law, SEC final rules, PCAOB Auditing Standards and the Sentencing Guidelines. For information on these documents, see Van Daelen and Van der Elst 2009, pp. 86–87.

3.4   LEGAL RISK MANAGEMENT ENVIRONMENT: TO BE CONTINUED . . .

Section 3.2 of this chapter began by stating that a short historical overview could deepen understanding of the current corporate legal framework of risk management. It went on to describe the development of internal control and risk management provisions over time. Section 3.3 discussed the legal risk management environment of the 21st century. Clearly, the content of this issue has significantly changed over the years. Although this chapter has focused on listed companies because internal control and risk management reforms specifically address publicly held companies, the reforms also affect non-listed companies and government governance. To discuss why and to what extent these provisions can be useful, this section will briefly go into the need for disclosure and enforcement. Since the legal risk management framework might need some revision, this section also aims to make clear what risk management provisions are already included in the legal risk management framework, questioning whether those provisions are in fact useful. In addition, this section will discuss the latest developments to see what the future might hold. Currently, there are arguably more questions than answers concerning risk management. Some issues that need a full and comprehensive analysis – and hence can obviously not be resolved yet – will be addressed below. They may give insight into the legal risk management movements that may prove significant in the years to come.

3.4.1 Level of Disclosure and Enforcement

Corporate frauds and failures have been a major issue for centuries, and it is safe to assume this will not change any time soon. For many decades policymakers and lawmakers have attempted to mitigate poor governance due to opportunistic behaviour and bad management. The separation of ownership and control that characterizes modern corporations was already described by Berle and Means at the beginning of the worldwide Great Depression. Shareholders, the owners of the capital and recourses, do not have direct influence on the firm. This enables managers, those who can decide how capital and recourses are spent, to pursue their own goals. According to Berle and Means, the separation of ownership and control implies shortfalls of competence and responsibility. Almost eighty years later they are proved to be right, as these problems are still shaping company law today.

From a company law perspective, there are two issues arising from the separation of ownership and control that need to be addressed: information asymmetry and enforcement. Shareholders have less – and less up-to-date – information about the company than its managers. This makes it difficult for shareholders to detect mismanagement early. After major corporate failures and frauds especially, additional disclosure requirements are issued in order to restore shareholders' and investors' faith and trust in the reliability of companies and the overall market. For example, in response to the Great Depression, US Congress enacted the Securities Act of 1933 and the Securities Exchange Act of 1934. After the corporate failures and frauds at the beginning of this millennium, the US SOX was enacted and the Dutch Tabaksblat Code was issued. However, disclosure requirements are only useful to shareholders or investors if companies are obliged to disclose the right amount of relevant information. This seems only logical, but gauging the correct level of disclosure is far from easy.[139] To be sure, the creation of many and cumbersome disclosure requirements will result in significant compliance costs for the company. It goes without saying that those costs will have an effect on shareholder wealth through, *inter alia*, dividend payments. Whether shareholders – as well as the company – can profit from disclosure provisions depends on the balance between the profits and the costs of the disclosure of information. Section 3.3 showed that the UK Combined Code only requires the board to report to the shareholders that it has reviewed the effectiveness of the overall internal control and risk management system. By contrast, the Dutch DCGC 2008 requires the board to give a description in the annual report of the design and effectiveness of the risk management and internal control systems for the main risks as well as information on major failings in and significant changes made to the systems. These differences are important in identifying an appropriate disclosure level. Does the UK provision provide enough information or does the Dutch provision provide the market with valuable additional information? Furthermore, if the information of the latter is considered more valuable, what is the effect on the compliance costs? And is the overall outcome more favourable?

A second, and at least as important, issue involves the level of enforcement. The current corporate governance movement is not likely to result in a desirable outcome if both public and private enforcement are weak. The choice between mandatory rules and self-regulation does not stand on its own. History shows that the level of enforcement is of the utmost importance for any rules to succeed. In the Netherlands the self-regulatory corporate governance recommendations of the Peters Committee had no substantive effect. By contrast, the recommendations of the UK Cadbury Committee brought significant changes in governance practices as well as an increase in the average performance of firms. Stronger shareholder rights combined with the Listing Rules containing an obligation for listed companies to disclose whether or not it complied with the code could explain this difference. At the time, in the UK the external auditor already had to review the statement of (non-)compliance and not applying the code opened up the possibility of litigation. Obviously, the market can

---

[139] See for a discussion of mandatory disclosure: Choi & Pritchard 2008, pp. 26ff.

only provide management with incentives to change if mechanisms are in place to facilitate punishing companies for poor governance.[140] If this is not the case, self-regulation to reduce frauds and risk management failures will be based on shaky foundations. The upshot is that the quality of enforcement of either laws or self-regulation is an essential element of corporate governance.[141]

After many decades of attempting to mitigate poor governance due to opportunistic behaviour and bad management, the recent financial scandals arguably show that the 21st century legal risk management framework too was unable to prevent this type of risk from materializing. In search of the correct levels of information disclosure and enforcement of risk management provisions, learning from the past and path dependency are issues to be taken into consideration. 'The strategy for reform is not to create an ideal set of rules and then see how well they can be enforced, but rather to enact the rules that can be enforced within the existing structure'.[142] Before addressing which rules fit the existing structure, it must first be clear what kind of risk management rules are included in the current legal risk management framework.

3.4.2   What Kind of Risk Management Rules do we Have?

The latest financial scandals once again show that the corporate governance framework, especially internal control and risk management, might have to be reconsidered. If the framework ought to give reasonable assurance that bad management and managers serving their own interests can be prevented, it is safe to say it has not succeeded in reaching the intended level. The framework does not seem to properly detect severe fraudulent behaviour in an early stage. It might even have led shareholders and other stakeholders to rely too much on the framework protecting their interests. Hence, one of the main questions relating to risk management, for academics as well as policymakers and lawmakers, is what kind of risk management provisions do we need? Since the legal risk management framework might need some revision, what risk management rules are already included in the legal risk management framework?

Companies currently face several types of risk management provisions at multiple levels. This is the result of years of issuing laws and codes.

---

[140]   De Jong, DeJong, Mertens & Wasley 2001.
[141]   La Porta, Lopez-de-Silanes, Shleifer & Vishny 1997, pp. 1131–1150; La Porta, Lopez-de-Silanes, Shleifer & Vishny 1998, pp. 1113–1155.
[142]   La Porta, Lopez-de-Silanes, Shleifer & Vishny 2000, pp. 3–27.

The outcome is that internal control and risk management provisions not only require public companies to have risk management systems in place, but also they must assess the systems, monitor their effectiveness, disclose information on them and disclose information on the actual risks the company is facing. An interesting question in this context is whether shareholders and other stakeholders can be protected by this mixture of provisions creating an incomplete framework. To be sure, an incomplete regulatory risk management framework does not have to be insufficient. The steps reflected at the first dimension of Tables 3.2 to 3.5 in Section 3.3 are the steps to be taken by companies in establishing their internal control and risk management framework. The regulatory framework does not have to provide requirements for every level. In fact, if the regulatory framework were to be completed for every level, it might result in too many cumbersome rules with too-high compliance costs. Analysing the impact of each provision is more important. For instance, is it necessary to require the board of directors to have, maintain, and monitor internal control and risk management systems in order to make sure that they do so? Or is risk management in this day and age an evident and fundamental constituent of the board's responsibility for managing the company? In other words, will directors manage the company's risks less thoroughly when there are no provisions that require directors to have, maintain and monitor a risk management system, but only provisions that require directors to report how they fulfil their task of managing the company's risks and to what extent their methods are effective?

A related issue is the role of business law regarding risk management provisions. The regulatory risk management framework shows that the focus is both on regulating elements of directors' duty and on ensuring transparency. Before building on the current rules, it might be useful to consider whether fraudulent behaviour and inadequate management can be prevented by trusting directors to fulfil their duty responsibly and with integrity – with sufficient mechanisms in place to enforce proper fulfilment of its duty – and by providing the company and its stakeholders with a coherent regulatory risk management framework that facilitates the audit committees' and external auditors' monitoring and requires reporting. These questions are relevant as they determine whether business law should continue regulating directors' duty, as well as ensuring transparency, or deregulate the first and proceed with the latter.

In addition, the EU regulatory risk management framework started to develop relatively late and is incomplete in several areas.[143] By the time the

---

[143]   Van Daelen & Van der Elst 2009, p. 93.

relevant directives had to be implemented, EU member states had already developed – and were building on – their national internal control and risk management frameworks with requirements in their national corporate laws and/or corporate governance codes. This necessitated EU member states to further complete their national framework with the inclusion of the EU provisions. Although the implementation of the EU directives achieved a measure of harmonisation, the EU member states' approaches to risk management do, at first sight, not fully match up (see Section 3.3). It is not yet clear whether these divergent approaches of EU member states will slow down the creation of a level playing field for companies within the EU.

REFERENCES

Allen, William T., Reinier R. Kraakman, and Guhan Subramanian (2007), *Commentaries and Cases on the Law of Business Organization*, 2nd Edition, New York: Wolters Kluwer/Aspen Publishers.

Arcot, Sridhar R. and Valentina G. Bruno (2006), 'In Letter but not in Spirit: An Analysis of Corporate Governance in the UK', available at http://ssrn.com/abstract=819784 (accessed 23 November 2009).

Banner, Stuart (2002), *Anglo-American Securities Regulations: Cultural and Political Roots 1690–1860*, Cambridge: Cambridge University Press.

Berle, Adolf A. and Gardiner C. Means (1932), *The Modern Corporation and Private Property*, New York: Harcourt, Brace and World, Inc.

Bratton, William W. (2002), 'Enron and the dark side of shareholder value', *Tulane Law Review, forthcoming*, available at http://ssrn.com/abstract=301475 (accessed 23 November 2009).

Choi, Stephen J. and Adam C. Pritchard (2008), *Securities Regulation: cases and analysis*, 2nd Edition, New York: Thomson/Foundation Press.

Coase, Ronald H. (1937), 'The nature of the firm', *Economica*, **4** (16), 386–405, available at http://www3.interscience.wiley.com/journal/119896447/issue (accessed 23 November 2009).

Cunningham, Lawrence A. (2002), 'Sharing accounting's burden: Business lawyers in Enron's dark shadows', *Boston College Working Paper*, available at http://ssrn.com/abstract=307978 (accessed at 23 November 2009).

Daelen, Marijn M.A. van and Christoph F. Van der Elst (2009), 'Corporate regulatory frameworks for risk management in the US and EU', *Corporate Finance and Capital Markets Law Review*, **1** (2), 83–94.

Fayol, Henri (1916), 'Administration industrielle et générale', *Bulletin de la Société de l'Industrie Minérale*, No. 10, 5–164, translated in Fayol, Henri (1949), *General and industrial management*, London: Pitman.

Fernald, Henry B. (1943), 'Internal auditing', *The Accounting Review*, **18** (3), 228–34, available at http://www.jstor.org/pss/240766 (accessed 23 November 2009).

Frentrop, Paul (2002), *Ondernemingen en hun aandeelhouders sinds de VOC: Corporate Governance 1602 – 2002*, Amsterdam: Prometheus.

Gaastra, Femme S. (2002), *De geschiedenis van de VOC*, 4th Edition, Zuthpen: Walburg Pers.

Harris, Ron (1994), 'The Bubble Act: Its passage and its effects on business organization', *The Journal of Economic History*, **54** (3), 610–27.

Heier, Jan R., Michael T. Dugan and David L. Sayers (2004), 'Sarbanes-Oxley and the culmination of internal control development: A study of reactive evolution', *American Accounting Association 2004 Mid-Atlantic Region Meeting Paper*, available at http://ssrn.com/abstract=488783 (accessed 23 November 2009).

Heijer, Henk J. den (2005), *De Geoctrooieerde Compagnie: de VOC en de WIC als voorlopers van de naamloze vennootschap*, Deventer: Kluwer.

Jensen, Michael C. and William H. Meckling (1976), 'Theory of the firm: Managerial behavior, agency costs and ownership structure', *Journal of Financial Economics*, **3** (4), 305–60.

Jong, Abe de, Douglas V. DeJong, Gerard Mertens and Charles E. Wasley (2001), 'The Role of Self-Regulation in Corporate Governance: Evidence from The Netherlands', *Erasmus Research Institute of Management Report Series Reference No ERS-2001-87-F&A*, available at http://publishing.eur.nl/ir/repub/asset/148/erimrs20020119130128.pdf (accessed 23 November 2009).

Keynes, John M. (1921), *A Treatise on Probability*, London: Macmillan.

Knight, Frank H. (1921), *Risk, Uncertainty, and Profit*, Boston, MA: Hart, Schaffner & Marx; Houghton Mifflin Company.

Kraakman, Reinier R., Paul Davies, Henry Hanssmann, Gerard Hertig, Klaus J. Hopt, Hideki Kanda and Edward B. Rock (2004), *The Anatomy of Corporate Law – A Comparative and Functional Approach*, Oxford: Oxford University Press.

La Porta, Rafael, Florencio Lopez-de-Silanes, Andrei Shleifer and Robert W. Vishny (1997), 'Legal determinants of external finance', *Journal of Finance*, **52**, 1131–1150.

La Porta, Rafael, Florencio Lopez-de-Silanes, Andrei Shleifer and Robert W. Vishny (1998), 'Law and finance', *Journal of Political Economy*, **106**, 1113–1155.

La Porta, Rafael, Florencio Lopez-de-Silanes, Andrei Shleifer and Robert W. Vishny (2000), 'Investor protection and corporate governance', *Journal of Financial Economics*, **58**, 3–27.

McCahery, Joseph A. and Erik P.M. Vermeulen (2008), *Corporate Governance of Non-Listed Companies*, Oxford: Oxford University Press.

Moeller, Robert R. (2005), *Brink's Modern Internal Auditing*, 6th Edition, Hoboken, New Jersey: John Wiley and Sons, Inc.

Moye, John E. (2004), *The Law of Business Organizations*, 6th Edition, New York: Thomson Delmar Learning.

Raaijmakers, Theo (M.)J.G.C. (2006) *Ondernemingsrecht*, Pitlo Deel 2, Deventer: Kluwer.

Ramsey, Frank P. (1931), 'Truth and Probability', *The Foundations of Mathematics and Other Logical Essays*, New York: Harcourt Brace.

Rayton, Bruce A. and Swuina Cheng (2004), 'Corporate Governance in the United Kingdom: Changes to the regulatory template and company practice from 1998–2002', University of Bath, School of Management, *Working Paper Series 2004.13*, available at http://www.bath.ac.uk/management/research/pdf/2004-13.pdf (accessed 23 November 2009).

Ribstein, Larry E. (2002), 'Market vs. regulatory responses to corporate fraud: A critique of the Sarbanes-Oxley Act of 2002', *Journal of Corporation Law*, **28** (1), available at http://ssrn.com/abstract=332681 (accessed 23 November 2009).

Ricklefs, Merle C. (1991), *A History of Modern Indonesia Since c.1300*, 2nd Edition, London: MacMillan.

Romano, Roberta (2005), 'The Sarbanes-Oxley Act and the making of Quack corporate governance', *Yale ICF Working Paper* **05** (23).

Savage, Leonard J. (1954), *The Foundations of Statistics*, New York: John Wiley & Sons, Inc.

Talbot, Lorraine E. (2007), *Critical Company Law*, Abingdon: Routledge-Cavendish.

Taylor, Frederick W. (1911), *The Principles of Scientific Management*, New York: Harper & Brothers.

Vries, Jan de & Ad van der Woude (2005), *Nederland 1500–1815: De eerste ronde van moderne economische groei*, Amsterdam: Balans.

Zeckhauser, Richard J. (1991), 'The Strategy of Choice' in *Strategy and Choice*, Massachusetts: MIT Press.

CODES AND GUIDELINES

Cadbury Committee (1992), *Report on the Financial Aspect of Corporate Governance*, London: Gee, (Cadbury Report).

Cohen Commission (1978), *Commission on Auditors' Responsibility: Report, Conclusions, and Recommendations*, New York: AICPA Inc., (Cohen Report).

Committee of Sponsoring Organizations of the Treadway Commission (COSO) (1992), *Internal Control – Integrated Framework*, New York: AICPA Inc., (COSO I Report).

Committee of Sponsoring Organizations of the Treadway Commission (COSO) (1996), *Guidance on Monitoring Internal Control Systems Internal Control Issues in Derivatives Usage*, New York: AICPA Inc.

Committee of Sponsoring Organizations of the Treadway Commission (COSO) (1999), *Fraudulent Financial Reporting: 1987–1997 – An Analysis of U.S. Public Companies*, New York: AICPA Inc.

Committee of Sponsoring Organizations of the Treadway Commission (COSO) (2004), *Enterprise Risk Management – Integrated Framework*, Executive Summary, New York: AICPA Inc., (COSO II Report).

Committee on Corporate Governance (2000), *The Combined Code – Principles of Good Governance and Code of Best Practice*, (Combined Code 2000).

Corporate Governance Code Monitoring Committee (2008), *Report on the Evaluation and Updating of the Dutch Corporate Governance Code*.

Corporate Governance Code Monitoring Committee (Frijns Committee) (2008), *The Dutch Corporate Governance Code – Principles of Good Corporate Governance and Best Practice Provisions* (2008 DCGC).

Department of Trade and Industry (2003), *Review of the role and effectiveness of non-executive directors* (Higgs I Report).

Final Report of the High Level Group of Company Law Experts (2002), *A Modern Regulatory Framework for Company Law in Europe*, Brussels.

Financial Reporting Council (FRC) (2003), *Audit Committees – Combined Code Guidance* (Smith Report).

Financial Reporting Council (FRC) (2003), *The Combined Code on Corporate Governance*, (Combined Code 2003).

Financial Reporting Council (FRC) (2005), *Internal Control – Revised Guidance for Directors on the Combined Code* (Turnbull II Report).

Financial Reporting Council (FRC) (2006), *Good Practice Suggestions from the Higgs Report* (Higgs II Report).

Financial Reporting Council (FRC) (2006), *The Combined Code on Corporate Governance*, (Combined Code 2006).

Financial Reporting Council (FRC) (2006), *UK Approach to Corporate Governance*.

Financial Reporting Council (FRC) (2008), *The Combined Code on Corporate Governance*, (Combined Code 2008).

Greenbury Committee (1995), *Directors' Remuneration – Report of a Study Group Chaired by Sir Richard Greenbury*, London: Gee, (Greenbury Report).

Hampel Committee (1998), *Committee on Corporate Governance – Final report*, London: Gee, (Hampel Report).

Minahan Committee (1979), *Report of the Special Advisory Committee on Internal Accounting Control*, New York: AICPA Inc., (Minahan Report).

Peters Committee (Committee on Corporate Governance) (1997), *Corporate Governance in Nederland – De Veertig Aanbevelingen* (Corporate Governance in the Netherlands – Forty Recommendations), (Peters Report).

Rutteman Working Group (1994), *Internal Control and Financial Reporting*, London: The Institute of Chartered Accountants in England and Wales (ICAEW), (Rutteman Report).

Tabaksblat Committee (Corporate Governance Committee) (2003), *The Dutch corporate governance code: Principles of good corporate governance and best practice provisions,* (Tabaksblat Code).

Treadway Commission (1987), *Report of the National Commission on Fraudulent Financial Reporting*, New York: AICPA Inc., (Treadway Report).

Turnbull Committee (1999), *Internal Control: Guidance for Directors on the Combined Code*, London: The Institute of Chartered Accountants in England & Wales (ICAEW), (Turnbull I Report).

EU LEGISLATION AND DOCUMENTS

Regulation (EC) No. 1606/2002 of the European Parliament and of the Council of 19 July 2002 on the application of international accounting standards, OJ L 243 of 11 September 2002 (IAS Regulation).

Directive 78/660/EEC of the Council of the European Communities of 25 July 1978 on the annual accounts of certain types of companies, OJ L 222 of 14 August 1978 (Fourth Directive)

Directive 83/349/EEC of the Council of the European Communities of 13 June 1983 on consolidated accounts, OJ L 193 of 18 July 1983 (Seventh Directive).

Directive 84/253/EEC of the Council of the European Communities of 10 April 1984 based on Article 54 (3) (g) of the Treaty on the approval of persons responsible for carrying out the statutory audits of accounting documents, OJ L 126 of 12 May 1984 (Eighth Directive).

Directive 2001/65/EC of the European Parliament and of the Council of 27 September 2001 amending Directives 78/660/EEC, 83/349/EEC and 86/635/ EEC as regards the valuation rules for the annual and consolidated accounts of certain types of companies as well as of banks and other financial institutions, OJ L 283 of 27 October 2001 (IAS 39 Directive).

Directive 2003/51/EC of the European Parliament and of the Council of 18 June 2003 amending Directives 78/660/EEC, 83/349/EEC, 86/635/EEC and 91/674/ EEC on the annual and consolidated accounts of certain types of companies, banks and other financial institutions and insurance undertakings, OJ L 178 of 17 July 2003.

Directive 2004/109/EG of the European Parliament and the Council of 15 December 2004 on the harmonisation of transparency requirements with regard to information about issuers whose securities are admitted to trading on a regulated market, OJ L 390 of 31 December 2004 (Transparency Directive).

Directive 2006/43/EC of 17 May 2006 of the European Parliament and of the Council on statutory audits of annual accounts and consolidated accounts, amending Council Directives 78/660/EEC and 83/349/EEC and repealing Council Directive 84/253/EEC, OJ L 157 of 9 June 2006 (Audit Directive).

Directive 2006/46/EC of 14 June 2006 of the European Parliament and of the Council amending Council Directives 78/660/EEC on the annual accounts of certain types of companies, 83/349/EEC on consolidated accounts, 86/635/ EEC on the annual accounts and consolidated accounts of banks and other financial institutions and 91/674/EEC on the annual accounts and consolidated accounts of insurance undertakings, OJ L 224 of 16 August 2006 (Amendment to Accounting Directives).

Commission Recommendation 2005/162/EC of 15 February 2005 on the role of non-executive or supervisory directors of listed companies and on the committees of the (supervisory) board, OJ L 52 of 25 February 2005.

Communication from the Commission to the Council and the European Parliament, Modernising Company Law and Enhancing Corporate Governance in the European Union – A Plan to Move Forward, [COM(2003) 284 final], 21 May 2003, (Commission's Plan to Move Forward).

4. Risk management in financial law

Christoph Van der Elst and Filip Bogaert

4.1 INTRODUCTION

Risk management is high on the agenda of all companies in the financial industry and even of many businesses. The financial crisis requires companies to develop policies assessing risk and providing reasonable responses to changing circumstances in a timely manner. The crisis illustrates that these strategies are distinguishing factors in whether a (financial) company survives or not.

As individual chapters in this book illustrate, risk management is embedded in different fields of research. This is logical, as it is related to doing business. Running a business implies taking risks. As long as businesses exist they are confronted with risk. This also applies to the financial industry. Although financial transactions have taken place for thousands of years, in the Western world it was not until during the Middle Ages that the need was felt to transfer large sums of money, in particular to finance the crusades. At medieval trade fairs money-changers issued documents that were redeemable at other fairs. These documents developed into bills of exchange. With the acceptance of endorsement of bills of exchange the documents were easier to trade. Specific institutions were needed to accept these endorsed bills of exchange. The documents decreased the need to hire armed guards and mitigated the risks of robbery. It required money to be kept in custody and supplying money in another place. Often goldsmiths kept such valuables as gold coins but also jewels in strongboxes. The goldsmiths could even charge people for keeping those deposits and later start lending the money to third parties and charge the lenders. As gold coins were heavy, the money-lenders started to issue credit notes which could be traded: the origin of paper money. Money-lenders soon found that more notes could be issued than the amount of gold coins and other assets deposited. They noticed that at any time only a small proportion of the gold they held was withdrawn. The mechanism fostered economic growth but contained a risk that the money-lenders could not perform when the gold deposits were reclaimed. Trust in the money-lenders and the convertibility of the paper into *real value* gold, silver and other valuables was crucial for the development of the financial industry. The principle of modern banking was established. Distrust in banks regularly caused severe financial crises. In the 1820s speculation in South American government securities caused many small regional banks in the United Kingdom to issue bank notes. When confidence in these banks ebbed in 1825, several small banks went bankrupt and panic caused a run on the banks, which was followed by several further bankruptcies. To restore confidence Peel's Act was passed. The Act forced banks to divide into two departments, one for issuing notes and one for the banking business.[1]

During the same era of the money-lenders local governments started to develop new methods of public finance. In the low countries *rentes*, a specific kind of annuities, were sold to the public. The success of these *rentes* depended on a well-established secondary financial market for these instruments as well as for other government-related financial instruments.[2] The first exchange for these instruments was established in Antwerp in 1531, which was later, after the Protestants were expelled from Antwerp in 1585, eclipsed by the Amsterdam exchange, which profited from the booming economy of the Dutch Republic of the United Provinces.

Around that period, new ventures were started: capital was gathered to buy vessels and overseas trading was fully explored. The British Russia Company was set up in 1553 and one of their three vessels returned from a commercial trip from Russia to England. The Company obtained a royal charter as *'one bodie and perpetuall fellowship and communaltie'* [3] as well as a monopoly on the trade with Russia. Financing these risky and long-term trading ventures required the pooling of funds which could only be raised via the sales of shares to hundreds or even thousands of investors. These investors together owned the joint stock, hence the name joint stock company. In the late 16th century other major joint-stock companies started, like the Levant Company and the East India Company in England and the most famous of all, the Dutch East India Company. The difference with these new forms of enterprises was the charter of incorporation. Whilst the other types of enterprises could be seen as partnerships with unlimited liability of all partners, these joint stock companies were considered as *bodies* with a legal status, separate from the members, meaning that the liability of the latter was limited to the amount the holder had

---

[1]   For an analysis of a number of banking crises, see Tilly 2008, p. 17, and Caprio and Honohan 2001, pp. 80–81.

[2]   Munro 2006, pp. 11–13.

[3]   Munro 2006, pp. 49–50.

Table 4.1　Overview of financial crises between the 15th and 20th centuries

Year	Commodities	Companies	Real Estate	Banks	Financial Assets
1400				Bardi & Peruzzi (Florence), 1348	
1500	Gold (New World), 1550s			Medici (Florence), 1492	Bourse loans (Antwerp), 1557
1600	Coins in Spain, 1618 **Tulips, 1640**	Dutch East India Co., 1636–40	Canals, elegant houses (Holland) 1636–40	Fugger (Augsburg), 1596	
1700		**South Seas (London), Companie d'Occident (Paris), 1720**		**Sword Blade (London), Banques Generale & Royale (Paris), 1720**	
		British and Dutch East India Co., 1772		British country banks, 1750s	British gilts in Amsterdam, 1763
	Sugar, coffee, 1799	Dutch East India Co., 1783 French canals, 1793		British country banks, 1793	Assignats (France), 1795
1800	Exports, 1810 and 1816		Biens Nationaux (France), 1825		
		British, French canals, 1820s	Chicago, 1830–42	British country banks, 1824	Foreign bonds, foreign mines, new companies, Britain, 1825
	Cotton in Britain, France; exports into Britain, 1836	British railroads, 1836	Chicago, 1843–62		Foreign mines, Britain, France 1850
	Sugar, coffee in Hamburg, wheat, 1857	British and French railroads, 1847	Chicago, US public land, 1853–77	Germany, 1850	
	Cotton, 1861	French and US railroads, 1857		Overend Gurney	

Table 4.1 (continued)

Year	Commodities	Companies	Real Estate	Banks	Financial Assets
	Gold (New York), 1869 Petroleum (US), 1871	US railroads, 1873		(London), 1866; Credit Mobilier (Paris), 1867	
		Panama Canal Company, France, 1888	Chicago, Berlin, Vienna, 1878–98	Germany 1870s	
	Copper (France), 1888; Petroleum (Russia), 1890s	US railroads, 1893	Argentine public lands; Chicago, 1890s	Union Generale (Paris), 1882	Foreign bonds, France; British discount houses, 1888
				Barings (London), 1890	
1900	Copper, US, 1907			Knickerbocker Trust (New York), 1907	
		Interna-tional Mercantile Marine, 1914 General Motors, 1920	US farmland, 1918–21	Creditanstalt, Austria), 1931	*Bills of Exchange, London, 1914* **1920s; German Reichsmark, French franc** Mergers, UK; foreign bonds, new shares, NY FDI, US Conglomerates, sterling, 1960s US dollar, 1973
			Florida, 1920s	500 US banks, 1932–3	
	Penn Central Railroad, 1970				
	Oil tankers, 1974				*LDC debt*
		Burmah Oil, 1974; Pertamina (Indonesia), 1975	US farmland 1970s		
	Gold, 1978–82	*Chrysler Auto, 1979*	US Southwest,	Banco Ambrosiano (Italy), 1982	
	Silver, 1980	California 1970s–80s	*US S&Ls, 1980s*		
	Coffee, cocoa etc., 1986			***Argentina, 1980–89 Chile, 1981***	**US dollar (1985) FDI in US, 1980s Junk bonds (US), 1989–90**

Table 4.1 (continued)

Year	Commodities	Companies	Real Estate	Banks	Financial Assets
				Japan, US 1980s–92	**Japanese shares, 1980s;**
			USREITs, offices, malls, hotels;	*Sweden 1990*	***Vietnamese credit cooperatives***
		PanAmerican Airways, 1991 Guinness Peat Aviation, 1992	Japan, Sweden 1980s	BCCI, 1991	Korean mergers, 1990s Emerging market shares, 1990s Romanian, Albanian Ponzi Schemes
	Copper, Japan 1996			***Mexico 1994*** Barings (Singapore), 1995	Derivatives (Orange Country; Metallgesellschaft, Ashanti Gold Mines), forex futures, options **Russian bonds, long-term capital management, 1998**
		Korean Chaebols; Thailand 1997	*Thailand, 1996–97*	*Indonesia, Republic of Korea, Malaysia, Thailand 1997–98*	High tech stocks, US dollar 1997
		Enron, Worldcom, *Parmalat,* HIH, etc. (2001–2003)		**Subprime mortgages, CDOs, credit crunch, Fannie Mae Freddie Mac, Lehman Brothers, AIG, Fortis, ING, Northern Rock etc. (2007-??)**	**Financial crises spill-over effect to the economy (2007-??)**

Note: Items in italics indicate government support and items in bold indicate a major crash.

Source: For 1400–1998: G. Caprio and P. Honohan, *Finance for Growth: Policy Choices in a Volatile World*, MPRA Paper No. 9929, March 2001, 80–81.

agreed to pay in buying the shares. The success of these companies could only be fostered if it was accompanied with a facility to trade the shares.[4] Stock exchanges like the Amsterdam Stock Exchange and the London Stock Exchange encouraged the establishment of companies – of which many remained unchartered – to increase their business.

In the UK a first speculative boom burst in 1719. The South Sea Company issued stock for financing short-term government debt and the exclusive right for trade with the Spanish colonies in South America. The directors of that company used both fair and unfair techniques to drive up the market price of the stock. This kind of *free market lunch* resulted in a run, offering many different kinds of ventures. Investors were eager to buy the shares of these companies. When a number of assessments were published, indicating that the business of the South Sea Company and other companies contained many unrealistic promises concerning dividends, it became clear that many of these ventures were focused on quick capital gains. Panicky behaviour resulted in a severe market correction and the passing of the *Bubble Act*. This Act prohibited raising capital by the issue of transferable shares in the absence of a Royal Charter or Act of Parliament.[5]

These two short presentations on the development of stock exchanges and banks show the importance of a reliable financial system and reliable financial institutions. The long list of financial crises over the last centuries[6] illustrates that Adam Smith's *invisible hand* and free trade are insufficient.

4.2   THE FINANCIAL SECTOR AND FINANCIAL SYSTEM

Both the financial system and the financial sector must be encouraged to limit excessive risks and reduce information and transaction costs. The financial sector can be defined as 'that part of an economy which offers and provides financial services to the other sectors of the economy. It consists of the central bank, other banks, non-bank financial institutions, organized financial markets and the relevant regulatory and supervisory institutions'.[7]

The financial system can be defined as 'the interaction between the

---

[4]   Frentrop 2002, pp. 66–68.
[5]   Cheffins 2008, pp. 137–140.
[6]   For an overview of a number of cases see Chapter 2.
[7]   Schmidt and Tyrell 2004, p. 21.

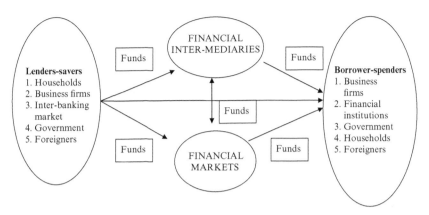

Figure 4.1   The financial system

supply of and the demand for the provision of capital and other finance-related services.'[8] Figure 4.1 illustrates how this financial system works. Parties can either directly or indirectly provide their excess liquidities to the market. Direct financing occurs when these parties provide the borrowers with the liquidities via the financial market. This is the case, *inter alia*, when a household buys a bond issued by the government offered on the market or when a foreigner acquires shares of a company (via the financial market). Indirect financing occurs when parties with excess liquidities deposit or invest this money in intermediaries that support the parties who are short of cash. Households that open a savings account or large (institutional) investors that fund private equity investors to finance buy-outs of firms are examples of indirect financing. Both the financial market and the financial intermediaries channel the funds from sectors with a surplus to sectors with a shortage of funds. It must be noted that financing can occur without the intervention of the financial market or the financial intermediaries. When a household directly provides a loan to a private company, the financial market is not necessarily involved.

The financial system with intermediaries and markets reduces the information asymmetry between supply and demand of capital; that is, of borrowers and lenders and provides for risk mitigating techniques. Before turning to examples of how risks in the financial system are mitigated, the most important risks in this system and the structure of financial law vis-à-vis these risks will be addressed in the next section.

[8]   Schmidt and Tyrell 2004, p. 21.

4.3   RISK AND FINANCIAL LAW

4.3.1   Risks *of* and *within* the Financial System

The financial system facilitates the channelling of funds from lenders to borrowers. The service results in risk-mitigation opportunities. Lenders cannot always observe the behaviour of borrowers. Borrowers know more about the project for which they tap capital and can engage in activities that are undesirable. The financial system pools the savings and enables the financing of large projects. At the same time the financial intermediaries mitigate the information-acquisition costs, as well as the monitoring costs of borrowers.

However, financial intermediation must be government-supported. Moral hazard, adverse selection, and information asymmetries are sources of risk that cannot be fully excluded without government intervention. Financial intermediaries that have incentives to engage in too many risky activities may fail to channel the funds in a prudent way. Government intervention is required at several levels. Firstly, the government provides the framework to protect property rights and to enforce contracts. The allocation of property rights ensures that people want to enter into (property) transactions. The government ensures that these transactions, embedded in contracts, can be enforced if one party fails to perform the conditions of that (transaction) contract. Secondly, the government can provide an information disclosure system that reduces the aforementioned problems of moral hazard, adverse selection and information asymmetries for both borrowers and financial intermediaries. Thirdly, financial intermediaries must guarantee their soundness. While the first and part of the second task of the government is not specifically aimed at the financial system, the third task and part of the second task as far as it is related to the transactions in the financial markets is specifically designed for the financial system.

Risk is often defined as the probability of an undesirable event or as the variability of future outcomes.[9] Risk should be separated from uncertainty. Uncertainty is commonly used to describe a state of not knowing whether a proposition is true or false, but the degree of uncertainty does not affect the degree of exposure to that proposition.[10] Risks in the world of financial services and markets have many different forms: the interest rates may rise, a creditor may fail to pay its debt, or the participants may

---

[9]   For an overview of these concepts, see Chapter 1.
[10]   Holton 2004, pp. 21–22.

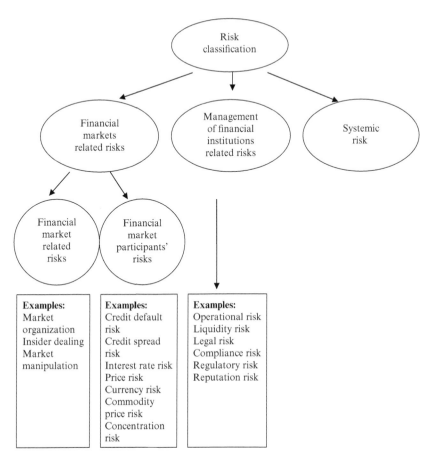

Figure 4.2 Risks in the financial system

default. Often risks are classified in two broad classes: business risks and financial risks. The first class, the business risks, is related to the nature of the firm's operational activities. The second class, the financial risks, arises from losses in the financial markets. Given the nature of the products and services in the financial industry, business risks are related to financial risks. Another classification is the distinction between systematic risk and unsystematic risk. The first class is related to the market, like the risk of inflation, recession or a bear market. The second is related to the company, organization or entity.

Figure 4.2 presents an overview of some of the most important risks of the financial system. Financial markets bring together many participants with complementary needs. When organizations enter into business relationships, and into particular financial relations, risks emerge. In the financial system several classes of risks can be identified.

Firstly, there are the risks that are related to the (functioning of the) financial market, like a failing market operator, the abuse of (inside) information, misleading investors, changes in the interest rates or a default of a borrower. Financial law is concerned with the trading places and in particular the integrity and the efficiency of the marketplace. IOSCO[11] identified several risks related to the market itself: the incompetence of the operator, an inefficient trading system, non-performance or a deficient review of the products traded. Market operators must have the competence and the ability to control the reliability of the market participants in order to make sure that the participants are treated fairly and in a consistent manner. Directly related to the well-functioning of the market are clearing and settlement systems, that is, the systems that guarantee that the transfer of ownership in return for payment is performed. It contains a number of stages – custody, confirmation, clearing and settlement – and each stage encounters operational and other risks, that is, risks that transactions are not properly executed or not brought to an effective end.

The market risk comes from the adverse movement of the (market) price of an investment or asset, and in particular of financial instruments. This risk can be systematic when there is an overall movement in the prices of assets and instruments in the economy, or unsystematic when it arises out of the price movement of a particular asset or instrument. The volatility of the prices and thus the market risk can be subdivided into a number of specific market risks: (equity) price risk, interest rate risk, currency risk and commodity price risk. The price risk is the risk of an adverse price movement of a financial instrument, like a share or bond. The interest rate risk is related to unexpected changes in the interest rate. A company or household that has borrowed on a variable interest rate is exposed to this type of risk. The currency risk stems from the change in the price of one currency against another. When a Eurozone investor acquires stock in an American listed entity the unsystematic risk of the investment is aggravated by the systematic risk of changes in the dollar/euro exchange rate.[12] The commodity price

---

[11] The International Organisation of Securities Commissions is an international standard setter for securities markets.

[12] Between the introduction of the euro in 1999 and the end of 2009, the USD/EUR exchange rate fluctuated between 1.20 (November 2000) and 0.63 (July 2008). If the investor had bought an American financial instrument of €10 in November 2000 and sold this instrument in July 2008 and the price of the financial instrument remained unchanged (in USD), he would only receive €5,25 in July

risk refers to risks of adverse movements of the future market values of a commodity.[13]

A second class of risks is related to the manipulative behaviour of the participants. Market manipulation and market trading on the basis of undisclosed information disturbs the efficient price formation process and investors' confidence. The credit default risk is the risk that the counterparty will fail to meet its obligations in accordance with the agreed terms and conditions. Related to the credit default risk is the credit spread risk. The rate that the bank charges on a loan will depend, to some extent, on the borrower's ability to repay, which is the risk of default. After the loan has been granted, the borrower's financial situation may change, while it is not necessarily possible to adjust the rate to reflect the new situation. This change in the quality of the loan increases the opportunity cost of the lender. Another risk that is related to the credit default risk is the concentration risk,[14] which refers to the famous statement *don't put all your eggs in one basket*. An investor runs the risk that it may invest too great a proportion of its funds in one particular asset, investment, or class of instruments.

Related to the former class of risks are those that can have an impact on the whole economy, the systemic risks. Systemic risk can be defined as[15]

the risk that (i) an economic shock such as market or institutional failure triggers (through panic or otherwise) either (X) the failure of a chain of markets or institutions or (Y) a chain of significant losses to financial institutions, (ii) resulting in increases in the cost of capital or decreases in its availability, often evidenced by substantial financial-market price volatility.

Systemic risk can be seen as a risk *to* the financial system, as opposed to financial risks *within* the financial system.[16]

Due to the interdependencies in the financial system, a bank run can be the start of a systemic risk crisis. The deposits that bankers hold and for which they pay interest are used to provide loans to others. When many depositors want to withdraw their funds, the banks experience a shortage of cash which might cause the bank to collapse. Bank failure can lower

---

2008 (€10/1,2 = US$8333 investment in November 2000 and US$8333*0,63 = €5,25 in July 2008)

[13] While the oil price hit a low of US$ 20 a barrel in 2001, the price soared to more than US$140 a barrel in 2008 and fell back to less than US$40 a barrel in February 2009.

[14] See Basel Committee on Banking Supervision 2006, p.3.

[15] Schwarcz 2008, p. 204.

[16] Schwarcz 2008, p. 207.

Table 4.2   Worldwide systemic risk banks

Country	Banking groups	Country	Banking groups
US	Bank of America Merrill Linch	Spain	Santander
		Italy	Banca Intesa
US	Citigroup	Italy	UniCredit
US	Goldman Sachs	Germany	Deutsche Bank
US	JP Morgan Chase	Netherlands	ING
US	Morgan Stanley	Japan	Mitsubishi UFJ
Canada	Royal Bank of Canada	Japan	Mizuho
		Japan	Nomura
UK	Barclays	Japan	Soumitomo Mitsui
UK	HSBC		
UK	Royal Bank of Scotland	**Country**	**Insurance groups**
UK	Standard Chartered	the Netherlands	Aegon
Switzerland	UBS	Germany	Allianz
Switzerland	Credit Suisse	UK	Aviva
France	BNP Paribas	France	AXA
France	Société Générale	Switzerland	Swiss Re
Spain	BBVA	Switzerland	Zurich

Source: Patrick Jenkins and Paul Davies, 'Thirty Groups on Systemic Risk List',
Financial Times, 30 November 2009, p. 1.

the level of confidence of the public in the financial industry and cause
other depositors to withdraw their money from other banks, causing these
banks to fail as well. During the Great Depression of the 1930s the number
of banks in the US decreased from approximately 24 000 in 1929 to 15 000
in 1933, mainly due to this type of failure. At the same time, the price index
fell by more than 30 per cent and the unemployment rate soared from 3
per cent to approximately 25 per cent.[17] In 2009 financial regulators from
all over the world, under the auspices of the Financial Stability Board,
identified 30 financial institutions which, if they failed for whatever reason,
could cause and/or contribute to a worldwide systemic risk. These financial institutions are included in Table 4.2. With four Swiss companies and
two Dutch companies on the one hand and the absence of any company
from China, Brazil or Russia on the other, it is clear that the size of the
country is no longer related to the importance of companies for the well-
functioning of the financial system.

---

[17]   Kohn 1991, p. 104.

Next, there are those risks that are related to the financial intermediaries and management of financial institutions, for example managers who breach the law. As risks that are related to the financial markets, risks related to the management of financial intermediaries are subdivided into several subtypes. First, the operational risk is defined by the Basel Committee on Banking Supervision as 'the risk of loss resulting from inadequate or failed internal processes, people and systems or from external events'.[18] The Basel Committee identified four causes of loss:

1. Internal processes (due to, for example, inaccurate transaction execution or errors in model specifications)
2. people (due to, for example, fraud or incompetence)
3. systems (due to, for example, program failure or breakdown or telecommunication system failure)
4. external events.

The Basel Committee includes the legal risk, which is the risk that somebody files a claim against the financial intermediary, as an operational risk. In a broader perspective legal risk includes compliance and regulatory risks, which is the inability to meet the (new) legal and regulatory requirements of both prudential supervision and the conduct of business supervision.

Reputation risk is the risk that the organization fails to meet expectations. The US Federal Reserve defines reputation risk as 'the risk to earnings and capital arising from negative publicity regarding an institution's business practices.'[19] This type of risk is regularly seen as the most important risk in business, as the Economist Intelligence Unit found in a survey of 269 senior risk managers.[20] The biggest source of reputation risk is compliance failure. Due to information asymmetries outsiders know less of the organization than insiders. Trust embodied in reputation alleviates this problem.

The liquidity risk is the risk of the inability 'to fund increases in assets and meet obligations as they come due'.[21] Liquidity is key to the financial industry. There is also a market component to liquidity risk. Unusually

---

[18]   Basel Committee on Banking Supervision 2001, p. 2.
[19]   Board of Governors of the Federal Reserve System, Interagency Statement on the Purchase and Risk Management of Life Insurance 2004, p. 14.
[20]   The Economist Intelligence Unit, *Reputation: Risk of risks*, December 2005, p. 2.
[21]   Basel Committee on Banking Supervision 2008, p. 2.

large (or small) transactions might not be executed due to an absence of counterparties interested in the trade at a fair market price.

4.3.2   Financial Law as a Risk Mitigating Mechanism

Many of the aforementioned risks are addressed in financial law. An important driver for new regulations is externalities, spillovers (of costs) to parties that are not directly involved. As a result of the information asymmetries and adverse selection, the intermediaries may take too much risk. The government mitigates many of these problems via regulatory interventions. Further, it wants to promote stability in the financial markets and avoid disruptions. This explains why much of the financial regulation was developed during periods of financial crises and debacles when the shortcomings of the systems were exposed. The American Securities Act, the Securities Exchange Act and the Sarbanes-Oxley Act are examples of that development. However, encouraging financial stability via regulations might be detrimental to efficiency, create confusion and overlap, and distort incentives in an undesirable manner. During periods of economic prosperity and innovation, many laws and regulations are considered to be cumbersome and deregulation periods provide new incentives for the development of the markets. During the 1980s and 1990s many countries experienced a financial regulations revolution. In 1999 the Gramm-Bleach-Bliley Act repealed the 1933 Glass-Steagal Act that prohibited the combination of banking activities with securities or insurance business thus providing the financial industry with, among other things, more convenience, less cost, and more product diversification.[22] In Japan, which had a system similar to that of the US, *keiretsu* groups allowed significant integration and in the 1980s the deregulation started with the abolition of ceilings on deposit interest rates. In the 1990s the European Financial Area and the introduction of the home country control, which allows financial institutions and financial instruments in the whole European area, boosted the development of a large European financial market. Via the Financial Services Action Plan the European Union further developed this integration process with common rules for securities and derivatives markets, raising capital, complementary pension funds, financial reporting and collateral.[23] More

---

[22]   For a short overview of the main changes, see Barth, Brumbaugh and Wilcox 2000, p. 22.

[23]   Communication of the Commission of 11 May 1999, entitled 'Financial Services: Implementing the Framework for Financial Markets: Action Plan', Com (1999) 232.

recently the European Commission has consolidated and further improved this system.[24]

For banking supervision the Basel Committee has divided the regulatory framework for safety and soundness into three pillars:[25]

1. minimum capital requirements
2. sound supervision review
3. market discipline via appropriate disclosure.

These three pillars to a large extent also capture the risks related to the overall regulatory financial framework. The first two pillars should be broadened and a fourth pillar should be added. These four pillars are:

1. sound capital requirements and investor compensation schemes
2. sound business organizations (financial institutions) with an appropriate risk-management system
3. sound organization of the financial markets including appropriate disclosure
4. sound supervision review.

Firstly, the financial intermediaries must not only be adequately funded, but in light of the inherent risk related to financing and limited by the non-existent mechanisms for savers to influence the decision-making processes of these financial intermediaries, this risk should be mitigated for these lenders via investor compensation schemes. Secondly, financial intermediaries should develop sound business organizations in order to be in control of all the business processes and activities. Thirdly, the financial market must be organized as such as to provide trust to the different participants and prevent fraudulent or even inappropriate behaviour. Finally, the market and the intermediaries require external monitoring. Each of these pillars will be briefly addressed in the next sections and relevant legislative measures will illustrate the tools and mechanisms in place to reach the pillars' objectives.

4.3.2.1 Capital requirements and investor compensation schemes
Many risks can be mitigated with the requirement for the financial intermediaries to maintain sufficient capital. Monitoring the activities of the

---

[24] For a discussion of the improvements, see Commission Green Paper of 3 May 2005.
[25] Basel Committee on Banking Supervision 1999, p. 12.

Table 4.3   Credit assessment for capital requirements

Credit assessment	AAA to AA−	A+ to A−	BBB+ to BB−	Below BB−	Unrated
Risk weight	20%	50%	100%	150%	100%

Source: Basel Committee on Banking Supervision, *International Convergence of Capital Measurement and Capital Standards*, June 2006, p. 22.

financial intermediaries, as well as the financial market, allows for the early detection of inappropriate behaviour. Supervision is also an important mechanism to mitigate the systemic risk. Finally, transparency of the financial intermediaries' activities provides other parties with the necessary information to take disciplinary action.

Over the last decades a large number of laws and regulations have been issued to strengthen the different pillars for both the financial intermediaries and the financial market. The first pillar regarding the financial position of financial intermediaries is structured differently for each type of financial intermediary. Under EU law a bank can only start its business activities if its initial capital and reserves amount to more than €5 million.[26] For each individual bank the total amount of required capital is calculated via a risk-weight approach. The Basel II framework, designed to establish minimum levels of capital[27] and copied in European legislation, provides capital in accordance with the quality of the borrower, which is the credit assessment. The credit assessment results in a risk assignment (Table 4.3). Very good borrowers will be provided with a high rating (AAA to AA−). The probability of default of this type of borrower is limited, hence the relatively low capital requirement for the bank. High risk corporations will be rated with a low rating (below BB−) or even remain ungraded. For these borrowers the bank might even be required to have more capital set aside than the amount of the loan.

Other types of financial intermediaries combine flexible initial capital requirements with additional capital requirements closely tied to the operations of the intermediary. Investment firms must have sufficient initial capital with regard to the nature of the investment services or activities in question.[28]

---

[26]   Directive 2006/48/EC, Article 9, paragraph 1.
[27]   Basel Committee on Banking Supervision, International Convergence of Capital Measurement and Capital Standards, June 2006, p. 333.
[28]   Directive 2004/39/EC, Article 12.

Capital requirements prevent financial intermediaries from defaulting if (some of) the borrowers default. However, investors remain vulnerable to the failure of financial intermediaries. In particular, small investors will not be aware of or may not be in the position to assess the financial intermediary's integrity and financial soundness. To increase confidence in the financial sector and to limit the risk of a run on a credit institution (and as a consequence default), compensation schemes have been developed. In the European Union, deposits are guaranteed by a protection scheme for an amount of up to €20 000,[29] which was recently increased to €50 000[30] and €100 000 from 2011 onwards. This type of protection for investors also has significant risks. First, there is a serious moral hazard that investors take less care in their investment decisions as a safety net is provided. This risk is mitigated via the threshold limitations, the types of investments that are covered as well as the types of protected investors. Next, the system only effectively offers protection to the extent that the investors consider the scheme as robust and reliable to effectively cover the losses in case of a default. In particular, the failure of a large financial institution causes serious doubts about the financial position of the compensation scheme. Finally, the compensation scheme needs reliable organization and supervision, which increases its costs.

4.3.2.2 Business organization

The second pillar, sound business organizations, is generally developed in corporate and business law.[31] The importance of the financial system requires far-reaching frameworks to limit problems of adverse selection, moral hazard and information asymmetries. It is reflected in many additional legal requirements.

In the EC Solvency II Directive,[32] a Directive that aims to ensure the financial soundness of insurance undertakings and to protect policyholders and the financial stability of the system, insurance companies are required to have an effective system of governance which provides sound and prudent management of the business. The persons who run the insurance company must be 'fit and proper': their professional qualifications, knowledge and experience must be adequate to enable sound and prudent management (fit), and they must be of good repute and integrity (proper). Insurance undertakings must have written policies in relation to at least

---

[29] Directive 94/19/EC, Article 7.
[30] Directive 2009/14/EC, Article 1.
[31] For an analysis, see Chapter 3 of this book.
[32] Solvency II Directive, Articles 41 to 46.

risk management, internal control, internal audit and, where relevant, outsourcing. They must ensure that those policies are implemented and reviewed at least annually. The policies must be subject to prior approval by the administrative or management body and be adapted in view of any significant change in the system or area concerned. The risk-management system must comply with a number of mandatory requirements. The system must comprise strategies, processes and reporting procedures necessary to identify, measure, monitor and manage continuously the risks both at individual and aggregate levels. Adequate reporting on the risks to which the undertakings are or could be exposed, and their interdependencies, is required. The risk-management system must be effective and well integrated into the organizational structure and in the decision-making processes of the insurance undertaking, with proper consideration of the persons who effectively run the undertaking or have other key functions. Further, the risk-management function must cover the following additional tasks:[33]

(a) to design and implement the internal model;
(b) to test and validate the internal model;
(c) to document the internal model and any subsequent changes made to it;
(d) to analyse the performance of the internal model and to produce summary reports thereof;
(e) to inform the administrative, management or supervisory body about the performance of the internal model, suggesting areas needing improvement, and up-dating that body on the status of efforts to improve previously identified weaknesses.

Further, Solvency II requires insurance undertakings to provide for an effective internal audit function. This function must be objective and independent from the operational functions. Reports are to be submitted to the administrative or management body.

According to Article 7 of MiFID level 2,[34] allowing investment firms and exchanges to operate throughout the EU, investment firms must have risk management policies, procedures and systems. The minimum requirements given in Article 7 are:

(a) to establish, implement and maintain adequate risk management policies and procedures which identify the risks relating to the firm's activities, processes and systems, and where appropriate, set the level of risk tolerated by the firm;

---

[33] Solvency II Directive, Article 44.
[34] Commission Directive 2006/73/EC.

(b) to adopt effective arrangements, processes and mechanisms to manage the risks relating to the firms' activities, processes and systems, in light of that level of risk tolerance;

(c) to monitor the following:

    (i) the adequacy and effectiveness of the investment firm's risk management policies and procedures;

    (ii) the level of compliance by the investment firm and its relevant persons with the arrangements, processes and mechanisms adopted in accordance with point (b);

    (iii) the adequacy and effectiveness of measures taken to address any deficiencies in those policies, procedures, arrangements, processes and mechanisms, including failures by the relevant persons to comply with such arrangements, processes and mechanisms or follow such policies and procedures.

Next, Article 6 of this Directive requires the appointment of a compliance officer who is responsible for the compliance function and for the reporting, at least annually, regarding this compliance function, any deficiencies regarding compliance and any appropriate remedial measures which have been taken. This compliance function should be empowered with authority, resources, expertise and access to all relevant information. The compliance officer may not be involved in the performance of services or activities he monitors. His remuneration must be set so as to prevent his objectivity from being compromised.

4.3.2.3 Financial market organization and disclosure

The third pillar is related to the organization of the financial markets and the financial intermediaries. The best possible environment for trading must be provided, limiting problems related to information asymmetries. Three broad areas of financial law address these problems:

1. The organization of the market
2. Transparency requirements
3. Insider information duties and market manipulation prohibition.

First of all, trading will only take place when participants have confidence in the reliability of the platform at which the trading occurs. In Europe the organization of a number of these markets is regulated in the MiFID Directive. Multilateral trading facilities (MTFs) are systems that are operated by an investment firm or market operator and bring together buyers and sellers in financial instruments. The competent national authority must authorize the MTFs. This authorization depends on the organizational structure and the facility's programme of operations. An important organizational requirement is related to the facility's risks. The authorization will only be granted to the facility if it has shown that it is adequately equipped 'to manage the risks to which it is exposed, to implement appropriate arrangements and systems to identify all significant risks to its operation and to put in place effective measures to mitigate those risks'.[35]

These trading facilities must also make sure that the market participants apply the market's rulebook. The markets must monitor the transactions and establish and maintain arrangements and procedures to monitor the behaviour of the participants.[36] As always, some market participants, often large professional parties, develop other systems outside the regular markets. A relatively recent phenomenon is the *dark pool*, a private trading system where professional parties also exchange trading information which might deprive the public of information thus decreasing market transparency.

Next to market organization, the second important condition is the disclosure of information allowing all financial market participants to assess and limit their risk exposure. When a borrower wants to tap the capital markets, he must disclose reliable and comparable information allowing investors to assess the risks involved when investing in the securities issued. It ensures investor protection and enhances market efficiency as well as the proper functioning of the securities markets. The first time an issuer taps the capital market, this information is gathered in a prospectus. This document must address the risk factors that are issuer or industry specific.[37]

Market efficiency and investor protection can only be guaranteed if issuers regularly inform the markets of their activities and the risks they encounter. To that end, issuers of securities that are traded on a European regulated market must provide in their annual reports a description of the principal risks and uncertainties that they face.[38]

Thirdly, and related to the first set of rules regarding transparency requirements, there are rules that mitigate information asymmetries via the prohibition to trade and forbidding false or misleading signals to the market. Persons who possess inside information are prohibited from acquiring or disposing of financial instruments to which that information relates.[39] These persons are in the first place all corporate incumbents but also third parties that by virtue of their professional duties or even

---

[35] Directive 2004/39/EC, Article 39 (b).
[36] Directive 2004/39/EC, Article 43.
[37] See the annexes to Commission Regulation (EC) No 809/2004. For an analysis of the disclosed risk factors, see van Daelen 2008.
[38] Directive 2004/109/EC, Article 4, paragraph 2 (c).
[39] Directive 2003/6/EC, Article 2.

criminal activities possess the inside information. These persons are also prohibited from disclosing this inside information to any other person or recommending or inducing any other person to acquire or dispose of the related financial instruments. Inside information is information[40]

> of a precise nature which has not been made public, relating, directly or indirectly, to one or more issuers of financial instruments or to one or more financial instruments and which, if it were made public, would be likely to have a significant effect on the prices of those financial instruments or on the price of related derivative financial instruments.

Issuers must take the necessary steps to make this inside information public as soon as possible to limit the periods of information asymmetry.

Financial markets can also be disturbed by conflicts of interests. For different types of market participants specific rules have been developed to mitigate these conflicts. Investment firms must establish, implement and maintain arrangements to prevent that transactions are entered into with or for clients when inside information or confidential information relating to the client or the transactions is involved. Next these firms must have written policies to address these conflicts.[41]

4.3.2.4 Supervision of financial markets and financial institutions

All previous pillars with their separate regulatory frameworks and rules must be effectively and adequately monitored and enforced. Supervision takes place at different levels and various methodologies are applied. First, there is a difference between *ex ante* and *ex post* monitoring. *Ex ante* monitoring is applied for many financial intermediaries. Before a bank can start its activities, it must submit a detailed file with information about the management of the bank such as the identities of the shareholders and the initial capital. Life and non-life insurance companies must, *inter alia*, submit a scheme of operations, possess a minimum guarantee fund that is run by persons with professional qualifications or experience, prove its solvency margins, and so on. Undertakings for collective investment in transferable securities (UCITS) must be authorized before they can start their activities. The management company of the UCITS must have a management team of good repute that is sufficiently experienced, and a programme of activities must be submitted. Occupational pension schemes will only be registered or authorized if they have submitted properly constituted rules

---

[40] Directive 2003/6/EC, Article 1.
[41] Commission Directive 2006/73/EC, Articles 12 and 22.

and are run by persons of good repute, and if technical provisions are computed and certified by an actuary or specialist.

Similarly, *ex ante* monitoring is applicable to initial public offerings of securities. These offerings must be accompanied by a prospectus that has been approved by the competent authorities.

Ex post monitoring is the monitoring procedure after the event, the behaviour or activity that took place. Most of the *ex post* monitoring is in the hands of the courts. Over the last few years, the financial system has experienced the developments of *ex post* administrative sanctions of supervisory authorities. The organization of the administrative procedure and the system of sanctioning are nationally organized. In the Netherlands, the supervisory authority has already sanctioned late disclosure of inside information, negligence in the duty of care of financial advisors and delay in notifying the presumptive evidence of insider trading. The public announcement of any kind of sanctioning is considered to cause significant reputational damage for financial market participants.

Another approach to supervision of financial markets and systems is related to the division of power of supervision. Over the last decades, the legislator has developed several levels of monitoring and supervision. The main levels of supervision and monitoring are:[42]

1. internal monitoring and compliance
2. monitoring via self-regulatory bodies (like MTFs)
3. private (institutionalized) monitoring (like credit rating agencies)
4. government supervision.

The first level of monitoring is structured within the financial market participants. Over the last few years, many new rules have been issued that require many financial intermediaries to establish internal control and compliance departments that must control its functioning. As was already discussed above, investment firms must appoint a compliance officer who is responsible for the compliance function, for the reporting deficiencies regarding compliance and for any appropriate remedial measures. This compliance function should be empowered with authority, resources, expertise and access to all relevant information.[43]

Secondly, market participants organize procedures and rules and can enforce these rules via the authorized system. MTFs must make sure that

---

[42] For an overview of the division of the supervisory responsibilities related to the securities markets in a number of countries, see Technical Committee of the International Organisation of Securities Commissions 1999, p. 32.

[43] See Section 4.3.2.2.

the participants in the market abide by the market rules. The markets must monitor the transactions and establish and maintain arrangements and procedures to monitor the behaviour of the participants.[44] The operator of the facility has the right and the power to suspend or remove the financial instruments that are traded but no longer comply with the rules of the market.[45]

Thirdly, in specific areas financial and company law requires market participants to submit information to other participants. Certified auditors check the financial information companies disclose to the market. Although the operations of external auditors are performed independently, since the debacles of Enron and WorldCom, new supervisory frameworks have been developed all over the world to monitor the work of these auditors.

Credit Rating Agencies issue creditworthiness opinions. These opinions are supposed to limit the information asymmetries between debt issuers and investors. In the US the credit rating agencies are registered as Nationally Recognized Statistical Rating Organizations (NRSROs). The American rules emphasize the importance of the integrity of the processes of rating agencies.[46] The European Union approved a regulation to require rating agencies to register and disclose the methodologies, models and key rating assumptions.[47] In the meantime, the industry itself is already disclosing a great deal of information on its procedures and work schedules to inform the market and the participants.

Finally, supervision by the government has also been further developed over the last decades. For a long period of time there has been a tendency to connect the supervision to a particular business or even part of the business, like banking and insurance whereas the securities market was to a large extent self-regulated. The result was a significant level of fragmentation of the supervision procedures, often justified by the specificities required to monitor that particular business.

The United States offers an excellent example of this fragmentation. US banks have to opt to be licensed by the federal government or by the individual states. At the federal level[48] several agencies monitor the banks:

1. The Board of Governors of the Federal Reserve System, the central bank of the United States, which is *inter alia* competent to monitor the engagements of bank holding companies in non-banking activities.

---

44   Directive 2004/39/EC, Article 43.
45   Directive 2004/39/EC, Article 41, paragraph 1.
46   For a discussion, see the Securities and Exchange Commission 2009.
47   Regulation No 1060/2009, Article 8.
48   Even state licensed banks can be submitted to some federal rules.

2. The Office of the Comptroller of the Currency, who licences or charters national banks.
3. The Federal Deposit Insurance Corporation, which provides insurance for deposits and acts as a receiver for failed banks. The Corporation also approves material actions of banks, like mergers and acquisitions.
4. The Office of Thrift Supervision who regulates the savings and loans associations.

The Securities and Exchange Commission, established by the Securities and Exchange Act in 1934, supervises the securities markets and sets, in particular, requirements for the disclosure of documents, the rules for market participants like broker dealers, the rules for the mutual fund industry and the investigation of violations. The supervision of the American insurance industry is almost entirely in the hands of the state governments.

The monitoring of the individual financial institutions and the monitoring of the risk of the financial system as a whole has been approached via micro- and macro-prudential supervision. At the European level, micro-prudential supervision is based on the principle of home country control, minimum prudential standards and mutual recognition. Macro-prudential supervision aims at mitigating common or correlated shocks and shocks that trigger unintended domino effects (knock-on effects). Both in Europe and the US, macro-prudential supervision still is under developed: the available warning systems have no mechanisms to ensure that timely and appropriate action is taken.[49] Although the monitors are not the originators of the financial crises of the last few years, it is generally argued that weak supervision did not prevent the excessive borrowing, the cheap credit and the too-complicated financial products.

Both in Europe and in the US, the economic crisis has shown clearly that the supervisory framework was insufficient to prevent the serious financial problems. At the moment of writing the supervision framework in the US is being restructured via a new agency, the Financial Institutions Regulatory Administration, which will combine the competences of four supervisory authorities. The consumer protection role of the Federal Reserve will be transmitted to a Consumer Financial Protection Agency. Next, a new Agency for Financial Stability will monitor the systemic risks.[50] In Europe, a new European System of Financial Supervisors with

---

[49] For an analysis, see the De Larosière Report, p. 85.
[50] Masters 2009, p. 9.

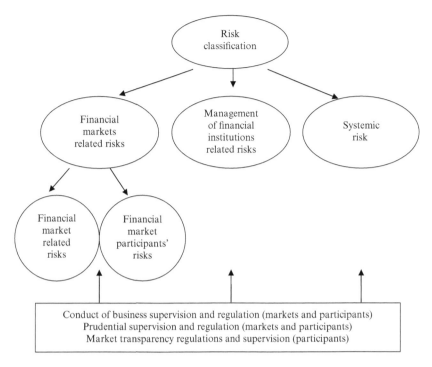

Figure 4.3   Financial law and risk assessment

three new European Supervisory Authorities in a network-oriented structure and a European Systemic Risk Board must prevent a similar financial
crisis to that of 2008 and 2009.[51] Figure 4.3 summarizes the impact of
financial law on financial markets and participants.

4.4   FINANCIAL LAW AS A RISK MANAGEMENT TOOL: CASE STUDIES

The previous sections provided an overview of the most common risks
in the financial system. A number of these risks will now be discussed
in more detail as well as the way in which these risks can be mitigated.
Furthermore, a number of legal instruments issued to address these risks
will be analysed. Finally, it will be shown in what way the mitigation may
result in new risks in some situations. In particular, a number of risks in

---

[51]   See the Commission proposal of 26 October 2009.

the banking industry will be addressed and two mechanisms that mitigate these risks will be explored in more detail: securitization and credit derivatives. In addition, the way in which risk spreading for collective investment schemes is conducted in a European context will be discussed.

4.4.1 The Traditional Deposit Bank: an Overview from a Risk Perspective

Traditional banking activity consists of the collection of numerous small deposits, which are later used to originate loans.[52] The banks (or originators) perform the role of an intermediary[53] who transfers money from economic entities with a surplus (households) to entities that are in need of cash (government and enterprises).[54]

It is important to note that the depositors can withdraw their deposits at any time by simple request, while the bank normally cannot reclaim the cash lent to its borrowers before the maturity of the loan. Additionally, the loans originated by the bank have a much longer maturity than the deposits. The deposits and the loans are the liabilities and the assets of the bank respectively so that the loans are funded by the deposits. In reality the balance sheet of the bank will of course look more complex because the bank has other sources of funding at its disposal, for instance equity and debt instruments, and the bank will also hold other assets.

As far as the loans are funded by the deposits, the balance sheet of the bank operates as a transformation device between the deposits and the loans.[55] In particular, the transformation mainly relates to:

1. The transformation of term: the deposits have a shorter maturity than the loans.
2. The transformation of scale: the origination of one loan requires various smaller deposits.
3. The transformation of risk: if the depositors originate loans themselves, their credit risk exposure will be much higher. As soon as the debtor fails to meet his obligations, the depositor will not receive any payment.

   Intermediation thus reduces the risk exposure of the depositors because the bank will screen and monitor the candidate borrowers and because the depositors fund a small part of the loans allowed by

---

[52] Schrans and Steennot 2003, p. 378; Scholtens and van Wensveen 2003, p. 18.
[53] Bhattacharya 1993, p. 3.
[54] Allen and Santomero 1997, p. 21; Diab and Boustany 2003, pp. 91–92.
[55] Scholtens and van Wensveen 2003, p. 18; Bhattacharya 1993, pp. 4–5.

the bank. The bank acts as a delegated monitor of the depositors[56] and has an advantage over the individual depositor because the monitoring costs are shared over multiple depositors. Furthermore, the insolvency of one debtor will hardly have any consequence for the individual depositors,[57] who are partly exposed to the credit risk.

The credit risk of the depositors is reduced because there is no direct contractual relation between the depositor and the borrower. Each party contracts with the bank, which acts as the intermediary.

4. The currency transformation: each time the funding and the loans are expressed in another currency, the bank takes on a currency risk.

The positive spread between the interest payments received on the loans and interests paid on the deposits are an income for the bank. The on-balance transformation process generates a number of risks.

Firstly, there is the risk of a maturity mismatch. The origin of this risk lies in the fact that various short-term deposits, which the bank has to repay at the first request of the depositors, are used to fund illiquid loans with a much longer maturity. Under normal market conditions the short-term interest rate is lower than the long-term interest rate and the bank will own a positive spread.[58] If, for instance, the interest rate structure inverts, the bank will have to pay a higher interest rate to the depositors than it collects from the loans. The bank can resolve this tension by liquidating (selling) the long-term assets or by obtaining long-term funding. The sale of the assets will only be possible as far as the bank holds a portfolio of liquid (exchange traded) assets. The loans do not meet that requirement.

The fact that a bank often owns illiquid assets with a long maturity is the source of a second problem. If the savers find a better investment or lose their trust in the banking system, they will withdraw their deposits. If the bank is not able to liquidate assets and to free up enough cash to repay its depositors, it will fail.

A bank that has liquid assets and that funds short- and long-term assets with short- and long-term liabilities, respectively, is a stable bank, but one without a large spread income. The management of the bank will have to find a sound equilibrium and have a sufficiently large capital base.

Furthermore, the bank is also exposed to what is understood as the risk of asset dilution. This risk refers to the situation where the bank is confronted with a value decrease of its assets. It is clear that this is a serious

---

56 Diamond 1984, p. 414.
57 Dombrecht and Plasschaert 1989, pp. 16–17.
58 Thakor 1992, p. 679.

threat to the bank. Asset ownership goes along with risk exposure and will either make the owner realize a gain or suffer a loss.

Traditionally, the following broad risk categories have been distinguished:

1. Interest (rate) risk
2. Currency risk
3. Market risk
4. Liquidity risk
5. Credit (default) risk.

The value of the bank's loan portfolio can be affected by a number of risks, the most important one being the credit risk. If a debtor becomes insolvent or goes into bankruptcy, it becomes less likely that the bank will receive a full repayment of the outstanding debt. This will negatively affect the value of the loan. Credit risk can be considered an important risk, but it is certainly not the only one. The value of a fixed loan will decrease as the interest rate increases.

Asset dilution undermines the financial position of the bank. Ultimately the bank will no longer be able to meet its obligations towards the depositors. The risk of asset dilution can be mitigated in several ways. The bank can diversify its assets portfolio by investing in different asset categories with a various risk profile or the bank can enter into hedge transactions. In addition, the bank can buy insurance or sell the asset.

The foregoing illustrates that a bank has to manage a wide variety of risks and that the depositors are indirectly exposed to the same risks. Different techniques are put in place to strengthen the trust of the depositors in the banking system. The Banking Act of 1933 in the US provides a good example. Firstly, a deposit insurance system was founded (Federal Deposit Insurance Corporation, FDIC), which guarantees to a certain extent the repayment of the deposits. Secondly, the Act introduced a formal distinction between commercial banks and investment banks by preventing commercial banks from underwriting securities, in other words: commercial banks were no longer allowed to take on certain asset exposures to minimize the risk of asset dilution.

4.4.2 Securitization

4.4.2.1 Introduction
In Section 4.4.1, the traditional banking business was explained and a concise overview was given of some of the risks attached to it. The business cycle of a typical deposit bank comprises two steps: the collection of the

funding and subsequently the origination of loans.[59] Funding is the bottleneck in the origination process because in the absence of funding it will be impossible to originate new loans.

The kind of loans the bank originates is decisive to assess the bank's risk exposure. If the bank exclusively originates mortgages with maturities up to 20 years which are exclusively funded by deposits, the bank is exposed to the maturity mismatch and the asset dilution risk. If, on the other hand, the bank originates credit card receivables with maturities of up to six months, the risk of a maturity mismatch will become much smaller.

In the early 1970s the technique of securitization was developed to resolve the aforementioned problems. In the next section a concise overview of the use and features of securitization will be provided.

4.4.2.2   Overview of the true sale securitization process

In a securitization transaction the bank sells a portfolio of financial assets (often loans) to a Special Purpose Entity (SPE), which pays the bank the transfer price (cash) in return.[60] The SPE collects the cash required to make the payment by issuing debt securities to investors (the capital market).[61] The SPE in its turn will repay the investors with the incoming cash flows of the loans, which consist of the periodical repayment of the principal and interest by the borrowers.[62]

Figure 4.4   Overview of the true sale securitization

The SPE can take the form of a trust, a partnership or a company and is the bank's counterparty in the securitization transaction. The SPE is intended to be bankruptcy remote. To meet this requirement two conditions have to be fulfilled:

1.   In the first place it must be avoided that, in case the bank goes into bankruptcy, the assets of the SPE fall into the bank's bankruptcy estate. Two structural arrangements are available:

---

[59]   Schrans and Steennot 2003, p. 378; Scholtens and Van Wensveen 2003, p. 18.
[60]   Wood 2007, p. 111.
[61]   De Vries Robbé 2008, p. 36.
[62]   Henderson and Scott 1988, p. 32.

a.   The assets are sold to the SPE by means of a *true sale*. Although other techniques are available,[63] the transfer of the loans is mostly done by an assignment.[64]

This is necessary to make sure the assets have left the estate of the bank and have entered the estate of the SPE. The way this is done guarantees the investors that (i) the SPE will remain fully and exclusively entitled to the cash flows generated by the loan portfolio after a contingent bankruptcy of the bank and that (ii) the SPE will remain able to timely repay the debt securities.[65]

b.   The SPE is constituted and structured in a way that it must not be consolidated by the bank. There are no formal links between the bank and the SPE.

2.   Secondly, structural measures have to be taken to minimize the chance that the SPE itself goes bankrupt because that would involve the investors of the SPE in costly[66] and lengthy bankruptcy proceedings. Therefore the scope of the SPE's activities is strictly limited to the issuance of debt securities and the acquisition of the loan portfolio.[67] The charter or bylaws of the SPE will forbid the undertaking of any other activity[68] to avoid the accumulation of debt.

Consequently, the SPE will neither employ staff nor have other assets or liabilities besides the debt securities and the acquired portfolio.[69] The servicing of the loan portfolio and the debt securities will be taken over by another party, often the bank.[70] This has multiple advantages. The bank has the required knowledge and means at its disposal to carry out the servicing. An additional advantage is that the borrower must not be notified of the assignment of the loan[71] as a result of which the commercial relationship between bank and borrower remains unchanged.

The transfer of the assets isolates the loan portfolio from the claims of the bank's creditors. Due to the bankruptcy remoteness of the SPE, the debt

---

63   For instance a trust of proceeds or a novation.
64   Wood 1995, p. 51; De Vries Robbé 2008, p. 21.
65   Tavkoli 2008, p. 40.
66   Gorton and Souleles 2005, pp. 1–2.
67   Deacon 2004, p. 1.
68   Fabozzi and Kothari 2007, p. 5.
69   Gorton and Souleles 2005, p. 2.
70   Wood 2007, p. 111.
71   In New York, England, Germany and Belgium the notice to the debtor is not strictly required for the validity of the assignment.

security investors are the SPE's only creditors[72] and are in the event of the SPE's insolvency fully and alone entitled to the proceeds of the loan portfolio.[73]

4.4.2.3 An alternative for the true sale securitization: funding transfer by means of secured lending

A securitization transaction was elaborated upon above, whereby the SPE used the cash collected by the emission of debt securities to buy loans from the bank (see Figure 4.4). However the SPE can also decide to simply lend the collected cash to the bank.[74] In this case the bank remains the owner of the loan portfolio and will normally pledge the assets on behalf of the SPE and/or its investors.[75] The bank must recognize the received cash as a new asset and recognize a corresponding obligation to repay the cash to the SPE as a new liability. The SPE has to derecognize the cash transferred to the bank and to recognize a new asset, namely the claim on the bank in repayment of the loan.

The following three figures provide an overview of the balance sheet of the bank and the SPE before and after securitization. Depending on which mechanism is used to transfer the funding from the bank to the SPE, the balance sheets look different after the transfer of the funding.

The two transactions look very similar, but have different characteristics and a different aim:

1. In *secured lending* securitization, the SPE lends the bank the collected cash, which the bank can use as an alternative source of funding. The ownership of the loan portfolio remains with the bank. Accordingly, the bank remains exposed to the asset-related risks. The secured lending transaction clearly does not qualify to lay off asset-related risks.
2. *True sale securitization* is based on the sale of the loan portfolio to the SPE. This kind of securitization also provides the bank with a funding alternative. The bank can apply the received cash in multiple ways. Firstly, the cash can be used to resolve a possible funding bottleneck and to restart a new cycle of loan origination. Secondly, the bank might also use the sale proceeds to repay some outstanding liabilities and to reduce the on-balance leverage.

---

[72] Kothari 2008, p. 1.
[73] Fabozzi and Kothari 2007, p. 4.
[74] Mastroeni 2001, p. 46.
[75] Meisner 2003, p. 6.

Bank	
Assets	Liabilities
Loans	Deposits

SPE	
Assets	Liabilities
Cash	Debt Securities

Figure 4.5   The balance sheet of the bank and the SPE before securitization

Bank	
Assets	Liabilities
Cash	Deposits

SPE	
Assets	Liabilities
Loans	Debt Securities

Figure 4.6   The balance sheet of the bank and the SPE after true sale securitization

Bank	
Assets	Liabilities
Loans	Deposits
Cash	Lending

SPE	
Assets	Liabilities
Lending	Debt Securities

Figure 4.7   The balance sheet of the bank and the SPE after secured lending

The use of the sale transfer mechanism leads to an asset exchange between the bank and the SPE. Together with the acquisition of the ownership of the asset portfolio, the SPE is exposed to the asset dilution risk. Since the SPE will repay the issued debt securities with the cash flows coming from the loan portfolio, the SPE investors ultimately bear the risk of asset dilution. In contrast with the secured lending technique, true sale securitization is eligible as a risk transfer mechanism and is thus much more relevant from a risk perspective.

True sale securitization provides the bank with an instrument to influence its income statement.[76] The sale of the loan portfolio enables the bank to recognize a gain or loss on the sold assets and to fix the moment of the gain/loss recognition. It's quite possible that securitizations are used to meet the accounting targets in a synthetic way.[77]

4.4.2.4 Credit enhancement

The bankruptcy remoteness of the SPE protects the investors from the competing claims of the SPE creditors and the bank against the cash flows generated by the loan portfolio. As a group the investors are exposed to the risk of asset dilution (including credit risk). Credit enhancement refers to the different techniques which are put in place to protect the holders of the debt securities (the SPE investors) against the insolvency of the SPE.[78] Credit enhancement is thus intended to mitigate the credit risk exposure of the investors. As will be shown later, credit enhancement *can,* but does not necessarily have to, reduce the risk exposure of *all* the debt securities holders. It is quite common that only the exposure of a (small) part of the investors is altered, while the exposure of the other part of the investors remains unchanged or even increases.

In most securitization transactions, the SPE will not issue one but several categories of debt securities with various risk profiles (see Figure 4.8). In this tranching and the creation of a cash-flow waterfall, each category has a different ranking in the receipt of the incoming principal and interest payments that the SPE receives on the loan portfolio.[79] More precisely, the incoming cash flow of the SPE will first be used to repay the holders of the securities with the highest ranking (the A securities). The holders of the subordinated B securities will only receive payment after the holders of the A securities. The same goes *mutatis mutandis* for the

---

[76] Karaoglu 2005, p. 3.
[77] Dechow and Shakespeare 2006, p. 2; Niu and Richardson 2004, p. 6.
[78] Wood 1995, p. 58.
[79] Fabozi and Kothari 2007, p. 2.

SPE	
Assets	Liabilities

Loans OR lending	Tranche A – low credit risk
	Tranche B – medium credit risk
	Tranche C – high credit risk
	Tranche D – junior tranche

Cash flow distribution

Figure 4.8   The segmented liability side of the SPE's balance sheet

holders of the subordinated C and D securities. The A class securities are called the senior tranches and carry the lowest level of (credit) risk, while the holders of the D class securities, the so-called junior tranche, bear the highest exposure to the credit risk.[80]

The junior tranche is obviously the most risky tranche and is often retained by the bank.[81] The size is configured in such a way that all the expected losses stemming from the loan portfolio are carried by the bank. The investors are thus only exposed to the more exceptional unexpected losses. The level of the expected losses will be estimated on the historical performance of the transferred asset pool. This practice means that the bank first transfers the assets (and risks) to the SPE but then takes back a part of the risks in the transferred assets in the form of debt securities.

The SPE will request a credit rating agency[82] to assign a credit rating to

---

[80]   GBRW 2000, p. 74.

[81]   GBRW 2000, p. 3.

[82]   There is an information asymmetry between the SPE and the investors with regard to the quality of the debt securities issued. The credit rating agency is a financial intermediary who tries to bridge the asymmetry by bringing information into the financial markets, which should result in a better (higher) pricing of the debt securities. After the outbreak of the financial crisis the credit rating agencies were strongly criticized because they had intervened at two stages in the securitization process. Firstly, they were paid by the banks to advise and structure the transaction to create as many debt securities with an outstanding credit rating ('the pre-rating assessment'). Next, the same credit rating agency was solicited to rate the debt securities that had been created on the basis of the structure formerly conceived by itself (see Crockett, Harris, Mishkin and White 2004, p. 49: '*Rating*

the various tranches. According to Moody's the credit rating will inform the investors of the level of risk associated 'with receiving full and timely payment of principal and interest on this specific debt obligation and how that risk compares with that of all other debt obligations.'[83] The more senior tranches will receive a better rating than the lower mezzanine and junior tranches. The level of credit risk and the credit rating is reflected in the amount of interest that the holder of a particular tranche receives. The higher the level of credit risk, the higher the risk premium (credit spread)[84] for the investor.

4.4.2.5 Excess spread

To be able to repay the investors, the incoming cash flows of the SPE have to match at least the outgoing cash flows of the vehicle. The SPE is able to calculate the correct amount of its liabilities to the investors and thus to determine the required amount of underlying loans to generate a sufficient incoming cash flow. The excess spread is the positive difference between the incoming and outgoing cash flows of the SPE.[85] The excess spread is deposited into an account of the SPE ('the spread account') and can be used for different purposes, including credit enhancement.

Excess spread serves as an additional protection for the holders of the debt securities because if one or more debtors of the underlying loans default, the decrease in the incoming cash flows will not immediately impede the SPE to timely repay its investors. Indeed, the first credit losses caused by defaults in the underlying portfolio are absorbed by the available excess spread. The level of protection depends on the amount of the excess spread.

Excess spread is the cheapest type of credit enhancement because it is

---

agencies are increasingly offering advice on the structuring of debt issues, usually to help secure a favourable rating'; Partnoy 2006, p. 73: *'Perhaps the starkest difference between credit rating agencies and other gatekeepers has been the increasingly substantial role that the agencies play in rating new structured finance issues, particularly credit derivatives').*

[83] See   www.moodys.com/moodys/cust/AboutMoodys/AboutMoodys. aspx?topic=rapproach.

[84] The credit spread is a quantitative expression of the credit risk that is calculated by comparing the Yield-To-Maturity (hereafter YTM) of the security issued by the SPE with the YTM of a comparable security issued by an industrialized nation with, of course, the same maturity and currency. The latter are assumed to be free of credit risk, whereas this is certainly not the case with securities issued by the SPE. The difference between the YTMs is called the credit spread and reflects the credit risk premium for the SPE investors (see Webber and Churm 2007, p. 533).

[85] Norton 1995, pp. 16–17.

composed of the incoming cash flows generated by the underlying assets. However, the use of excess spread as credit enhancement has the disadvantage that there is not much credit enhancement available at the inception of the transaction. At the end of the securitization, the available excess spread usually accrues to the bank. The bank is thus once again exposed to the risks of the transferred assets. If none or only a small number of the debtors of the loans defaults, there will be a considerable amount of excess spread available at the end of the securitization transaction, allowing the bank to pick up a gain on the assets as they were never transferred to the SPE.

4.4.2.6   The cash collateral pool

The cash collateral pool is a bank account with cash and serves the same purpose(s) as a spread account. The only difference lies in the source of the cash. While the excess spread consists of the incoming cash flows received by the SPE, the cash collateral account is funded by a subordinated loan granted by the bank or another credit institution[86]. Whether the grantor of the subordinated loan will receive a full repayment at the end of the program depends on the volume of the credit losses suffered by the SPE. If many debtors of the transferred loans default, the SPE will have to use the cash collateral pool to service the outstanding debt securities and will not be able to repay the subordinated loan to the bank in full. In those circumstances, the bank that has granted the loan will suffer a loss due to the materialization of credit risk related to the transferred assets. In spite of the transfer, the bank will continue to be exposed to losses caused by the transferred assets. A part of the credit risk flows back to the bank in the form of the subordinated loan.

4.4.2.7   Overcollateralization

Overcollateralization is the credit enhancement technique whereby the nominal value of the loan portfolio is higher than the nominal value of the issued debt securities.[87] Overcollateralization is achieved by selling assets to the SPE under their fair value. Usually, the amount of overcollateralization that is not used to offset credit losses within the asset pool of the SPE will be returned to the bank, which is again indirectly exposed to credit losses.

---

[86]   Macours 2002, p. 3.
[87]   Ugur and Erkus 2007, p. 240.

4.4.2.8 Credit insurance and guarantees

Both these techniques comprise an engagement of a (third) party to reimburse the SPE for the losses suffered by the materialization of credit risk.[88] In most cases the amount of the protection is limited. In cases where the protection is provided by the bank, there is clearly a return of the transferred credit risk.

4.4.2.9 The influence of the accounting rules

The question of whether the bank will be able to remove assets and risks from the balance sheet by means of securitization will strongly depend on the accounting rules. The removal of assets will only be possible to the extent that the legal transaction is recognized by the applicable accounting rules as a sale. The accounting rules are applied to the economic substance, which makes the legal qualification of the transaction less relevant. The fact that the securitization transaction is legally considered to be a true sale does not guarantee that the accounting rules will follow the legal qualification. To accomplish a transfer of assets and risks, the applicable accounting rules (1) must consider the loan portfolio and the cash (sale proceeds) as transferred and (2) may not constrain the bank to consolidate the SPE as a subsidiary.[89] To this end the bank and SPE must account for the securitization as follows (compare Table 4.3 and Figures 4.3 and 4.4).

The bank must:

1. derecognize the loan portfolio, which is transferred to the SPE
2. recognize the sale proceeds received from the SPE as an asset
3. not consolidate the SPE as a subsidiary.

The SPE must:

1. derecognize the cash proceeds paid to the bank
2. recognize the loan portfolio as an asset.

At this moment two major Generally Accepted Accounting Principles (GAAPs) exist: IFRS is applied in the EU[90] and in many other countries,[91] while US GAAP is applicable in the US. Both frameworks contain rules

---

88   Brewer and Iseley 1990, pp. 127–139; Wood 1995, p. 58.
89   Jeffrey 2002, pp. 341–351.
90   IAS Regulation.
91   For an overview, see Deloitte, available at http://www.iasplus.com/country/useias.htm (accessed 31 December 2009).

applicable to (1) the (de)recognition of cash and the loan portfolios and (2) consolidation. Especially with regard to the qualification of the transfer mechanism as a sale or secured lending, the IFRS and US GAAP provide detailed guidance. The classification includes the following criteria.

1.   Have the assets been transferred?
2.   Have the rights to the cash flows generated by the assets been transferred?
3.   Has the Originator retained or transferred all or a part of the risks related to the assets?
4.   Who has control[92] over the assets?

Both frameworks prescribe that the derecognition of the loan portfolio is only allowed as a consequence of a bankruptcy remote true sale that results in the isolation of the assets on the balance sheet of the SPE.[93] With regard to consolidation the frameworks have a different approach. Both contain a set of general consolidation principles, but US GAAP provides a consolidation exemption for the so-called Qualified SPEs (QSPEs). QSPEs are SPEs that meet certain criteria which emphasize the passive nature of the SPE. The exception is intended for SPEs that operate as a passive holding shell around the acquired assets. In practice almost all the securitization SPEs will comply with the QSPE prerequisites. IFRS does not have a comparable exception.[94] The IFRS consolidation principles are clarified in SIC-12, which addresses the criteria on the basis of which the bank should consolidate the SPE under the consolidation principles of IAS 27. However, SIC-12 has often been criticized because of its vagueness.

Consolidated financial statements are prepared by combining the financial statement of the bank with the financial statement of the SPE by adding together the assets, the liabilities, the equity, the income and the expenses,[95] after which some adjustments are made (*inter alia* elimination of intergroup transactions).

Previously, true sale securitization was realized by a transfer of the assets (the loan portfolio) from the bank's balance sheet to that of the

---

[92]   The control commonly refers to the power to sell or pledge the assets. If the SPE is supposed to have acquired the full ownership of the assets, it should be entitled to sale and/or pledge them. Sometimes the bank has a call option to buy back the transferred assets, which prohibits the SPE to sell or pledge the assets.

[93]   Financial Accounting Standards Board 2002, pp. 27–28.

[94]   For an overview of the securitization accounting under IFRS and USGAAP see Rosenblatt, Johnson and Mountain 2005, pp. 1–96.

[95]   Bonham, Curtis, Davies, Dekker, Denton, Moore, Richards, Wilinson-Riddle, Williams, Wilson 2006, p. 396.

SPE. If the bank is obliged to consolidate the SPE, the assets of the two entities will be put together on the bank's consolidated balance sheet and the previously transferred assets will reappear.

Thus, as soon as the bank has to consolidate the SPE, the securitization transaction will not – from a group perspective – entail a transfer of credit risk, because the consolidation process will neutralize all the effects of the preceding asset transfer. To accomplish a risk transfer the securitization transaction must therefore have an off balance sheet nature, in the sense that the bank is fully entitled to derecognize the transferred assets and is not obliged to consolidate the SPE.

If the accounting rules do not allow a derecognition of the loan portfolio by the bank and a recognition of the loan portfolio by the SPE, the transfer mechanism between the bank and the SPE must – at least from an accounting perspective – be considered as secured lending. Therefore the bank will have to recognize the cash received from the SPE as an asset, but will also have to recognize the obligation to repay the cash as a liability. Accordingly, the SPE must recognize its claim on the bank as an asset. It is clear that this transaction does not entail a shift of assets[96] and risks and therefore cannot be used for the transfer/mitigation of credit risk. The technique of the secured lending only serves the purpose of funding.[97] US GAAP reserves the consolidation exemption to SPEs which acquire assets by means of a true sale.

4.4.2.10   The legal position of the investors

Section 4.4.2.2, showed that off-balance securitization, in contrast to an on-balance transaction, shifts credit risk to the SPE and consequently its investors. From the investors' point of view, this is an important aspect. If the value of the loan portfolio fully dilutes due to the realization of credit risk, all the assets of the SPE are swept away. For the investors this means that they will not receive any payment if no external credit enhancement has been put in place. Indeed, the credit risk is absorbed by the SPE and its investors. The debt securities issued in an off-balance securitization program are referred to as Asset Backed Securities (ABS).

In an on-balance sheet transaction, the loss is taken by the bank, which is obliged to repay the loan to the SPE notwithstanding the realization of the credit risk. The bank will repay the loan with its other assets and the SPE investors will not suffer any loss as the technique of the secured lending provides the SPE investors with full recourse to all the assets of

---

96   Grossmann and Stöcker 2008, p. 51.
97   Burmeister, Rudolf, Sigl and Will 2008, p. 24.

the bank.[98] In most secured lending transactions the bank will pledge some assets (the loan portfolio) in favour of the SPE and its investors. In this way, the SPE has a double recourse and even becomes a preferential creditor of the bank.

4.4.2.11 The recharacterization of the sale as secured lending

The overview of the structural aspects of true sale securitization showed that notwithstanding the – pretended – '*true sale*' of the loan portfolio to the SPE, the bank continues to be involved. The servicing of the assets, the retention of the junior tranche and the supply of credit enhancement expose the bank to the gains and losses caused by the transferred assets. More than once this conclusion has raised the question of whether a true sale has taken place, because a sale normally entails that the seller is no longer exposed to the possible losses or gains of the assets sold.

On the basis of the foregoing findings some transactions based on a true sale were recharacterized by the US courts as secured lending.[99] The recharacterization risk is not limited to securitization transactions, but is also associated with other transactions which are based on a sale mechanism such as a repo or a sale and lease back.

The recharacterization risk has far-reaching consequences for the position of the creditors of the SPE (the investors) and the bank. If the transaction is considered to be secured lending, the assets will be part of the bankruptcy estate of the bank and serve at least theoretically as mutual collateral for all the creditors of the bank. Consequently, the recharacterization procedures are often initiated by the bank's creditors. A recharacterization of the transaction by the courts weakens the position of the SPE investors because they lose their exclusive rights (proceeds of) the loan portfolio.

4.4.2.12 Securitization: a technique to shift, veil or accumulate risk?

Traditionally, true sale securitizations are seen to shift risk from the bank to the capital market (the SPE investors) and to function as a bridge

---

[98] Poulain 2003, p. 1.

[99] Aicher and Fellerhoff 1991, p. 181; Kravitt, 1995, Section 5–56.12. See also 813 F.2d 266, 271 (9th Cir. 1987), available on http://bulk.resource.org/courts.gov/c/F2/813/813.F2d.266.85-2714.85-2698.html; Major's Furniture Mart Inc. v. Castle Credit Corp. 602 F.2d 538, 544 (3d Cir. 1979); CF Motor Freight v. Schwartz, 215, B.R., 947 (Bankr. E.D. Pa. 1997); Fireman's Fund Ins. v. Grover, 813 F.rd 266, 251–272 (9th Cir. 1987); National Discount Co v. Evans, 272 F. 570, 573–74 (6th Cir. 1921); Ryan v. Zinker, 164 B.R. 224 (Bankr. E.D.NY. 1994); Rechnitzer v. Boyd, 40 B.R. 417, 422 (Bankr. C.D. CAL 1984); Castle Rock Indus. Bank v. S.O.A.W. Enters, 32 B.R. 279, 282 (Bankr. W.D. Tex 1983).

between them. The analysis of the details of the transaction structure indicated that at least part of the transferred risk flows back to the bank, for example by the retention of the first loss piece, which represents the expected losses of the transferred assets.

Furthermore, securitizations transform and cut the asset-related risk in multiple untraceable liquid pieces (the debt securities). This practice increases the links between the participants in the financial system. Under certain conditions the spreading of the credit risk can thus also facilitate the spreading of problems over the financial system. In addition, it is not always clear who ultimately holds the debt securities and is exposed to the risks.

Regulated financial entities have to reserve a certain amount of regulatory capital consistent with their level of risk exposure. The transfer of the loan portfolio by the bank to an SPE will allow the bank to free up or reduce its regulatory capital. In principle, securitization SPEs are not regulated and do not have to hold regulatory capital. Securitization can, in theory, procure a transfer of risk from regulated entities to unregulated entities. The logical consequence is that the total amount of regulatory capital decreases in the financial system as a whole. In a certain sense, the process erodes the protection against systemic risks.

The bank provides the true sale securitization with credit enhancement. From time to time banks support their SPEs that are experiencing problems beyond their formal engagements. This practice is called *implicit recourse*.[100] In doing so, the bank takes back a certain amount of risk beyond the predefined level. This voluntary and undocumented recourse commitment of the bank cannot be found in the bank's financial statement and can mislead the bank's creditors and shareholders.[101] As a consequence, this source of risk has not been included in the amount of regulatory capital. Recent research seems to indicate that ABS investors rely on the fact that the bank will provide implicit recourse[102] if the SPE should experience problems. In order to avoid reputational damage, the bank has a strong incentive to avoid the failure of the SPE.

4.4.3 Credit Derivatives

Credit derivatives are a recent financial innovation. A credit derivative can roughly be defined as a transaction, based on a change in the

---

[100] Vermilyea, Webb and Kish 2008, p. 1199.
[101] Schipper and Yohn 2007, Vol. 21, p. 21.
[102] Gorton and Souleles 2005, p. 4.

creditworthiness of a (third) party.[103] The most important feature of credit derivatives is the possibility to transfer the credit risk generated by certain assets without the necessity to transfer the assets (hereafter the 'reference obligation') themselves. Every obligation to pay[104] implies a credit risk and can be used as a reference obligation like (a portfolio of) loans, bonds, commercial paper or shares. Now that credit risk is sold over the counter and on the markets, market participants have the opportunity to take on credit exposure without having to buy assets. These features gave credit risk the status of an autonomous risk that can be traded, priced and, most importantly, managed.

The notion of credit derivatives covers a number of products which all more or less serve the same purpose, but nevertheless have different structural characteristics[105]. A credit derivative generally meets the following criteria:[106]

- – it is an individually negotiated OTC[107] transaction or a note structure;
- – between two parties, one of which can be referred to as the buyer of protection/seller of risk and one which can be referred to as the seller of protection/buyer of risk;
- – whereby the value of at least one of the obligations is based on performance by a third party (reference entity) or parties under specific debt obligations (reference obligations) or on a change in the creditworthiness of the reference entity;
- – which obligations are often, but not necessarily, triggered by the occurrence of one or more credit events.

The best known credit derivatives are the credit default swap (CDS), the total return swap (TRS) and the credit linked notes (CLN).[108] These derivatives will be briefly discussed.

A CDS is a bilateral contract. The buyer that seeks protection pays a fee, the swap premium, to the seller who sells protection in return for the right to receive a payment conditional upon the default of the reference obligation or the reference entity.[109] The CDS can be settled in different ways:[110]

---

[103]   Hudson 2000, p. 7; Batten and Hogan 2002, p. 251.
[104]   Batten and Hogan 2002, p.253.
[105]   Batten and Hogan 2002, p. 253.
[106]   Hudson 2000, p.10.
[107]   An OTC (Over The Counter) transaction is a private trade of financial instruments that does not take place on an exchange. The parties trade directly with each other or via a network of intermediaries (dealers).
[108]   Kiff and Morrow 2000, p. 3.
[109]   Anson, Fabozzi, Choudhry and Chen 2004, p. 48.
[110]   Hudson 2000, p. 11.

1) Physical settlement: the protection seller pays the protection buyer the value of the reference obligation before the contingency in cash and receives the reference obligations or other specified assets.[111] Physical settlement is used in most cases.[112]
2) Cash settlement: The protection seller pays a fixed amount ('digital settlement') or the difference between the value of the reference obligation before the contingency and the market value of the reference obligation after the contingency.

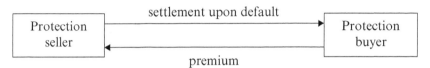

Figure 4.9   The credit default swap

The parties specify, among other things, the reference obligation, the reference entity, the way of settlement, the premium and the credit event. The credit event identifies the circumstances that will be considered as a default of the reference obligation or the reference entity. Generally the credit event does not only include bankruptcy but also contains rating downgrade, restructuring, and cross acceleration.[113]

The second type of credit derivative is the TRS. The total return[114] of a reference obligation includes all the cash flows generated by the obligation as well as the value appreciation or depreciation.[115] The swap buyer (the buyer that seeks protection) agrees to transfer the total return of the reference obligation to the swap seller (the seller that sells protection) in exchange for the payment of a floating rate by the swap seller.[116] The amount of the floating rate depends on (1) the credit rating (creditworthiness) of the debtor, (2) the value and the credit risk of the reference obligation, (3) the funding costs of the swap buyer and (4) the amount of the regulatory capital the swap buyer has to reserve.[117] The reference

---

[111]   Morgan and Riskmetrics 1999, p. 13.
[112]   Nomura fixed income research 2006, p. 3.
[113]   Cross default refers to the occurrence of a credit event with respect to another outstanding debt of the reference entity.
[114]   Bowler and Tierney 2000, p. 17.
[115]   Anson, Fabozzi, Choudhry and Chen 2004, p. 99.
[116]   Choudhry 2002, p. 793.
[117]   Choudhry 2002, p. 797.

obligation remains on the balance sheet of the swap buyer, which means that the swap buyer must continue to fund the reference obligation. The floating rate payments (LIBOR +/− spread) to the swap buyer are a reimbursement for its funding costs.

The swap payments (floating rate) usually take place every four to six months. The change-in-value payments may be made at maturity or on an interim basis.[118] As with the CDS, physical settlement is also possible for the TRS. In this case the swap buyer will transfer the reference obligation to the swap seller, who will in return pay the value of the reference obligation at the inception of the swap.[119]

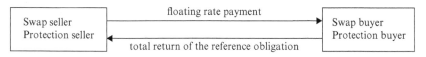

Figure 4.10   The total return swap

The result of TRS is that the swap seller obtains asset exposure to the reference obligation without having to invest in the reference obligation. The swap buyer in its turn is no longer exposed to the economic risks of the reference obligation. In comparison with the CDS, the buyer of a swap transfers all the economic risks of the reference obligation, while the CDS buyer only obtains protection against the dilution of the reference obligation due to a credit event that is explicitly mentioned in the transaction documentation.[120]

Both the CDS and the TRS offer the buyer an unfunded protection.[121] The buyers are only protected against the credit risk of the reference obligation to the extent that the protection or swap seller effectively fulfils its obligations. The buyers that seek protection are thus exposed to counterparty risk. The TRS differs from the CDS and the other credit derivatives as the payment streams between the parties do not depend on the manifestation of a credit risk. All the risks generated by the reference obligation are transferred to the swap seller. The swap seller obtains off-balance asset exposure because the reference obligation remains on the balance sheet of the swap buyer and only the cash flows representing the total return are exchanged between the parties. The advantage for the swap seller lies in

---

[118]   Morgan and Riskmetrics 1999, p. 18.
[119]   Batten and Hogan 2002, p. 257.
[120]   Jobst 2007, p. 204.
[121]   Jobst 2007, p. 204.

the fact that it can obtain asset exposure (gain or losses) without having to fund and invest in the reference obligation.

There are many similarities between a cash-settled credit derivative and an insurance contract. Notwithstanding the similarities, credit derivatives and insurances may not be put on a par. The most important difference is that a valid insurance contract requires an insurable interest. Such a requirement does not apply to credit derivatives. Therefore it is possible and valid to buy credit protection by means of a credit derivative even if the protection buyer is not exposed to credit risk. Credit derivatives are said to make the markets more complete. The parties can devise the credit-risk related products they want and can take on credit exposure to a certain reference entity or reference obligation in situations where it is not possible to create real asset exposure.

The possibility to underwrite a credit derivative without asset ownership can also be a source of problems. When Dana Corporation filed for bankruptcy it had about US\$2 billion in bonds outstanding. At the same time there was more than US\$20 billion of CDS in notional amount referencing the company. Most of the CDS required the physical settlement of bonds. As a consequence, the bond prices rose suddenly after the bankruptcy filing.[122] In other cases the bond price started to rise after a bankruptcy filing owing to the fear of shortage in the deliverable obligations.

Credit Linked Notes[123] are securities with a fixed maturity that are issued by the protection buyer, who is exposed to credit risk by the fact that he owns the reference obligation. The protection seller will buy the notes and pay the price. The protection seller will periodically receive coupons (interest payments). The repayment of the principal depends on whether a credit event happens with respect to the reference obligation. If there is no manifestation of credit risk, the protection seller will receive full repayment of the principal. The performance of the notes is linked to the performance of the reference obligation. Just like the CDS, the CLN requires a definition of the credit event and will not protect against other market risks.

The CLN gives the protection buyer a funded protection on the basis of the payment made by the protection seller at the beginning of the transaction. The last mentioned party bears the counterparty risk in this structure.[124] The CLN has some advantages, but in practice its application is limited to credit institutions that have a good credit rating and a large

---

[122] Nomura fixed income research 2006, p. 1.
[123] Anson, Fabozzi, Choudhry and Chen 2004, pp. 119–121.
[124] Batten and Hogan 2002, p. 256.

portfolio of reference obligations because of the cost of the emission of the securities.[125]

Credit derivatives facilitate altering the credit risk exposure of an asset portfolio. If the credit risk is managed by a sale of assets the risk profile of the whole portfolio changes[126] because all the risks are influenced by the asset sale. In contrast to an asset sale, the contracting of a credit derivative does not require any collaboration or notification to the debtor of the reference obligation. Credit derivatives are thus more discrete and do not influence the commercial relationship between the owner of the reference obligation and the debtor.[127] The credit derivatives make it possible to create short positions in credit risks, allowing an entity to obtain credit protection and speculate on a credit event without having real asset exposure. Credit derivatives are the building blocks of many structured finance products.[128]

Of course, the concept of credit derivatives also has certain limitations. The candidate protection buyer will have to find a counterparty that is willing to contract and take on the credit risk. If unfunded derivatives are involved the counterparty must have a good creditworthiness, otherwise the protection buyer will be exposed both to the credit risk of the reference obligation and to the counterparty risk.

4.4.4   Collective Investment Schemes

Small investors have direct access to large parts of the capital markets. However, the limited resources of time and capital make direct participation in the capital market expensive. A collective investment scheme mitigates these problems. They operate by collecting funds from investors and invest the funds in securities and other types of assets. The collective investment schemes benefit from economies of scale, lower the transaction costs and mitigate information deficiencies. However, collective investment schemes generate risks, in particular due to agency costs and the limited resources for small investors to monitor the risks attaching to the behaviour of fund managers like:

1. loss of benefits through excessive costs and abusive trading practices
2. incompetence in fund management

---

[125]   Batten and Hogan 2002, p. 257.
[126]   Morgan and Riskmetrics 1999, p. 6.
[127]   Kolb and Overdahl 2003, p. 168.
[128]   Amato 2005, p. 56.

3. fraudulent diversion of assets from the fund
4. corporate governance risks
5. liquidity and redemption risks for the investors.[129]

Regulation mitigates or at least reduces these risks: in particular rules relating to asset allocation; portfolio shaping general disclosure; and business organization. The specificities of the regulatory requirements are related to competence and conflict-of-interest risks, which cannot be addressed through disclosure and contracting.[130]

In the European Union the risks of collective investment schemes are addressed in the 1985 UCITS Directive, repealed by Directive 2009/65/ EC.[131] The Directive aims to liberalize access of the schemes in the European Union, to support investor protection and to mutually recognize the schemes in the European Union. Collective investment schemes are undertakings, the sole object of which is the collective investment in transferable securities and/or in other liquid financial assets.

An important risk for collective investment schemes (and for investors funding the scheme) is concentration risk. Financial law mitigates this risk by imposing risk- spreading rules and disclosure of the investment policies. The liquidity risks are covered through the prohibition of investing in instruments other than transferable securities, units of other UCITS, deposits, financial derivative instruments and certain types of money market instruments. Next, the management of the investment scheme must employ risk management tools to monitor and measure the positions and contributions to the overall risk profile of the portfolio. In addition, UCITS may invest no more than 5% of its assets in transferable securities or money-market instruments issued by the same body. There are a number of exceptions, in particular and *inter alia* to mimic a stock or debt securities index, for securities guaranteed by the government and bonds issued by a credit institution.

The management of UCITS might use the investment scheme for strategy oriented behaviour in the issuer in which it invests. The approach of acquiring stakes in issuers to influence the behaviour of the investee is outside the function of the investment fund. As the management of the investment scheme must focus on the efficient investment over efficient management of issuers, this agency cost is mitigated via the prohibition to acquire any shares carrying voting rights, which would enable it to

---

129 Moloney 2008, pp. 234–235.
130 Frankel and Cunningham 2006, p. 240.
131 Directive 2009/65/EC.

exercise significant influence over the management of an issuing body. However, this approach creates new legal risks. The Directive does not provide any guidance as to what should be considered *significant influence* nor does it provide any harmonizing rules. The European Council only issued a Recommendation that, in countries where percentage limits are introduced, the supervisory authorities must ensure that the limits are observed by the management.

4.5 CONCLUSION

Reliable financial institutions and reliable financial markets are pivotal for the economy. Both the financial institutions and markets are encouraged to limit excessive risk taking that may impair this reliability. The financial intermediaries must guarantee their soundness and monitoring of the market and the market transactions must reduce the likelihood of inappropriate market behaviour. The monitoring frameworks were developed over the years and each financial crisis added new layers of legislation and regulation as well as new techniques to mitigate the risks that triggered the crisis. However, these techniques often contained new risks which were not fully acknowledged. Both the financial environment and the instruments used became more complex. The latest financial crisis illustrates this phenomenon. In the last chapter of this book we give our view on the future of the race to reduce and control excessive risk-taking behaviour.

REFERENCES

Aicher, Robert D. and William J. Fellerhoff (1991), 'Characterization of a transfer of receivables as a sale or a secured loan upon bankruptcy of the transferor', *The American Bankrupcy Law Journal*, 181–225.

Allen, Franklin and Anthony M. Santomero (1997), 'The theory of financial intermediation', *Journal of Banking and Finance*, **21** (12), 1461–1485.

Amato, Jefferey D. (2005), 'Risk aversion and risk premia in the CDS market', *BIS Quarterly Review*, 55–68.

Anson, Marc J., Frank J. Fabozzi, Moorad Choudhry and Ren R. Chen (2004), *Credit Derivatives: Instruments, Applications and Pricing*, Hoboken, New Jersey: John Wiley & Sons, Inc.

Barth, James R., Dan Brumbaugh and James A. Wilcox (2000), 'The repeal of the Glass-Steagall and the advent of broad banking', available at http://www.occ.treas.gov/ftp/workpaper/wp2000-5.pdf (accessed 22 December 2009).

Batten, Jonathan A. and Warren P. Hogan (2002), 'A perspective on credit derivatives', *International Review of Financial Analysis*, **11** (3), 251–278.

Bhattacharya, Sudipto (1993), 'Contemporary banking theory', *Journal of Financial Intermediation,* **3** (1), 2–50.

Bonham, Mike, Matthew Curtis, Mike Davies, Pieter Dekker, Tim Denton, Richard Moore, Hedy Richards, Gregory Wilinson-Riddle, Matt Williams, Allister Wilson (2006), *International GAAP 2007. Generally Accepted Accounting Practice under International Financial Reporting Standards,* London: LexisNexis.

Bowler, Troy and John F. Tierney, 'Credit derivatives and structured credit', *Deutsche Bank, Fixed Income Research,* 2000, 17. http://www.classiccmp. org/transputer/finengineer/%5BDeutsche%20Bank%5D%20Credit%20Derivat ives%20and%20Structured%20Credit.pdf (accessed 8 February 2010).

Brewer, Russell B. and Linda S. Iseley (1990), 'Credit enhancement for asset-backed securities', in Jess Lederman (ed.), *The Handbook of Asset-backed Securities,* New York: Institute of Finance.

Burmeister, Ralf, Franz Rudolf, Claudia Sigl and Frank Will (2008), 'Covered bonds as a funding tool', in ECBC, *European Covered Bond Fact Book,* available at http://ecbc.hypo.org/Content/Default.asp?PageID=367 (accessed 8 February 2010).

Caprio, Gerard and Patrick Honohan (2001), *Finance for Growth: Policy Choices in a Volatile World,* New York: Oxford University Press.

Cheffins, Brian R. (2008), *Corporate Ownership and Control,* New York: Oxford University Press.

Choudhry, Moorad (2002), 'Credit Derivatives', in Frank J. Fabozzi (ed.), *The Handbook of Financial Instruments,* Hoboken: John Wiley & Sons, Inc.

Crockett, Andrew, Trevor Harris, Frederik S. Mishkin and Eugene White (2004), *Conflicts of interest in the financial services industry: What should we do about them? Geneva Reports on the World Economy 5,* Geneva: International Center for Monetary and Banking Studies.

Daelen, Marijn M.A. van (2008), 'Risk Management Solutions in Business Law: Prospectus Disclosure Requirements', available at ssrn.com/abstract=1287624 (accessed December 31, 2009).

Deacon, John (2004), *Global Securitisation and CDOs,* Chichester: John Wiley & Sons, Inc.

Dechow, Patricia M. and Catherine Shakespeare (2006), 'Do managers time securitization transactions to obtain accounting benefits?', available at http://ssrn. com/abstract=928741 (accessed 22 December 2009).

Deloitte, Use of IFRSs plus by Jurisdiction, available at http://www.iasplus.com/ country/useias.htm (accessed 31 December 2009).

Diab, Nasri A. and Iyad H. Boustany (2003), *La titrisation des actifs,* Paris: LGDJ.

Diamond, Douglas W. (1984), 'Financial intermediation and delegated monitoring', *Review of Economic Studies,* **51** (3), 393–414.

Dombrecht, Michel and Sylvain Plasschaert (1989), *Het financiewezen in België,* Deurne: MIM.

Fabozzi, Frank J. and Vinod Kothari (2007), 'Securitisation: the tool of financial transformation', *Yale ICF Working paper,* available at http://papers.ssrn. com/sol3/papers.cfm?abstract_id=997079&rec=1&srcabs=994575 (accessed 22 December 2009).

Frankel, Tamar and Lawrence A. Cunningham (2006), 'The mysterious ways of mutual funds', *Annual Review of Banking and Financial Law,* **25** (1), 235–293.

Frentrop, Paul (2002), *Corporate Governance 1602–2002 – Ondernemingen en hun aandeelhouders sinds de VOC,* Amsterdam: Prometheus.

Gorton, Gary and Nicholas S. Souleles (2005), 'Special purpose vehicles and securitization', *Working paper research department federal reserve bank of Philadelphia*, available at http://papers.ssrn.com/sol3/papers.cfm?abstract_id=713782 (accessed 22 December 2009).

Grossmann, Ralf and Otmar Stöcker (2008), 'Overview of covered bonds', in ECBC, *European Covered Bond Fact Book*, available at http://ecbc.hypo.org/Content/Default.asp?PageID=367 (accessed 22 December 2009).

Henderson, John and Jonahtan P. Scott (1988), *Securitisation,* Cambridge: Woodhead – Faulkner.

Holton, Glyn A. (2004), 'Defining risk', *Financial Analyst Journal*, **60** (6), 19–25.

Hudson, Alistair (ed.) (2000), *Modern Financial Techniques, Derivatives and Law*, The Hague, London, Boston: Kluwer Law International.

Jeffrey, Peter (2002), 'International harmonization of accounting standards, and the question of off-balance sheet treatment', *Duke Journal of Comparative & International Law,* **12** (2), 341–351.

Jobst, Andreas A. (2007), 'A primer on structured finance', *Journal of Derivatives and Hedge Funds*, **13** (3), 199–213.

Karaoglu, Emre (2005), 'Regulatory capital and earnings management in banks: the case of loan sales and securitizations', *FDIC Center for financial research Working paper,* available at http://www.fdic.gov/bank/analytical/cfr/2005/wp2005/CFRWP_2005_05_Karaoglu.pdf (accessed 22 December 2009).

Kiff, John and Ron Morrow (2000), 'Credit derivatives', *Bank of Canada Review*, 3–11.

Kohn, Meir (1991), *Money, Banking, and Financial Markets*, Chicago: Dryden.

Kolb, Robert W. and James A. Overdahl (2003), *Financial Derivatives*, Hoboken, New Jersey: John Wiley & Sons, Inc.

Kothari, Vinod (2008), 'Back on to the balance sheet: the future face of securitisation', available at http://www.vinodkothari.com/The%20Future%20Face%20of%20Securitization%20Viinod%20kothari.pdf (accessed 8 February 2010).

Kravitt, Jason H.P. (1995), *Securitisation of Financial Assets*, New York: Aspen Law & Business Publishers, 5–56.12.

Macours, Kristof (2002), 'Effectisering vanuit bancair perspectief', *Bank. Fin.*, 3–12.

Masters, Brooke (2009), 'Dodd seems to be right Hercules for supervision task', *Financial Times* 11 November 2009, p. 9.

Mastroeni, Orazio (2001), 'Pfandbrief-style products in Europe', *Bis Paper No 5,* available at http://www.bis.org/publ/bppdf/bispap05b.pdf (accessed 22 December 2009).

Meisner, Norbert (2003), 'The market for covered bonds in Europe', *Deutsche Bank Global Markets* Research, 2003, available at http://pfandbriefverband.info/d/internet.nsf/0/CA48735357A27B24C12571E9003778AD/$FILE/eur_li_lued_meisner_covered_bonds.pdf (accessed 22 December 2009).

Moloney, Niamh (2008), *EC Securities Regulation*, Oxford: Oxford University Press.

Morgan, and RiskMetrics (1999), *The J.P. Morgan guide to credit derivatives*, available at: http://www.investinginbonds.com/assets/files/Intro_to_Credit_Derivatives.pdf (accessed 22 December 2009).

Munro, John H. A. (2006), 'Entrepreneurship in early-modern Europe (1450–1750): An exploration of some unfashionable themes in economic history', *Working paper University of Toronto*, available at: http://repec.economics.utoronto.ca/files/tecipa-257-1.pdf (accessed 22 December 2009).

Niu, Flora and Gordon D. Richardson (2004), 'Earnings quality, off-balance sheet risk, and the financial-components approach to accounting for transfers of financial assets', *Working paper, W. Laurier University and University of Toronto*, available at: http://papers.ssrn.com/sol3/papers.cfm?abstract_id=628261 (accessed 22 December 2009).

Nomura fixed income research (2006), *CDS recovery basis: issues with index auctions & credit event valuations*, New York: Nomura Securities International inc., available at http://www.securitization.net/pdf/Nomura/CDSRecovery_12Apr06.pdf, (accessed 22 December 2009).

Norton, Joseph J. (1995), *International Asset Securitisation*, London: Lloyd's of London Press.

Partnoy, Frank (2006), 'How and why credit rating agencies are not like other gatekeepers', *San Diego Legal Studies Research Paper Series*, available at: http://papers.ssrn.com/sol3/papers.cfm?abstract-id=900257 (accessed 22 December 2009).

Poulain, Annick (2003), 'European structured covered bonds: Moody's rating approach', *Moody's Investors Service*, 2003, 1, available at: http://ec.europa.eu/internal_market/bank/docs/regcapital/realestate/200307-comments/moodys%20rating%20approach_en.pdf (accessed 22 December 2009).

Rosenblatt, Marty, Jim Johnson and Jim Mountina (2005), 'Securitization accounting', available at http://www.securitization.net/pdf/Publications/SECAccounting_Jul05.pdf (accessed 22 December 2009).

Schipper, Katherine and Teri L. Yohn (2007), 'Standard-setting issues and academic research related to the accounting for financial asset transfers', *Accounting horizons*, **21** (1), 59–80.

Schmidt, Reinhard H. and Marcel Tyrell (2004), 'What Constitutes a Financial System in General and the German Financial System in particular?', in Krahnen, Jan P. and Reinhard H. Schmidt (eds.), *The German Financial System*, Oxford: Oxford University Press.

Scholtens, Bert and Dick van Wensveen (2003), *The theory of financial intermediation An essay on what it does (not) explain*, Vienna: Suerf.

Schrans, Guy and Reinhard Steennot (2003), *Algemeen deel van het financieel recht*, Antwerp, Groningen, Oxford: Intersentia.

Schwarcz, Steven L. (2008), 'Systemic risk', *Georgetown Law Journal*, **97** (1), 193–249.

Tavkoli, Janet M. (2008), *Structured Finance & Collateralized Debt Obligations*, Hoboken, New Jersey: John Wiley & Sons, Inc.

Thakor, Anjan V. (1992), 'Maturity transformation', *The New Palgrave Dictionary of Money and Finance*, London: MacMillan.

The Economist Intellence Unit (2005), *Reputation: Risk of risks,* available at: http://www.acelimited.com/NR/rdonlyres/2B964DD5-F93E-47C3-BA44-999A0B AEAD40/0/RISK_REPUTATION_REPORT.pdf (accessed 12 January 2010).

Tilly, Richard H. (2008), 'Banking crises in comparative and historical perspective: the nineteenth century', available at: http://www.ibf-frankfurt.de/BankhistArchiv_1-2008_Tilly.pdf (accessed 22 December 2009).

Ugur, Ahmet and Hakan Erkus (2007), 'Securitisation: a basic finance tool of financing for the firms', available at http://www.e-sosder.com/dergi/22220-246.pdf (accessed 22 December 2009).

Vermilyea, Todd A., Elisabeth R. Webb and Andrew A. Kish (2008), 'Implicit recourse and credit card securitizations: what do fraud losses reveal?', *Journal of Banking & Finance*, 2008, **32** (7), 1198–1208.

Vries-Robbé, Jan J. de (2008), *Securitization Law and Practice*, Alphen aan den Rijn: Wolters Kluwer.
Webber, Lewis and Roham Churm (2007), 'Decomposing corporate bond spreads', *Bank of England Quarterly Bulletin*, available at: http://www.bankofengland. co.uk/publications/quarterlybulletin/qb070403.pdf (accessed 22 December 2009).
Wood, Philip R. (2007), *Project Finance, Securitisations, Subordinated Debt*, London: Sweet & Maxwell.
Wood, Philip R. (1995), *Title Finance, Derivatives, Securitizations, Set-off and Netting*, London: Sweet & Maxwell.

CODES AND GUIDELINES

Basel Committee on Banking Supervision (1999), *A new capital adequacy framework*, Basel: Bank for International Settlements.
Basel Committee on Banking Supervision (2001), *Working Paper on the Regulatory Treatment of Operational Risk*, Basel: Bank for International Settlements.
Basel Committee on Banking Supervision (2006), *Studies on credit risk concentration: an overview of the issues and a synopsis of the results from the Research Task Force project*, Basel: Bank for International Settlements.
Basel Committee on Banking Supervision (2008), *Liquidity Risk: Management and Supervisory Challenges*, Basel: Bank for International Settlements.
Financial Accounting Standards Board (2000), *Statement of Financial Accounting Standards No. 140: Accounting for transfers and servicing of financial assets and extinguishments of liabilities, a replacement of FASB Statement No. 125,* available at http://www.fasb.org/pdf/aop_FAS140.pdf (accessed 22 December 2009).
GBRW (2000), 'Study on asset-backed securities: impact and use of ABS on SME finance', available at http://siteresources.worldbank.org/ EXTECAREGTOPPRVSECDEV/Resources/EU_study_on_ABSs_impact_ on_SME_finance.pdf (accessed 12 January 2010).
Securities and Exchange Commission (2009), Release 34–59342, *Amendments to Rules for Nationally Recognized Statistical Rating Organizations*, available at: http://www.sec.gov/rules/final/2009/34-59342.pdf (accessed 22 December 2009).
Technical Committee of the International Organisation of Securities Commissions (1999), *Supervisory Frameworks for Markets*, Madrid: IOSCO.
The High-Level Group on Financial Supervision in the EU (The De Larosière Group) (2009), *Report* (De Larosière Report).

US LEGISLATION AND DOCUMENTS

Case Law

The Woodson Company, 813 F.2d 266, 271 (9th Cir. 1987), available at http://bulk. resource.org/courts.gov/c/F2/813/813.F2d.266.85-2714.85-2698.html;

Major's Furniture Mart Inc. v. *Castle Credit Corp.* 602 F.2d 538, 544 (3d Cir. 1979);
CF Motor Freight v. *Schwartz*, 215, B.R., 947 (Bankr. E.D. Pa. 1997);
Fireman's Fund Ins. v. *Grover*, 813 F.rd 266, 251–72 (9th Cir. 1987);
National Discount Co v. *Evans*, 272 F. 570, 573–74 (6th Cir. 1921);
Ryan v. *Zinker*, 164 B.R. 224 (Bankr. E.D.NY. 1994);
Rechnitzer v. *Boyd*, 40 B.R. 417, 422 (Bankr. C.D. CAL 1984);
Castle Rock Indus. Bank v. *S.O.A.W. Enters*, 32 B.R. 279, 282 (Bankr. W.D. Tex 1983).

EU LEGISLATION AND DOCUMENTS

Regulation (EC) No 1606/2002 of the European Parliament and of the Council of 19 July 2002 on the application of international accounting standards OJ L 243 of 11 September 2002 (IAS Regulation).

Commission Regulation (EC) No 809/2004 of 29 April 2004 implementing Directive 2003/71/EC of the European Parliament and of the Council as regards information contained in prospectuses as well as the format, incorporation by reference and publication of such prospectuses and dissemination of advertisements, OJ L 149 of 30 April 2004.

Regulation (EC) No 1060/2009 of the European Parliament and of the Council of 16 September 2009 on credit rating agencies, OJ L 302 of 17 November 2009.

Directive 94/19/EC of 30 May 1994 of the European Parliament and of the Council on deposit guarantee schemes, OJ L 135 of 31 May 1994.

Directive 2003/6/EC of 28 January 2003 of the European Parliament and of the Council on insider dealing and market manipulation, OJ L 96 of 12 April 2003 (Market Abuse Directive).

Directive 2004/39/EC of 21 April 2004 of the European Parliament and of the Council on markets in financial instruments amending Council Directives 85/611/EEC and 93/6/EEC and Directive 2000/12/EC of the European Parliament and of the Council and repealing Council Directive 93/22/EEC, OJ L 145 of 30 April 2004.

Directive 2004/109/EC of 15 December 2004 of the European Parliament and of the Council on the harmonisation of transparency requirements in relation to information about issuers whose securities are admitted to trading on a regulated market and amending Directive 2001/34/EC, OJ L 390 of 31 December 2004.

Directive 2006/48/ECof 14 June 2006 of the European Parliament and of the Council relating to the taking up and pursuit of the business of credit institutions, OJ L 177 of 30 June 2006.

Commission Directive 2006/73/EC of 10 August 2006 implementing Directive 2004/39/EC of the European Parliament and of the Council as regards organizational requirements and operating conditions for investment firms and defined terms for the purposes of that Directive, OJ L 241 of 2 September 2006.

Directive 2009/14/EC of 11 March 2009 of the European Parliament and of the Council amending Directive 94/19/EC on deposit-guarantee schemes as regards the coverage level and payout delay, OJ L 68 of 13 March 2009.

Directive 2009/65/EC of 13 July 2009 of the European Parliament and of the

Council on the coordination of laws, regulations and administrative provisions relating to undertakings for collective investment in transferable securities (UCITS) (recast), OJ L 302 of 17 November 2009.

Directive 2009/138/EC of the European Parliament and of the Council of 25 November 2009 on the taking-up and pursuit of the business of Insurance and Reinsurance (Solvency II) (recast) OJ L 335 of 17 December 2009.

Commission proposal of 26 October 2009, No. COM(2009) 576 final, for a directive of the European Parliament and of the Council Amending Directives 1998/26/EC, 2002/87/EC, 2003/6/EC, 2003/41/EC, 2003/71/EC, 2004/39/EC, 2004/109/EC, 2005/60/EC, 2006/48/EC, 2006/49/EC, and 2009/65/EC in respect of the powers of the European Banking Authority, the European Insurance and Occupational Pensions Authority and the European Securities and Markets Authority, available at http://ec.europa.eu/internal_market/finances/docs/committees/supervision/20091026_5 6_en.pdf (accessed 22 December 2009).

Commission Green Paper of 3 May 2005, No. COM (2005)177, Green Paper on Financial Services Policy (2005–2010).

Communication of the Commission of 11 May 1999, No. COM (1999)232, Financial Services: Implementing the framework for financial markets: Action Plan.

5. Risk management in taxation

Ronald Russo

5.1 HISTORICAL DEVELOPMENT

For a company, taxes in principle constitute costs. Costs are generally to be minimized, within the limitations of the relevant laws. This also applies to taxes. The relevant tax laws define the obligations of the taxpayers: generally this entails administrative obligations and the actual payment of taxes due. Governments regard taxation, amongst other things, as a principal source of finance for the public sector, whereby every company has to pay its fair share of the total tax burden. Tax laws are the means by which governments practically implement the shift of funds from private companies to the public domain. Taxation is a major factor in determining the net result of a company. As will be described below, it is not always easy to determine the exact amount of taxes due in the commercial accounts of a company. The risk that the amounts are not correct and the management of this risk will be discussed in this chapter.

The oldest taxes are generally considered to be custom duties and some forms of indirect taxes[1] levied from producers or importers of goods. These taxes were treated as part of the cost price and in this way the public paid their taxes without exactly knowing how much as they were hidden in the price of the product. Apart from the obscurity of the amount of tax actually paid, taxes on consumption were also felt not to evenly spread the tax burden, as persons with more income do not proportionately consume more. It was felt to be unjust that people paid roughly the same amount of tax regardless of their income. As a reaction to this, at the end of the nineteenth and the beginning of the twentieth century, personal income taxes were developed and indirect taxes were reduced, so the people became more aware of how much they contributed to the public finances in the form of taxation.[2] Taxing the income of corporate entities instead of just

---

[1] See section 5.3.1 for the distinction between direct and indirect taxes.
[2] See Ydema 2006.

taxing distribution of profits or taxing the shareholder came even later.[3] To view a corporate entity as a separate person with the ability to pay taxes on its profit apparently took some time.

The different ways in which corporate taxation is viewed by companies on the one hand (cost reduction) and governments on the other (means of funding) tended to lead to tension when interpreting the tax laws. Companies spent more and more time and effort to minimize their tax burden; governments reacted to tax planning schemes by making anti-abuse legislation. Tax legislation also had to contend with an ever more complicated financial and business world. New financial instruments need new treatment in tax laws (or at least, this has to be considered by the legislator).

As a result of these developments, the amount and complexity of tax laws has increased. Examples of legislation of this sort are: special rules for controlled foreign companies (CFCs); extensive rules for interest/royalty payments between related parties; detailed rules to avoid unintended use of the participation exemption, and so on. Disputes on how to apply these complicated laws in specific cases increased, as did the impact of these disputes.[4]

Primarily for the purpose of informing stakeholders, it became necessary to manage the risks related to taxation. The commercial accounts, the main source of information for stakeholders,[5] must give a true and fair view of the liabilities of the company, including its tax liabilities. Managing tax risks on a case-by-case basis is felt to be inadequate at the moment.[6] In practice, especially larger, listed companies tend to move from management of individual risks to being in control of the risks. This development is also visible in relation to tax issues.

5.2   INTRODUCTION

In general, all issues related to the tax position of a company are primarily the responsibility of its tax department. In practice, it may vary between a completely staffed department to one person from the financial administration designated for this purpose. Obviously, the relative size of the department in the company to a large extent determines its influence.

---

[3]   See Verburg 1984, section 2.5, in the Netherlands not until 1940.
[4]   See Freedman 2008, pp. 7–99, part II: Statutory Anti-Avoidance Provisions Old and New, where diverse authors address the anti-avoidance problems for diverse countries.
[5]   See Cox 2008, p. 33.
[6]   See Rabenort 2007, p. 341.

The tax department is usually permitted or obliged to call in external tax consultants to assist in solving specific problems. In fact, the tax department will fulfil the company's tax obligations to the government. Another responsibility of the tax department is the tax position in the commercial accounts. In both cases the tax department operates as the representative of the board of the company.

The external auditor for the commercial accounts of the company will contact the tax department of the company, again as representative of the board, to determine the impact of taxes on the accounts. The supervisory board has its own responsibility concerning the tax position and policy of the company[7] and to that end will also liaise with the tax department and the external auditor.[8] In practice, however, it seems that supervisory boards do not pay overly much attention to the tax strategy of companies.[9]

Risks in terms of tax law can be categorised into two main groups:[10]

1. Has the company fulfilled all formal requirements for all relevant taxes?

    There are requirements that apply to most taxes and specific requirements for each separate tax. An example of a requirement for nearly all taxes is that certain administrative demands concerning the accounts must be met. The tax authorities must be able to check the information that is given to them (usually in tax returns) against the primary documents. Examples of specific requirements are the filing of a tax return for a specific tax or giving detailed information on a specific issue, for instance a merger.

2. Are the amounts of taxes payable as mentioned in the commercial accounts correct?

    In the commercial accounts the taxes paid and payable constitute costs, as mentioned before. The board of the company and its external auditor have the responsibility that the commercial accounts give a true and fair view of the results and equity of the company. As taxes usually have a large impact on the results of a company, the board must be able to manage and/or control this figure.[11]

---

[7] According to the Tabaksblat Code III 5.4. See section 3.2.3 for the formal aspects of this Code.

[8] Grotenhuis 2008.

[9] See Van der Ende 2008, p. 107.

[10] Johnston 2006, p. 24, has two more groups: integration with the business and management of tax as a cost. This issue will be addressed again in section 5.4 in this chapter.

[11] For a general overview of the tax burden in 2010, see PricewaterhouseCoopers 2010, the global picture.

Both groups of risk must be managed and controlled by the board of a company. In general, especially with bigger companies, the board of a company will have to rely on administrative systems and procedures for its management and control. This is often accomplished by applying a Business Control Framework (BCF) or Enterprise Control Framework (ERM). Most companies now have a Tax Control Framework (TCF) specifically for taxes, which is part of the BCF.

The TCF of a company is currently the main instrument to manage and control tax risks. It entails a review of the complete corporate structure for each entity belonging to the group, a plan of where and when tax obligations have to be met and whose responsibility it is that the necessary actions to meet with the obligations are carried out correctly. Before looking in more detail at a TCF, the relevant taxes and the obligations they entail will be discussed below.

5.3 TAXES

5.3.1 General

Taxes exist in many different forms. For the purpose of this book various ways of categorizing taxes will be viewed below.[12]

Traditionally, taxes have often been divided into direct taxes and indirect taxes. The difference is that direct taxes are economically borne by the entity from which it is levied, while indirect taxes are meant to be borne by another party, for instance a customer of the entity. In this sense corporate income tax is an example of a direct tax, and value added tax (VAT) an example of an indirect tax.

Another important distinction between taxes is on whose initiative they are levied. As regards corporate income tax, the tax authorities usually send out tax forms that have to be filled out and returned by the taxpayer within a certain time. The tax authorities review the tax form and determine the tax to be paid on that basis. This system differs fundamentally from the system where the taxpayer takes the initiative to fill out and send a form to the tax authorities, including the calculation of the amount of tax payable. This is the system currently in use for VAT within the EU. The first system implies that the tax authorities actively review the forms prior to determining the amount of taxes to be paid. This limits the power

---

[12] For more information about classification of taxes, see Hofstra and Niessen 2002, Chapter 2.

of the tax authorities to amend the tax payable if at a later time it is discovered that the amount is not correct. In the second system, the tax authorities have nothing to do with the calculation of the tax to be paid, so there are fewer limitations when later amendments are required. The two systems are theoretically different, but in practice they converge. Owing to the increased workload of the tax authorities and government cutbacks, the active review of all tax forms in the first method has been replaced by a selection of risk categories and focusing a review on them (and conducting a random review of the rest). In practice, although theoretically the first system, it more closely resembles the second system.

Yet another distinction often made is between taxes that relate to a specific timeframe versus taxes that focus on transactions. Again corporate income tax is a good example of the first category. A good example of the second category is real estate transfer tax. This tax is only due when the ownership of real estate is transferred and has nothing to do as such with a timeframe. There is also another clear distinction here: corporate income tax is always due and not dependent on the actions of the taxpayer, whereas the liability to real estate transfer tax only arises if and when real estate is transferred. In terms of management of the tax risks involved, the different sorts of tax pose their own requirements. If for a certain tax it is required to return a tax form, the company is merely obliged to react by filling out and filing the relevant form. If a transaction triggers taxation, the company will have to act on its own initiative, for instance by reporting the transaction and asking for the relevant forms (which then have to be filled out and filed). To make sure the appropriate actions and reactions take place, the administrative organisation of the company must encompass all eventualities. In effect this is the TCF.

5.3.2 Specific Taxes

5.3.2.1 Corporate income tax

In practice, corporate income tax is by far the most important tax and also the most visible one in the commercial accounts. Many conclusions can be derived from the amount of tax in the commercial accounts. If it is too high, analysts could conclude that the company does not work tax efficiently. If it is not high enough, analysts might suspect that the company is too tax driven and runs a higher risk of later disagreements with the tax authorities with all the costs that involves. It might also be concluded that the company is not prepared to pay its fair share resulting in reputational damage.

The tax accounts are almost never identical to the commercial accounts, but the divergence varies from nation to nation. This difference is often referred to as the book-tax gap. It is safe to say that the commercial accounts and the tax accounts have many aspects in common, regardless of whether there is a formal link between the two. Where the accounts are no more than a record of what has happened in reality, there can be no difference between the commercial accounts and the tax accounts. The cost price of an article, the wages paid to an employee: these are facts that are basically the same for both sets of accounts.[13]

Differences appear if due to a specific (tax) legal requirement, for example, certain costs are not deductible or certain income is not taxable. The differences have many sources. For many governments tax law can be a tempting instrument to guide economic or investment behaviour. These so-called tax expenditures have nothing to do with tax accounting as such, but they create differences between the commercial accounts and the tax accounts. Another source can be the cohesion or inner structure of the tax system: the wish to tax profits in a corporate environment only once. The company that earns the profit is taxed; if it distributes the profit to a corporate shareholder, this dividend is generally not part of the taxable profit of that shareholder. This system, known as participation exemption, has a sound theoretical background but also creates differences between commercial accounts and tax accounts.

Essentially, there are two possible situations: the situation where there is a formal dependency between the commercial accounts and the tax accounts and the situation where such a dependency does not exist. In practice, all systems have elements of both, but lean more to one or the other end of the spectrum. A third category can also be distinguished: no formal dependency, but material dependency. This could be defined as the situation where the financial accounts can be seen as a starting point for tax accounting, but in practice separate tax accounts exist. Within the European Union, the following image emerges:[14]

It is noteworthy that, in spite of the practical formal dependency that exists in Germany, there are many specific points where the tax accounts differ from the commercial accounts. It is the same in the Netherlands: although there is material independency, there is a material link on the basis of case law.[15]

---

[13] On the issues mentioned here still much debate is possible, for instance which costs should be included in the cost price or whether or not recognition as an asset is mandatory. In many cases, however, the outcome of the discussion will be the same for the commercial accounts and the tax accounts.

[14] See Essers, Raaijmakers, Russo, Van der Schee, Van der Tas and Van der Zanden 2009, pp. 32–33.

[15] See Dutch Supreme Court 8 May 1957, BNB 1957/208.

Table 5.1   The relationship between tax accounts and commercial accounts

Formal dependency	No formal dependency	
	Material dependency	**Material independency**
Austria	Greece	Denmark
Belgium	Hungary	Netherlands
Cyprus	Ireland	Slovenia
Czech Republic	Latvia	
Finland	Malta	
Poland	Sweden	
France	UK	
Germany		
Italy		
Lithuania		
Luxembourg		
Portugal		
Slovakia		
Spain		

The differences between the commercial accounts and the tax accounts can be permanent or temporary. Permanent differences are fundamental differences: something constitutes a profit for the commercial accounts, but not for the tax accounts or vice versa. The most important example of this is the participation exemption. Temporary differences are timing differences: the commercial profit and the taxable profit are identical, but they are attributed to different years. An example is depreciation on an asset in three years commercially and in five years for taxation purposes. After five years, the same depreciation will have been effectuated and there is no longer a difference between taxable profit and commercial profit on this point. During the period of depreciation however, there is the timing difference.

When calculating the corporate tax burden for the commercial accounts, the commercial profit is adjusted for permanent differences and then submitted to the appropriate rate. Temporary differences are accounted for under the heading 'deferred tax'. The amount of corporate tax, adjusted with the deferred tax is the actual amount of corporate tax (cash tax) to be paid over a certain period.

A main activity of the tax department in relation to corporate income tax is to collect the commercial accounts of all companies belonging to the group and adjusting these accounts to draw up the tax accounts. The first step is to do this with the single accounts. The consolidation for the commercial accounts is not automatically the same as for the tax accounts. Therefore the commercial consolidations cannot automatically be used for the tax accounts so separate tax consolidation (if applicable) must follow.

Corporate income tax is usually levied on the basis of a tax return form that has to be filed. In practice the above-mentioned activities boil down to completing this form. The filled-out form leads to the amount of corporate tax to be paid (which is relevant for the commercial accounts). The result of this activity can also be used for the other tax issues in the commercial accounts: calculating the tax burden and the amount of deferred tax.

The formalities for the corporate income tax are not very complicated in principle. The tax form has to be filed correctly within a certain period. As this period is always after the year it relates to, companies are usually required to pay estimated corporate income tax assessments. The tax authorities estimate the corporate income tax due in a tax year (usually based on previous years) and the company can pay in the course of the year. This has to be monitored closely, for if the results of the company deviate significantly from the estimated results, the assessment has to be adjusted. This monitoring is also the responsibility of the company's tax department: it has to take action when necessary. When the tax form has been filed and the tax authorities deviate from the form in their final assessment, the tax department will have to analyse the deviation and report to the board whether or not to challenge the assessment. As the challenge usually must be made within a certain time, this has to be monitored as well. In these cases there is also a possible impact on the commercial accounts or even on the share price, if the potential payment is such that the stock market has to be informed.[16]

5.3.2.2 Value added tax (VAT)

VAT in the EU is governed by the Directive of November 28, 2006, PbEU L347 (the VAT Directive) which to a large extent defines the VAT taxation in the different Member States. Differences in VAT in the Member States are limited to situations in which the VAT directive offers a choice or where Member States have not yet amended their national laws.[17] In principle, VAT should not be an issue for companies, provided that the company is taxable for VAT purposes.[18] In that case, the company must charge VAT on all sales and pay it to the tax authorities but may recover

---

[16] See Hanlon 2008, pp. 129–131 and Macdonald 2008, pp. 133–135.

[17] In this last case direct appeal on the Directive is possible.

[18] The fact that VAT has different rates could in these cases still be a problem, but I will not go into this issue.

all VAT on incoming invoices. The company has an administrative burden but its results are not touched by VAT.

Problems arise when a company is wholly or partially exempt from VAT. This also means that all or part of the VAT on incoming invoices may not be recovered. The VAT in these cases is nothing more than costs for the company (and costs must of course be minimized, see section 5.1). Good examples of exempt companies are banks and insurance companies, usually big financial institutions. Other problem categories are formed by companies whose clients are wholly or partially private persons and companies that cannot recover VAT, for example government institutions. In these cases, the VAT (co)determines the price of the product.

VAT must be charged on the sales of a company (sales of goods and/or services), usually on a monthly basis.[19] The VAT on incoming invoices may be recovered, also on a monthly basis. The administrative requirements therefore differ from those for corporate income tax. On the one hand they are simpler; on the other hand they need to be produced must faster. The tax department usually plays no major role here: the relevant data come directly from the financial administration. In fact, all accounting software is prepared for the monthly VAT return. The tax department steps in only if problems occur.

The formalities concerning VAT are the proper (usually monthly) reporting to the tax authorities and subsequent payment of the amounts due. As with corporate income tax the assessments of the tax authorities need to be monitored by the tax department, especially if they deviate from the reported amounts.

5.3.2.3 Other taxes

In this section some of the taxes that generally have less of an impact on the accounts will be discussed. The list is by no means complete; for instance custom duties and local taxes will not be mentioned.

5.3.2.3.1 Dividend withholding tax (DWT) DWT is in principle due when a company distributes its profits to a shareholder. The shareholder can credit the DWT paid against the taxes due on the dividend received. For a corporate shareholder dividends received are often exempt because a participation exemption is applicable. If a company distributes dividends to a shareholder to whom the participation exemption is applicable, there is usually no obligation to withhold DWT.

---

[19]   See the VAT Directive, Article 252: the term can vary but can be no longer than one year.

DWT is more complicated if the company and its shareholder do not belong to the same country/tax jurisdiction. Then it is not a national matter, but one of attributing taxation rights to nations. The nation of the shareholder will usually not allow the crediting of DWT against taxes due unless this issue is addressed in a tax treaty. Most treaties limit the rights of the nations to levy DWT and make crediting of DWT mandatory.

All EU Member States have some form of participation exemption,[20] as this is required under a directive (July 23 1990, PbEG L225, the Parent-Subsidiary Directive). DWT is also covered by this directive in cases that the recipient of the dividend can apply the directive. In these cases no DWT is due.

DWT is due on all distributions of profits, whether they are formally designated as such or not. If, for instance, a subsidiary company provides services to a parent company without this parent paying at arms' length compensation, this is deemed to be a distribution of profit on which DWT is due (and possibly also corporate income tax). This is the problem known as transfer pricing: related parties who do business must do this at arms' length.

5.3.2.3.2   Real estate transfer tax (RETT)   RETT is due when the ownership of real estate is transferred. In some countries (for instance the Netherlands) it is not only due when legal ownership is transferred, but also if economic ownership is transferred. For transactions within a group exemptions are usually applicable if certain conditions are met, with a claw-back provision if the conditions are later altered.

As far as formal requirements are concerned, the company must actively inform the tax authorities that a transfer has occurred, file the appropriate form and pay the tax due. If an exemption is applicable, this usually has to be claimed on the form. The tax department will usually be responsible for this and (in case of an exemption) for monitoring that the claw-back provisions do not become applicable.

5.3.2.3.3   Wage withholding tax (WWT)   WWT is levied from employers on the wages paid. Legally they pay WWT for their employees, who can usually offset WWT against their personal income tax. WWT is a relatively easy way for governments to obtain revenue, for instance because there are far fewer employers then there are employees. Economically WWT can be viewed as costs for a company, going on the premise that employees are only interested in their net wage. From this point of view employees shift

---

[20]   See Endres et al. 2006, section 7.1.2.

the burden of WWT to the employer: the company. Regardless of whether the legal or the economical viewpoint is adopted, in practice WWT can be a real burden for a company. If, for instance, the tax authorities find that not enough WWT was paid by the company, the company could hold its employees liable for the surplus. In practice this is not so easy and can cause such uproar and/or administrative complications that the company may be better off just paying without charging its employees.[21] In this case there is no discussion that the payment constitutes costs for the company. In practice WWT can be quite important financially, depending on the number of employees. If, for instance, the WWT paid by a company was €10 a month per employee short, the impact for thousands of employees over a period of five years (the normal legal term for the tax authorities in the Netherlands to make a reassessment) can be enormous.

5.4 TAX CONTROL FRAMEWORK

5.4.1 General

As mentioned in section 5.2 many companies are no longer satisfied with managing the tax risks on a case-by-case basis, but they try to be in control of the tax risks.[22] A tax risk can be defined as any occurrence within tax strategy, operational activities or tax returns that leads to a negative effect on the tax goals or commercial goals of the company or leads to unexpected or unacceptable financial or reputational damage.[23] The definition is wide: not only a direct influence of tax positions on the commercial accounts, but also indirect influence such as reputational damage are included. In this sense, the risks are wider than the traditional risks (all formal requirements met and correct amounts of tax in the commercial accounts, see section 5.2).

Controlling tax risks as defined above is almost impossible if the company does not have a Business Control Framework and, as part of that, a Tax Control Framework (TCF). The TCF can be defined as the total of all processes and control measures used by a company to control its tax risks.[24]

As such the TCF is as much the domain of the (internal) accountant

---

[21]   This can cause further problems as usually the payment will have to be grossed up. This problem will not be explored at this point.

[22]   See Van der Laan and Weerman 2008, pp. 1269–1278.

[23]   Rabenort 2007, p. 341.

[24]   Van der Laan, Van Rosmalen, De Mare, Van Loon 2007, p. 50.

as of the tax department. Designing process and control measures is accountancy work. Knowledge of the specific tax laws and regulations is the domain of the tax department. The TCF is therefore a joint venture between the two. Both also need to be in contact with the rest of the company for the TCF to be fully reliable. For instance, if the group acquires a new entity, this entity must be integrated within the group on many levels, including in the TCF. To ensure the best possible control, the tax department, the internal accountant and management should confer prior to the actual acquisition.

If a TCF is in place, the external auditor can audit the TCF instead of all issues separately. In turn, a tax department will preferably not do work an external auditor has already done. For instance, if the external auditor has reviewed the commercial profit, the tax department may use this to determine the taxable profit. This is not always free of risk, since the external auditor will not correct anything that is not material.[25] Because an issue that is not material for the current commercial accounts may very well be material after tax scrutiny, the external audit may not be sufficient. For example, a mistake in the WWT may be immaterial in the current year, but the tax authorities may recover the WWT for this year, and also for past years (five years in the Netherlands). The tax authorities may also impose a penalty (sometimes more than 100%) for not paying the correct amounts in the previous years. These facts may add up to an effect that is material after all.[26]

The position of tax risk management in commercial accounts of listed companies can usually be found in the category Financial Risks; for an example see the Philips Annual Report 2008, p. 96.

5.4.2   TCF in Practice

How does a TCF work in practice and how is it set up? The big accounting firms have apparently put much effort into the development of TCFs in general and the implementation in specific companies.[27] For the general set-up of a TCF as part of the Business Control Framework see section 2.1.8 in Chapter 2. Suffice it to state here that a TCF is usually based on the COSO model; for an example see Philips Annual Report 2008, p. 94.

---

[25]   A rule of thumb as to what is material: 5–10% of normalised result before tax, 3–6% of equity, according to Van der Laan, Van Rosmalen, De Mare, Van Loon 2007, p. 56.

[26]   See Van der Laan, Van Rosmalen, De Mare, Van Loon 2007, p. 57 for further examples.

[27]   Type TCF as a search word on the website of any major accounting firm and you will see many references.

Table 5.2   Audit of tax model

Risk analysis	Figure analysis	Risk assessment	Scope programme	Review / check	Final review	Report
Preparation				**Implementation**		**Report**

Specifically for the TCF an 'audit of tax' should take place for each separate tax, as described by Van der Laan et al.[28] They have the following model for the audit of tax:

In the first stage (risk analysis) the relevant risks must be described. There are specific risks and general risks. Specific risks include risks on transactions, operational risks, compliance risks and financial accounting risks. General risks include portfolio risks, management risks and reputational risks.

The second stage (analysis of the figures) consists of determining the tax burden, cash tax and deferred tax (the general analysis) and an analysis of specific topics. Such topics can be the total amounts of interest paid and received, and dividends paid and received, and so on.

In the third stage the outcome of the first two stages is combined. The measures to contain the risks (internal and/or external procedures) are assessed and, if necessary, amended. The outcome of this stage is that the areas that need attention or that contain a specific risk are identified for further investigation.

In the fourth stage the areas that might have a material effect are identified and audited. The more reliable the internal control systems, the more likely it is that a factual audit will not be necessary.

The fifth and sixth stages contain the review, which should take place periodically in the course of the year and not just at the end, hence the division in review (in the course of the year) and final review (at the end of the year).

The last stage contains the report of the work that has been done and its results. It should be understandable for any professional, not just (tax) auditors or advisors.

As already mentioned, the stages described above should be followed for each tax as each one poses its own problems. VAT for instance must focus more on transactions in general, the applicable rates and the matches and mismatches for (intra group) cross-border transactions. It is of course possible to use another model, but basically it will need the same kind of structure and lead to the same information.[29]

---

[28]   See Van der Laan, Van Rosmalen, De Mare, Van Loon 2007, p. 60.
[29]   For another model, see Hoyng and Van der Reijden 2009, pp. 22–33.

If a TCF is in place, an 'audit of tax' (based on the TCF) is performed for all taxes and the outcome is reported. Does that mean that the tax risks are under control? This is a legitimate question because in the process of gathering the relevant information not all information can be exact. Sometimes a situation must be assessed by the tax department and/or the external consultant and the outcome is subject to a certain margin of error.[30]

This uncertainty is reflected in the commercial accounts of a listed company. Looking at, for instance, the Philips Annual Report 2008, (p. 108) fiscal risks are mentioned in some detail: transfer pricing uncertainties, uncertainties on general service agreements, disentanglements and acquisitions, permanent establishments and treatment of losses. No financial details on the (potential) size of the risks are given, but they must have influenced the overall tax position as presented in the annual report.

5.4.3   The Influence of Assessments on the Reliability of a TCF

In the process of the 'audit of tax' or the drafting of the TCF, the tax department must make many decisions on a detailed level. Sometimes these decisions are of a technical nature – for example: is this commercial intercompany debt also a debt for tax purposes – and soluble on a technical level. (Case 1.) However, it could be that the solution is not so straightforward: it may be possible to have a genuine difference of opinion on whether in these specific circumstances the debt in question is acceptable as a debt for tax purposes. (Case 2.) A step further is to purposefully look for the boundaries (in legal rules or case law) of what is possible for taxation purposes. (Case 3.)

In each of the three cases mentioned above the tax department must assess the situation, which will have an impact on the cash tax: if the debt is acceptable for tax purposes, the interest is generally deductible. Fluctuations in the value of the debt will in this case also affect the tax base. If the debt is not acceptable, the interest is not deductible and may possibly be classed as dividend, triggering DWT. The impact of both scenarios on the cash tax can be significant.

The assessment of the risk can be quite different for the three cases. The first case presents the fewest problems: it is a matter of having the technical skills (or hiring them externally) to make the assessment one way or the other. The level of risk involved is minimal. In the second case the risk is significantly higher as it is not soluble with technical skills only. The risk

---

[30]   See Rabenort 2007, p. 343.

can be material and should be controlled (for instance by conferring with the tax authorities on this specific issue, see section 5.2). In the third case the risk is highest, but it is a risk that is inherent to the strategy chosen by the board of the company.[31] The risk as such cannot be controlled, only identified. The conclusion must be that generally assessments of the second and third categories as described above have a negative influence on the reliability of the TCF as a means of risk control and from that point of view should be avoided.

The issue in the third case brings us to the more general issue of tax risk management in relation to tax planning. A definition of tax planning for the purpose of this subject is 'any action by a company designed to lower the overall tax burden of the group'. The real difficulty arises when one tries to define where the exact borderline is between tax planning within the boundaries of the law (acceptable) and tax avoidance (not acceptable). Further distinctions are possible; for instance should 'within the boundaries of the law' be interpreted as the letter of the law (and case law) or the spirit of the law?

5.4.4 TCF and Tax Planning

In itself it is perfectly legitimate for a group of companies to seek a structure in which the tax burden is limited as much as possible. As is evident from the previous section, the difficulty lies in establishing what is acceptable planning and what is unacceptable avoidance.[32] If the acceptability is not limited to the letter of the relevant laws, the answer to this question is to a large degree determined by ethics. This is not strange as corporate governance in general is based on ethics. For tax professionals, however, this is not a familiar field to deal with.[33] The choices to be made in this field should be made by the board of the company and not the tax department. A company must have an explicit tax strategy.[34] The board decides on this, as well as on the overall strategy of the company, but it must base its decisions on information of the professionals. In that sense the tax department could play its role again, but only by advising the board on the nature and extent of specific risks.[35]

---

[31] The risk appetite, the amount of risk the board is willing to take, see section 2.1.8. in Chapter 2.

[32] See Self 2008, pp. 151–156.

[33] See Duff 2008, pp. 197–205.

[34] See Simonis 2008, pp. 5–27, who also discusses the corporate governance code relating to tax policy of a company.

[35] See Happé 2008, p. 162.

In terms of risk management and the TCF the consequences of tax planning must be qualified and quantified. This is not always possible as has been explained above. The impossibility is usually connected to issues where the boundaries between tax planning and tax avoidance are not clear. For some companies this is in itself a reason not to go through with a certain structure. The policy may be to steer clear of the boundaries and stay well within the limits of what is acceptable.[36] A company may try to manage the risk by contacting the relevant tax authorities on the issue in question (seeking an advance ruling).[37] In that way the tax risk of the transaction may be ascertained long before the tax return is filed. The problem is that the tax authorities are not usually bound to cooperate and, if they do cooperate, they may take a different point of view to the transaction than the company. Another problem is that a tax authority will demand full disclosure prior to deciding on a request for a ruling. This is understandable as the tax authorities have an information disadvantage in their relationship with companies, especially with international groups. Full disclosure might not be advisable for the company from a business point of view or even be impossible because of contractual or legal obligations. If it is not possible to obtain a ruling the potential risk that the structure will not have the desired effect must be quantified. This result must be reported to the board, which can then decide whether and how to report this information in the commercial accounts. Of course the external auditor will also have an influence on the final decision. For an example of such information see the list of tax risks from the Philips Annual Report 2008 as mentioned at the end of section 5.4.2.

5.4.5   Formal Aspects of a TCF

The formal status of a TCF is that it is part of the business control framework of the company. On the basis of this model the board of the company declares that it is in control. The business control framework as a whole can be scrutinized by the external auditor as part of the audit of the annual accounts. However, it was made and is maintained by the employees of the company. Focusing on the TCF, the question can arise whether the audit of tax as mentioned in section 5.4.2 should be performed or at least supervised by a 'tax assurance provider' who is

---

[36]   See Avi-Yonah 2008, pp. 137–139, who argues that this should be the policy on the basis of corporate social responsibility and doubt on this point of view by Fraser 2008, pp. 139–150.

[37]   For an example of such a fictitious conference between a company and the tax authorities, see Kuiper 2008, pp. 1439–1443.

independent of the company and/or the external auditor. He can advise the external auditor on the tax position of the company on the basis of his report. Independence from the company would seem necessary for the tax assurance provider in order to obtain an objective result.[38] However, it could also be argued that the TCF and the tax assurance provider as an employee of the company, form a quality system, a sort of certification. For this certification to be accepted some sort of monitoring system or certification system would seem to be necessary. At present there is discussion in the Netherlands on setting up such a certification system. The general idea is to establish a register of certified 'tax assurance providers'. To be admitted to the register the tax assurance provider must comply with a number of requirements on experience and (permanent) education and will be subject to penalties if his work is not satisfactory. One of the most important issues is that the tax authorities would have to accept reports of the registered tax assurance providers to give the register the status it would need in practice.

The independence of a tax assurance provider from the external auditor is not currently mandatory, but seems advisable since there is a better guarantee for objectivity if the auditor and tax assurance provider do not belong to the same firm.

5.5 RECENT DEVELOPMENTS

5.5.1 General

There are a few recent developments that are expected to be important in the ongoing evolution of risk management in taxation. The first issue is the growing role of ethics in the field of taxation and the influence it has or should have on taxation of companies: the question of whether a specific company contributes its fair share to the income of governments of countries in which it does business. The second issue is that risk management in taxation has primarily been viewed as a responsibility or a tool for companies. Governments and, as part of them, the tax authorities also use risk management to determine which companies to submit to a tax audit. Both developments can lead to a new way of interaction between companies and governments, where relationships are based on trust in the here and

---

[38] If the provider is an employee of the company, the external auditor will have to audit his report. If the provider is independent, the external auditor can, in principle, just use the report.

now rather than fear of tax audits over past years. This new approach has been adopted in various countries. In the Netherlands it is known as horizontal supervision in combination with enforcement covenants between tax authorities and companies or organizations. A last development is the European tendency to work towards unity in various taxes. This has been accomplished to a large extent in the field of VAT and customs, but is still in its first stages in the field of corporate income taxation.[39] However, there is a technical outline of a common consolidated corporate tax base in the EU (CCCTB) which could be a basis for a European corporate income tax. All developments mentioned will be discussed and their influence on tax risk management explored.

5.5.2   Fair Share

As described in section 5.1 companies have long had one aim in their tax strategy: minimizing tax cost. This was done by looking for the boundaries in the laws, integrating tax havens into the structure of the group, and seeking tax arbitrage.[40] The goal of a tax haven in the group is to place deductions in countries with high tax rates and drop the profits in countries with low or even zero tax rates. Tax arbitrage tries to take advantage of mismatches between the tax systems of different countries. In this way it can for instance be possible to claim depreciation on an asset in two jurisdictions; this is called a double dip. Tax authorities reacted to this behaviour by devising and implementing ever more complicated anti-abuse legislation. Thus a negative spiral of structuring and legislation was created. Legislation, especially anti-abuse legislation is often complicated. It is clear that certain types of behaviour are undesirable for a government, but to capture this in words that are not open to diverse interpretations is difficult. The fact that the major companies have become more and more international organisations makes it especially difficult for tax authorities and judges to adequately assess the situations that are created. These developments can leave a very grey area when it comes to the scope of legislation and a lack of clarity as to where the boundaries are.

Since the accounting scandals at the beginning of this century (Enron, WorldCom, Parmalat, Ahold)[41] that usually also involved aggressive tax

---

[39]   The two most important European Directives in the field of corporate income taxation are the Parent-Subsidiary Directive and the Merger Directive.

[40]   See Happé 2008, pp. 159–160.

[41]   See section 3.2 in Chapter 3 for more information on these scandals.

devices, there has been a gradual change in thinking.[42] Following the emphasis on stricter corporate governance the big accounting firms began to reconsider their policy on tax risk management and the idea of fair share emerged:[43] a company must pay its fair share of tax in the countries in which it operates.[44] 'Fair play' is the term reserved for tax planning that stays within the limits of the legislation and does not have the ethical component that 'fair share' possesses.[45] The notion that a company must pay its fair share can also be found in publications of the IMF,[46] in which it is noted that globalization of the economy had a significant effect on the tax revenue, caused by fiscal termites (such as off-shore financial centres and tax havens etc.) which gnaw at the foundations of the tax systems. If both the companies and the tax authorities subscribe to the notion of fair share, it may be possible to break the negative spiral and construct a new way of dealing with each other.[47]

5.5.3 Horizontal Supervision

Horizontal supervision was an experiment of the Dutch tax authorities that started in 2005, but has now become the official policy. It was started as an attempt to create a new way of dealing with companies, especially big international companies. The premise for the experiment was that both parties (tax authorities and companies) have an interest in better relations. The tax authorities are faced with the hard fact that it is impossible for them to check each individual tax return in detail. In practice they work with a selection of risk groups that are monitored more closely. The rest is monitored at random. The companies find it hard to keep their tax risk management under control: if the tax liability cannot be accurately calculated because it is not clear whether or not the tax authorities are going to accept the tax strategies of the company, this is ultimately a bad thing for the share value. It seems that the premise is fulfilled. The solution was that both parties do not interact on the basis of aggression or mistrust and fear of retribution in later years, but on the basis of trust. Both must adhere to the notion (and trust the other party to do so) that the company must pay its fair share: no more and no less.[48]

---

[42] Schep 2002, p. 1109.
[43] See Landolf and Symons 2008, p. 6.
[44] See Happé 2008, p. 162 and his references to publications of the big accounting firms.
[45] See Poolen 2009, p. 19.
[46] See Tanzi 2000.
[47] See Hartnett 2008, pp. 179–181 and Hickey 2008, pp. 183–185.
[48] See Stevens 2009, pp. 6–13 and Happé 2009, pp. 5–15.

5.5.3.1   Practical implementation of horizontal supervision

In their publication of 21 March 2008 the Dutch tax authorities give their view on horizontal supervision and TCF.[49] The idea is that a company and the tax authorities make a deal: the enforcement covenant.[50] In this covenant parties strive to work effectively and efficiently on the basis of transparency, understanding, and trust. They strive for permanent insight in the current tax risks of the company and quick decision on ruling requests. Furthermore, the covenant contains agreements on specific issues of the company. Often it will contain agreements on old issues, so that parties can start with a clean slate. Notwithstanding the covenant, the tax authorities can still monitor the books and/or tax returns of the company (the normal vertical supervision), but in principle they will not audit issues that have already been audited by other internal or external parties. The principal object of the monitoring is the TCF. The TCF and its quality are very important for the tax authorities as a criterion for assessing the degree to which a company is in control of its tax risks.[51]

The advantages of horizontal supervision for the tax authorities are that they can monitor a big company at relatively little expense in terms of personnel.[52] A complete tax audit of a big company might take years and the potential gain for the tax authorities is by no means certain. Another issue is that a problem or a different point of view in a specific case is recognized much sooner and can be dealt with without disturbing the existing relationship: the parties agree to disagree on this point and ultimately seek the decision of a third party (a tax court or arbitration).

The advantages for the company are that they are much more in control of their tax liabilities. They cannot structure the group as aggressively as in the past, but the consensus at this point seems to be that this ultimately is not the best way to attain long-term share value anyway.[53] Problems can always be discussed with the tax authorities and dealt with quickly. It must be noted at this point that obviously not all issues (in fact the majority of the issues) are related to tax avoidance. It is often simply the road through

---

[49]   Belastingdienst 2008.

[50]   There are also covenants with organizations of companies or professionals (who work for small and medium-sized enterprises) which will not be discussed, see www.belastingdienst.nl/convenanten. For literature see Kastein and Koper 2009, p. 129; Verbakel and Van der Kamp 2009, p. 185.

[51]   Van der Laan and Weerman 2008, p. 1270, pose the question of whether it is necessary for a company to have a TCF prior to entering horizontal supervision. Their conclusion is that it is not, provided the tax authorities trust the company to establish a working TCF.

[52]   See Stevens 2009, p. 9.

[53]   See Essers 2009, pp. 13–17.

the jungle of international business, economic developments, different legal issues, and so on, that contains unknown or unforeseen obstacles that may have an impact on the tax and/or commercial accounts. In terms of risk management in taxation it is a vast improvement to be able to confer with the tax authorities on such an issue and get a timely response.

Other tax authorities have shown initiatives in the same general direction as horizontal supervision: a relationship with companies based on trust and dialogue and focused on the present instead of the past.[54] As it is all quite recent, it is too early to tell whether this approach will be followed by more countries.

5.5.3.2 Risks of horizontal supervision

As is usually the case, good developments also carry risks. In the case of horizontal supervision the risks have been the subject of a number of publications.[55] The main risk the authors seem to recognize is what happens to companies that do not want horizontal supervision. The whole concept of horizontal supervision is that it is not mandatory, but what are the consequences for a company if it does not comply. The risk is that for no other reason than not going along with horizontal supervision, the company will be classed as a risk from the point of view of the tax authorities and that the company will be more liable to vertical supervision and denied the benefits of horizontal supervision. An example is that a company that has a covenant is entitled to receive a quick response on a ruling request. Does this mean that a company without a covenant will not be answered at all or that the tax authorities will take substantially more time to answer? Is the answer more likely to be negative for a company that does not have a covenant? From the point of view that all companies must be treated equally (equality principle) this possible development causes a great deal of concern.

Another concern is the fact that the covenants are based on transparency, which means that the company must report all possible tax issues to the tax authorities at once. The conditions concerning timing and circumstances under which an issue must be reported can be a source of disagreement between the parties.

---

[54] See Happé 2009, p. 158 about Australia and Freedman, Loomer and Vella 2008, p. 81 about the UK and even the Cape Town Communique OECD forum on tax administration, January 11, 2008 as mentioned by Van der Laan and Weerman 2008, p. 1277.

[55] Zwemmer 2008, pp. 1213–1215, Van Herwijnen 2008, pp. 793–795, Bellingwout 2008, pp. 1309–1311, Gribnau 2008, pp. 1325–1336, Barmentlo 2009, pp. 17–22, De Jager 2009, pp. 22–26, Van der Enden 2009, pp. 1107–1113 and Van der Geld 2009, pp. 2–5.

A last major concern is the fact that companies who spend money on their internal control and have a good TCF, in a sense buy the expectation that the tax authorities will not audit them. A tax audit, apart from the possible outcome, is an expensive affair for a company as resources and people have to be committed to the project. Companies who cannot invest to the same degree are then likely to be 'punished' with more audits. It is also a bit worrying that a company will be able to steer a tax audit. If, for instance, the debtors of a company are reviewed by the external auditor for the purpose of the commercial accounts, the company might ask them to do a tax review as well in a separate report. This report will in principle prevent the tax authorities from auditing this point themselves.

It is too early to tell whether, or to what extent, these risks will manifest themselves as horizontal supervision has only started recently as an experiment with big companies. Organizations of companies and professionals as well as scholars will closely monitor these possible risks.[56]

5.5.4   CCCTB

At present there is no common European corporate income tax. In the past this fact has influenced the behaviour of companies as well as governments and continues to do so. Companies have sought the most tax efficient places to show profits: the country with the lowest corporate income tax rates. Countries have tried to compete with each other in the hope of luring investors by lowering the rate of corporate income tax. This has led to a rat race to the bottom with tax rates in the European Union. However, the rates are not the only deciding factor for the tax burden: it is the tax base combined with the rate that gives a more complete picture.[57] With this in mind it was decided to explore the possibility of having a common tax base in the European Union.[58] A working group of the European Committee was formed: the CCCTB WG.[59] The aim was wider than just having one tax base. As the name of the working group implies the aim was to draft a common consolidated corporate tax base. The intention was that a company should be able to calculate its consolidated taxable

---

[56]   The first signs from the big companies seem to be positive, see Schmit 2009, pp. 33–35. The tax authorities are also positive, see Poolen 2009, pp. 16–22.

[57]   See Essers 2007, pp. 741–742.

[58]   Informal meeting of Ecofin September 2004 and prior to that the 2001 report 'Towards an Internal Market without Tax Obstacles'.

[59]   For more information on CCCTB, see the EU website: ec.europe.eu/taxation_customs/taxation/company_tax/common_tax_base/index_en.htm.

profit from all its EU-companies and submit this in one tax return in the country of the parent company. This is called a 'one stop shop' and would give big companies a considerable advantage. Instead of calculating and submitting tax returns in each EU member state in which they are active, they could have just one return. As a result of the consolidation, transfer pricing problems in the EU would also be a thing of the past. The EU member states would then have a sharing mechanism to attribute the corporate income tax that the country of the parent has received to member states where the subsidiaries are located.

Although the potential benefits are huge, it is clear that it is an enormous task to create and implement the CCCTB as described above. The European Committee seems to have taken the view that a policy of getting there one step at a time is the best approach. The WG has published an outline of a CCCTB,[60] which could be used as a basis for a European corporate income tax. The step-by-step approach towards the CCCTB is evident for instance in a report on the activities of the CCCTB WG in May 2007. In this report it is stressed that the CCCTB will not include the applicable rate. There is obviously hope that if the rates remain the domain of the national government there will be less opposition to the CCCTB and that the rate will follow later. Another point is that the CCCTB is not mandatory: companies would be able to choose between the CCCTB and the national corporate tax system. Again the hope would be that they all choose the CCCTB in the end.

The CCCTB was originally to be based on the IFRS, but this soon proved to be difficult politically. The IFRS are not made by governments but by the International Accounting Standards Board (IASB) and the thought that this board could influence corporate tax revenue through the IFRS is too much for many governments. In practice however the IFRS proved to be the common language between the members of the CCCTB WG,[61] so that on many points the influence of the IFRS on the outline of the CCCTB is apparent.[62]

At the moment it is not clear when a CCCTB will be adopted but it seems probable that in one form or another it will be eventually. If so, it will take the form of a directive. What influence will a CCCTB have on tax risk management? Within the EU many problems for companies with cross-border activities would disappear. Unclear situations often exist, for

---

[60] WP 57, see the EU website of the mentioned above.
[61] See Neale 2008, pp. 37–45.
[62] For more details see Essers, Raaijmakers, Russo, Van der Schee, Van der Tas and Van der Zanden 2009, pp. 30–31.

instance in the field of transfer pricing, and that would then cease to exist within the EU. This would make it easier to manage and to be in control of the tax risks. On the other hand, the CCCTB would pose a new situation that would have its own problems that would need to be solved and this could mean new risks to be assessed.[63] On the whole, and after the initial problems that inevitably come with a new system have been solved, the CCCTB will probably have a positive effect for companies, according to Business Europe Task Force.[64]

5.6   CONCLUSIONS

1. Taxes usually have a material impact on the results of a company. The risk connected to errors in this part in the commercial accounts must be properly managed.
2. Due to the complexity of tax legislation, managing tax risks on a case-by-case basis is generally felt to be inadequate.
3. The consensus seems to be to manage the risk connected with taxation by being in control. This is achieved by setting up and maintaining a Tax Control Framework (TCF) as part of the Business Control Framework.
4. The TCF may not always be reliable when too many assessments are involved in the outcome. In this respect much depends on the risk appetite of the company.
5. A development for companies is that they seem to shift their focus from complication to avoid taxation to paying their fair share. A development for tax authorities is to seek more cooperation with companies and build on the work already done by other parties such as external auditors. In the Netherlands this has resulted in the development of horizontal supervision, in which the company and the tax authorities deal with each other in present time on the basis of trust. The TCF and its quality play an important role in horizontal supervision as it is the basis for the board of the company to state it is in control of its tax liabilities.
6. The development and implementation of a CCCTB will eventually lead to a better control of the tax risk within a company in the EU.

---

[63]   See Simonis 2009, p. 19.
[64]   Andersson 2007.

REFERENCES

Avi-Yonah, Reuven (2008), 'Aggressive Tax Behaviour and Corporate Social Responsibility', in Freeman, Judith (ed), *Beyond Boundaries: Developing approaches to tax avoidance and tax risk management*, Oxford: Oxford University Centre for Business Taxation, pp. 137–139.

Barmentlo, Dick G. (2009), 'Horizontaal toezicht en vierde tranche AWB: spagaat tussen vertrouwen en beboeting', *Vakblad voor de CB-adviseur, 1/2* 2009, pp. 17–22.

Bellingwout, Jaap W. (2008), 'Horizontaal Ideaal', *Weekblad voor Fiscaal recht*, 137 (6789), pp. 1309–1311.

Cox, Tim (2008), 'Stake holder communication', *International Tax Review, Tax management in companies (2nd edition)*, Tax Reference Library 44, available at: http://www.pwc.com/en_GX/gx/tax-management-strategy/pdf/pwc_tax_management_in_companies.pdf (accessed 11 January 2010).

Duff, David G. (2008), 'Relationships, Boundaries, and Corporate Taxation: Compliance and Avoidance in an Era of Globalisation', in Freedman, Judith (ed), *Beyond Boundaries: Developing approaches to tax avoidance and tax risk management*, Oxford: Oxford University Centre for Business Taxation, pp. 197–205.

Ende, Eelco M.E. van der (2008), in Pheijffer, Marcel and Fred van Eenennaam, *Commissaris van Nu: Gevaarlijke gedachten voor Commissarissen*, Assen: Van Gorcum.

Ende, Eelco M.E. van der (2009), 'Horizontale Mythes. Van horizontaal naar fiscaal systeemtoezicht', *Weekblad voor Fiscaal recht*, 138 (6826), pp. 1107–1113.

Endres, Dieter et al (2006), *The Determination of Corporate Taxable Income in the EU Member States*, Alphen aan de Rijn: Kluwer.

Essers, Peter H.J. (2007), 'CCCTB dreigt aan vlijt ten onder te gaan', *Weekblad voor Fiscaal recht*, 136 (6727), pp. 741–742.

Essers, Peter H.J. (2009), 'Horizontaal toezicht: een stille revolutie die haar eigen kinderen verslindt?', *Vakblad voor de MKB-adviseur*, 1/2, pp. 13–17.

Essers, Peter H.J., Theo Raaijmakers, Ronald Russo, Pieter van der Schee, Leo van der Tas, Peter van der Zanden (2009), *The influence of IAS/IFRS on the CCCTB, Tax Accounting, Disclosure, and Corporate Law Accounting Concepts*, Alphen aan de Rijn: Kluwer Law International.

Fraser, Ross (2008), 'Aggressive Tax Behaviour and Corporate Social Responsibility: A Response', in Freeman, Judith (ed), *Beyond Boundaries: Developing approaches to tax avoidance and tax risk management*, Oxford: Oxford University Centre for Business Taxation, pp. 139–150.

Freedman, Judith (ed) (2008), *Beyond Boundaries: Developing approaches to tax avoidance and tax risk management*, Oxford: Oxford University Centre for Business Taxation, pp. 9–77.

Freedman, Judith, Geoffrey Loomer and John Vella (2008), 'Moving Beyond Avoidance? Tax Risk and the Relationship between Large Business and HMRC', in Freeman, Judith (ed), *Beyond Boundaries: Developing approaches to tax avoidance and tax risk management*, Oxford: Oxford University Centre for Business Taxation, pp. 81–100.

Geld, Jan A.G. van der (2009), 'Horizontaal toezicht', *Tijdschrift voor Fiscaal Ondernemingsrecht*, 101, pp. 2–5.

Gribnau, Hans (J.)L.M. (2008), 'Belastingmoraal en compliance', *Weekblad voor Fiscaal recht*, **137** (6790), pp 1325–1336.

Grotenhuis, Aertjan (2008), *Fiscalist achter de schermen vandaan*, Deventer: Kluwer.

Hanlon, Michelle (2008), 'Analysing the Impact of Tax Avoidance', in Freeman, Judith (ed), *Beyond Boundaries: Developing approaches to tax avoidance and tax risk management*, Oxford: Oxford University Centre for Business Taxation, pp. 129–131.

Happé, Richard (2008), 'Multinationals, Enforcement Covenants, and Fair Share', in Freeman, Judith (ed), *Beyond Boundaries: Developing approaches to tax avoidance and tax risk management*, Oxford: Oxford University Centre for Business Taxation, pp. 157–176.

Happé, Richard H. (2009), 'Handhavingsconvenanten: een paradigmawisseling in de belastingheffing', *Tijdschrift voor Fiscaal Ondernemingsrecht*, 101, pp. 5–15.

Hartnett, Dave (2008), 'Boundaries, Behaviour and Relationships: The Future', in Freeman, Judith (ed), *Beyond Boundaries: Developing approaches to tax avoidance and tax risk management*, Oxford: Oxford University Centre for Business Taxation, pp. 179–181.

Herwijnen, P.A. van (2008), 'Horizontaal toezicht- een science fiction', *Weekblad voor Fiscaal recht*, **137** (6774), pp. 793–795.

Hickey, Loughlin (2008), 'Relationships and Boundaries: The Future', in Freeman, Judith (ed), *Beyond Boundaries: Developing approaches to tax avoidance and tax risk management*, Oxford: Oxford University Centre for Business Taxation, pp. 183–184.

Hofstra, Henk J. and René E.C.M. Niessen (2002), *Inleiding tot het Nederlandse belastingrecht*, Deventer: Kluwer.

Hoyng R. and E. van der Reijden, 'Belastingadvies in nieuw perspectief', *Tijdschrift voor Fiscaal Ondernemingsrecht*, 101, pp. 22–33.

Jager, Jan C. de (2009), 'Horizontaal toezicht zorgt voor kwalitatief hoogwaardig fiscaal proces', *Vakblad voor de CB-adviseur*, 1/2, pp. 22–26.

Johnston, Angus (2006), 'The explosion of tax risk', *International Tax Review*, 10, pp. 24–26.

Kastein, Jeroen and Bas Koper (2009), 'De rol van de intermediair in horizontaal toezicht voor ondernemingen', in Kamerling, Robert N.J. & Roy Kramer, *Tax Assurance in beeld, deel 6: TaxAssuranceEssays IV*, Breukelen: Nyenrode Tax Academy Press, pp. 129–150.

Kuiper, Jurgen G. (2008), 'Horizontaal toezicht en de Harvard-onderhandelingsmethode', *Weekblad voor Fiscaal recht*, **137** (6793), pp. 439–1443.

Laan, R. van der, M Rosmalen, G de Mare and E van Loon, Audit of tax: 'Waar gaat het naar toe? Waar kan het naar toe? Waar moet het naar toe?' in Kamerling, Robert N.J. & Roy Kramer, *TaxAssuranceEssays*, Nyenrode Business University, June 2007, p. 50.

Laan, R.A. van der and A.J.K. Weerman (2008), 'Tax Control Framework: van risicogericht naar 'in control': het werk verandert voor ons allemaal', *Weekblad voor Fiscaal recht*, **137** (6788), pp. 1269–78.

Landolf, Urs (H.) and Susan Symons (2008), 'Applying corporate responsibility to tax', *International Tax Review, Tax Reference Library 44, Tax management in companies (2nd edition)*, pp. 6–14.

Macdonald, Graeme (2008), 'Analysing the Impact of Tax Avoidance: A Response', in Freeman, Judith (ed), *Beyond Boundaries: Developing approaches to tax avoid-

ance and tax risk management, Oxford: Oxford University Centre for Business Taxation, pp. 133–135.

Neale, Thomas (2008), 'CCCTB: how far have we got and what are the next steps', in Lang, Michael et al (eds), *Common Consolidated Corporate Tax Base,* 53, Vienna, Austria: Linde, pp. 37–45.

Philips (2008), Philips Annual Report 2008, available at: http://www.philips.com/about/investor/financialresults/annualreports/index.page (accessed 2 February 2009).

Poolen, Theo W.M. (2009), 'Horizontaal toezicht vanuit het perspectief van de Belastingdienst', *Tijdschrift voor Fiscaal Ondernemingsrecht*, 101, pp. 16–22.

PriceWaterhouseCoopers (2010), *Paying taxes 2010*, available at: http://www.pwc.com/gx/en/paying-taxes/pdf/paytax-2010.pdf (accessed 12 January 2010).

Rabenort, M. (2007), 'Van Symptomatisch Tax Risk Management naar Tax Control', *Maandblad voor Belastingrecht en Belastingpraktijk*, 76 (10), pp. 341–45.

Schep, A.W. (2002), 'Enron en de ethiek van de belastingadviseur', *Weekblad voor Fiscaal recht*, 131 (6491), pp. 1107–9.

Schmit T.P.M., Ter uitleiding: enkele korte aantekeningen over horizontaal toezicht vanuit het perspectief van het bedrijfsleven, *Tijdschrift voor Fiscaal Ondernemingsrecht*, 101, pp. 33–5.

Self, Heather (2008), 'Acceptable Tax Avoidance?', in Freeman, Judith (ed), *Beyond Boundaries: Developing approaches to tax avoidance and tax risk management*, Oxford: Oxford University Centre for Business Taxation, pp. 151–156.

Simonis, Paul H.M. (2008), 'Over corporate governance, jaarrekeningenrecht en horizontaal toezicht', *Weekblad voor Fiscaal recht*, 137 (6747) pp. 5–27.

Simonis, Paul H.M. (2009), 'CCCTB: some Observations on Consolidation from a Dutch Perspective', *Intertax*, 37 (1), pp. 19–39.

Stevens, Leo G.M. (2009), 'Horizontaal toezicht: de noodzaak van vertrouwen', *Vakblad voor de CB-adviseur*, 1/2, pp. 6–13.

Stevens, Leo G.M. (2009), 'De noodzaak te vertrouwen', *Vakblad voor de CB-adviseur*, 1/2, p. 9.

Tanzi, Vito (2000), 'Globalization, Technological Developments, and the Work of Fiscal Termites' *IMF Working Paper*, 00/181, available at http://papers.ssrn.com/sol3/papers.cfm?abstract_id=880256 (accessed 12 January 2010).

Verbakel, René and Koos van der Kamp (2009), 'Knelpunten van horizontaal toezicht bij middelgrote ondernemingen (MGO's)', in Kamerling, Robert N.J. and Roy Kramer, *Tax Assurance in beeld, deel 6: TaxAssuranceEssays IV*, Breukelen: Nyenrode Tax Academy Press, pp. 185–202.

Verburg, J. (1984), *Vennootschapsbelasting,* Deventer: Kluwer.

Ydema, Onno I.M. (2006), 'Historische kanttekeningen bij bestedingsbelastingen', *Maandblad voor belastingrecht en belastingpraktijk*, 75 (5), pp. 189–206.

Zwemmer, J.W. (2008), 'Horizontaal Toezicht', *Weekblad Fiscaal Recht*, 137 (6638), pp. 1213–1215.

CODES AND GUIDELINES

Andersson, Krister (2007), *Comments on document CCCTB/WP/057*, On behalf of the Business Europe Task Force on CCCTB, available at: http://ec.europa.eu/

taxation_customs/resources/documents/taxation/company_tax/common_tax_
base/UniceComments_WP061.pdf (accessed 12 January 2010).
Belastingdienst (2008), *Horizontaal toezicht: samenwerken vanuit vertrouwen*,
available at: http://download.belastingdienst.nl/belastingdienst/docs/horizon-
taal_toezicht_samenwerken_vertrouwen_dv4031z1ed.pdf (accessed 12 January
2010).
Committee of Sponsoring Organizations of the Treadway Commission (COSO)
(2004), *Enterprise Risk Management – Integrated Framework,* Executive
Summary, New York: AICPA Inc., (COSO II Report).
Tabaksblat Committee (Corporate Governance Committee) (2003), *The Dutch
corporate governance code: Principles of good corporate governance and best
practice provisions,* (Tabaksblat Code).

EU LEGISLATION AND DOCUMENTS

Directive 2006/112/EC of the Council of the European Communities of 28
November 2006 on the common system of value added tax, OJ L 347 of 11
December 2006 (VAT Directive).
Council Directive 90/434/EEC of 23 July 1990 on the common system of taxation
applicable to mergers, divisions, transfers of assets and exchanges of shares
concerning companies of different Member States, OJ L 225 of 20 August 1990
(Merger Directive).
Directive 90/435/EEC of the Council of the European Communities of 23 July
1990 on the common system of taxation applicable in the case of parent com-
panies and subsidiaries of different Member States, OJ L 225 of 20 August 1990
(Parent-Subsidiary Directive).

LEGISLATION AND DOCUMENTS IN THE NETHERLANDS

Case Law

Dutch Supreme Court, 8 May 1957, BNB 1957/208.

6. Risk management interconnections in law, accounting and tax

Marijn van Daelen, Christoph Van der Elst and Arco van de Ven

6.1 INTRODUCTION

The problems that occurred at the turn of the century and the recent financial scandals brought internal control and risk management issues into the spotlight. Although the previous chapters have shown that risk management is not a new feature of businesses and corporate governance, it is currently high on the corporate agenda. Academics, policymakers and lawmakers, as well as practitioners, focus on risk management discussions. Many papers and books are written on the subject. However, a comprehensive approach in accounting, and business, financial and tax law to risk management is non-existent. These fields are all interrelated and describe and require particular behaviour within organizations.

The multidisciplinary approach of this chapter can give insight into the overall influence of risk management on companies and on society as a whole, taking the corporate governance discussion to a higher level. The previous chapters have provided an elaborate account of the development of risk management in business, financial and tax law, and accounting at EU level, within some EU member states and in the US. The previous chapters have also explored current risk management discussions and reforms in order to identify possible future directions. This chapter aims to set forth new insights derived from a multidisciplinary approach. Building on the previous chapters, Section 6.2 will explore risk management developments from a multidisciplinary approach and convey how these developments are connected. Section 6.3 will then analyse the interconnections between law, accounting and tax and will present the risk management landscape businesses are facing. Section 6.4 will conclude with a discussion of some of the challenges and problem areas risk management faces.

6.2 EXPLAINING THE DEVELOPMENT OF RISK MANAGEMENT

Internal control and risk management have significantly changed over the years and different views have been developed. These developments are somehow connected and will here be aligned in a new perspective. This section will explore risk management developments from a multidisciplinary approach by describing the development stages of risk management practices.

6.2.1 Stage 1: Birth of the Regulated Markets, Corporations and Professions

In the period up to the Great Crash of 1929 many corporate law and tax law rules, as well as accounting frameworks were developed. Companies became separate legal entities with limited liability, and corporate laws such as the British Companies Act were adopted and amended. The financial markets developed and stock exchanges and banks began to play an increasingly important role in society. In the wake of the industrial revolution and the emergence of large industrial corporations, the management of organizations professionalized.

Further back in time, the development of trade required the safe transfer of large amounts of money. Money was kept in custody and traders were charged for keeping the deposits. The custodians started lending the money to third parties and charged the lenders. The money-lenders started to issue credit notes and soon realized that more notes could be issued than would be covered by the value of the assets deposited. These money-lenders noticed that at any given time only a small proportion of the gold they held was being withdrawn. The mechanism fostered economic growth but contained the risk that the money-lenders could not perform if there were to be a run on them. Next, local governments started to develop new methods of public finance incorporated in instruments that started to be traded on stock exchanges, and people became familiar with counterparty risk. A financial system that facilitated the channelling of funds from lenders to borrowers was developed. It was soon found that financial intermediation required government support; moral hazard, adverse selection, information asymmetries are sources of risk that cannot be fully excluded without government intervention.

It was not only the beginning of the trade in government notes. The VOC became the first multinational corporation in the world. The company separated ownership from control. It is argued that early corporate boards were an imitation of town councils. These councils consisted of members who were involved with merchant guilds.[1] In a guild, decisions were taken jointly by the executive officers and the guild members of a plenary meeting that took place at least once every year. The members elected the officers.[2] The directors of companies engaged in risky activities, which could, and did, result in corporate failures, such as those of the South Sea Company and the Mississippi Company. Governments intervened and issued acts forbidding companies to be established without government consent in order to mitigate fraudulent behaviour. In the 19th century the government approach switched towards the development of a legal framework for corporations; the first companies acts were enacted. Governments prescribed regulations for managing the company, and directors were responsible for running the company and were accountable towards other corporate stakeholders. Professional management started to develop and issues of how to control organizations gained prominence. Risk as a topic in business was recognized in the opening decades of the 20th century.

Both the financial markets and corporate stakeholders required reliable counterparty information. It was soon realized that some kind of control of the disclosed information was necessary, and this awareness marked the start of the development of the accounting and auditing profession. At the end the 19th century accounting associations – the first of which was the Society of Accountants of Edinburgh – were founded and the regulation of the accounting profession was boosted by the foundation of the American Association of Public Accountants (AAPA), later renamed as the American Institute of Accountants (AIA). The professionalization process was further supported by the launch of accounting journals. Through discussions within the accounting profession a shared vision developed of generally accepted accounting and auditing principles among members of the accounting profession. The importance of accounting and accounting organizations was recognized by governments and accounting regulation began to be issued. The call for transparency was supported in the UK with adjustments to the British Companies Act, which required companies to keep detailed accounting records and demanded publication and audit of the balance sheet and the profit and loss statements of companies.

By the time of the financial crisis of the late 1920s and 1930s corporate

---

[1] Gevurtz 2004, pp. 41–58.
[2] Reference is also made to the College of Cardinals, whose members became the Pope's counsellors and in 1059 were granted the power to elect the Pope (decree of Nicholas II).

law, financial law, accounting and audit were well established. Risk was an acknowledged impact factor, not least because the business and financial world had been confronted with a number of fraud cases. As yet, though, there was no debate on the development of risk management processes nor was internal control on reporting an issue; risk and fraud were considered elements of business.

6.2.2   Stage 2: Reporting to Stakeholders

The stock market crash in 1929 triggered the Great Depression and brought different accounting and auditing irregularities into the spotlight. Different stakeholders should be protected against risks caused by organizations. Mandatory reporting and safeguards to assure the reliability of the reports were central in addressing these financial risks.

In a number of countries investor confidence was restored via the establishment of a supervisory agency monitoring the financial markets and the financial industry, for instance, the SEC in the US and the Banking Commission in Belgium. The supervisory agency was responsible for companies filing and disclosing more reliable information to the public and for ensuring that parties acting as financial intermediaries treated the investors fairly and honestly and put their interests first.

Internationally, the Bank of International Settlements was established. Originally its main task was to manage the post-World War I administration and distribution of the German annuities payable as reparations. The bank soon developed as a platform for cooperation of the central banks to maintain financial stability. Another major initiative of this bank was the post-World War II Bretton Woods system. This international monetary system provided fixed exchange rates of all important currencies against the dollar. The dollar had a rate of $35 per ounce of gold. The dollar was backed by gold and the system-affixed exchange rates was universally considered to be a trustworthy system.

The Securities Exchange Act of 1934 required disclosure and audit of financial information. It also paid some attention to internal control, by stipulating that auditors had to devote appropriate attention to the system of internal check and internal control. From the Great Depression onwards an increasing standardization occurred of what information should be made transparent and how it should be audited. Committees emerged, such as the Committee on Auditing Standards and the Committee on Accounting Procedures of the AIA, which issued the first US accounting standards. Later, a new standard setting body, the Accounting Principles Board (APB), was founded. From a regulatory perspective, compliance with the standards of, for instance, the Committee on

Accounting Procedures and the APB was made only on a voluntary basis. It took time and effort for the generally accepted accounting and auditing principles of the accounting professionals to be formalized. At the end of this stage, non-compliance with the formalized Generally Accepted Accounting Principles (GAAP) had to be disclosed in the annual financial statements and auditors had to report non-compliance in their audit opinions. Internal control was seen as one of the elements the external auditors must consider.

Income taxes already existed in most countries. Financing wars was often the triggering event that introduced this type of tax. The UK launched an income tax for the first time in 1799 to finance the war against Napoleon. In the UK, Addington's 1803 Act already required the self-employed to pay income taxes. Farming profits were also taxed. President Lincoln introduced income tax in 1862 to finance the American Civil War. For many years resistance against this type of tax was strong and in many countries income taxes were repealed after hostilities had ceased. As governments gradually became responsible for the welfare of their citizens, other kinds of taxes became insufficient to cover all expenses. Income taxes were introduced to stay (in the US in 1913) or maintained[3] (in the UK) and were gradually expanded both in importance and in range of application. In the US corporate taxation became an important issue after World War II due to the sharp increase in the tax rate.[4] Corporations started programmes to improve tax avoidance schemes – tax management became an issue. Appropriate and adequate information was required to manage tax risks. In the UK in 1965 income tax for individuals was separated from corporate income tax. Companies were required to restructure their tax administration to comply with legal requirements and manage tax risks.

In short, whilst information disclosure standards were being developed, no formal frameworks, techniques or schedules were available to produce this kind of information. Companies only had to make sure that reliable and ever more standardized information was published or available for tax purposes. Whether the information was collected effectively and efficiently was not yet an issue. Risk management was not much more than the acceptance that certain risks were necessary to generate the required levels of return. Table 6.1 summarizes the developments of this stage.

---

[3]   In the UK politicians frequently promised to abolish income tax after the elections were won, but the government never did. As the tax was very low at the end of the nineteenth century (less than 1%), it was not a priority issue.

[4]   Hines 2001, p. 10.

Table 6.1   Developments in stage 2: reporting to stakeholders

Date	Topic	Developments
Great Depression (Dow Jones from 831 to 41)		
1930	Bank of International Settlements	Originally managing the German post-World War I payments, later monitoring the Bretton Woods system
1933–34	Securities Act and Securities Exchange Act	Disclosure and audit of financial information A system of internal check and internal control for audit purposes
1939	Committee on Auditing Procedures	First Permanent Committee on Accounting Procedures of the AIA
1939	Committee on Auditing Standards	First Permanent Committee on Auditing Standards
1950	Accounting Principles Board	Foundation of Accounting Principles Board
1965	UK	Finance Act
1965	Generally Accepted Accounting Principles	Non-compliance of GAAP to be disclosed in audit opinions

6.2.3   Stage 3: Codification of Reporting Requirements

The economic effect of the oil crisis (1973–74) sharpened the focus on internal control of organizations. New standard-setting bodies, such as the Financial and Accounting Standards Board (FASB) and International Accounting Standards Committee (IASC), emerged because of the lack of substantial support from authorities. The accounting standards developed into a more rules-based approach. The Basel Committee was established to encourage convergence towards supervisory standards and guidelines in the banking industry. It called upon national authorities to implement its recommendations but had no supranational supervisory authority. Investigations into foreign bribes and fraudulent reporting prompted lawmakers to concentrate on the internal organization and functioning of firms. For example, the US audit-oriented approach changed with the 1977 FCPA requiring reporting companies to keep books, records, and accounts and to maintain a system of internal accounting controls in order to control management activities.

Europe woke up. In many countries regulatory frameworks on reporting were published. Often these accounts were also used as tax accounts.

However, the differences in accounting rules between the countries were huge and any comparison was almost impossible. In 1978 the Fourth European Company Law Directive[5] was issued and notwithstanding many optional arrangements, it harmonised the reporting standards in the EU member states to a large extent. The directive demanded the annual accounts to comprise a balance sheet, profit and loss account and notes on the accounts. In all member states the accounts must provide a true and fair view of the company's assets, liabilities, financial position and profit and loss. It also requires companies to disclose important events that occurred after the end of the financial year and its estimated future development in a narrative report. The latter can be considered a very preliminary assessment of the risk environment in which the company is operational. Similar rules were provided for consolidated accounts in 1986. The 1978 version of the directive contained no specific requirements for processing the accounts. The responsibility for establishing the accounts is left to the member states and companies itself. The member states must also determine the responsibility for the publication of the accounts. The directive itself only requires that the accounts are duly approved. In most countries it is the board of directors that is responsible for establishing and publishing the accounts. The board is also in charge of the procedures to accomplish this. The directive is silent on how this duty has to be carried out.

The accounts of the larger companies must be audited. The audit must be performed by certified auditors who organized themselves in self-regulatory bodies in most countries. Associations such as the IFA and the AICPA issued statements on auditing. The audit required an external professional to verify the reliability of the accounts. Account reliability in turn is influenced by the system used to develop the accounts. Consequently, the financial reporting system is checked indirectly. The AICPA also established the Cohen Commission and the Minahan Committee. The reports of these commissions highlighted the importance of internal control and the role of the auditor, management and the board.

More comprehensive narrative reporting was developed by the SEC. In 1980 the SEC clarified the 1968 Management's Discussion and Analysis of Financial Condition and Results of Operations (MD&A).[6] It required a discussion of the 'known trends or any known demands, commitments, events or uncertainties that will result in or that are reasonably likely to result in the registrant's liquidity increasing or decreasing in any material

---

[5] Directive 78/660/EEC, Article 54 (3) (g).
[6] SEC Release 6231 of 1980.

way'.[7] It also required disclosing 'known trends or uncertainties that have had or that the registrant reasonably expects will have a material favorable or unfavorable impact on net sales or revenues or income from continuing operations'.[8] The report had to focus 'specifically on material events and uncertainties known to management that would cause reported financial information not to be necessarily indicative of future operating results or of future financial condition'.[9] In clarifying that financial reporting should also cover *known trends and uncertainties*, the SEC requires the assessment of certain types of risks. This shift to risk assessment and disclosure also shows in the 1987 report of the Treadway Commission, which recommended that management identify and assess the factors that could lead to fraudulent financial reporting.

The awareness of the importance of appropriate internal control and risk management systems increased, but this was due to the introduction of requirements that necessitated some kind of organizational system and control framework. However, the growing attention to internal control did not yet lead to legislation requiring companies to report on internal control or to have an independent audit of their internal control systems. The most important developments of this stage are summarized in Table 6.2.

Table 6.2   Developments in stage 3: codification of reporting requirements

Date	Topic	Developments
Oil Crisis (Dow Jones from 985 to 578)		
1973	FASB	Foundation of the Financial Accounting Standards Board
1973	IASC	Foundation of the International Accounting Standards Committee
1974	Basel Committee	Committee of central bankers that provides supervisory standards and guidelines for the banking industry
1976	Foreign bribes	SEC and Senate Foreign Relationship Committee documented that more than 200 large US corporations had secret funds to

---

[7]   17 CFR 229.303.a–3–ii.

[8]   17 CFR 229.303.a–3–ii.

[9]   SEC Interpretation 33–6835 of 1989. It was later copied by IOSO 2003, p. 3: 'The purpose of MD&A-type disclosure is to provide management's explanation of factors that have affected the company's financial condition and results of operations for the historical periods covered by the financial statements, and management's assessment of factors and trends which are anticipated to have a material effect on the company's financial condition and results of operations in the future.'

Table 6.2   (continued)

Date	Topic	Developments
Oil Crisis (Dow Jones from 985 to 578)		
		pay bribes. This triggered a call to regulate, assess, report and attest internal control of organizations
1977	FCPA	Maintain a system of internal accounting controls in order to control management activities
1978	Fourth EU Company Law Directive	The directive provides a partially harmonized financial reporting framework
1978	Cohen Commission	Report on the external auditor's responsibility for reporting on internal controls
1979	Minahan Committee	Report providing guidance on internal control for management and boards among other
1980	SEC	Clarification of MD&A
1987	Treadway Commission	Report on fraudulent financial reporting

6.2.4   Stage 4: Corporate Governance Movement

Reporting as a means to enhance corporate governance was central to the first stages. Regulation and reporting on how organizations should manage and control their business was limited. The corporate governance movements show improvement of this kind of regulation and reporting. The savings and loan crisis of 1987 focused attention on the risks of financial institutions. Guiding principles of capital adequacy were imposed through the Basel I Capital Measurement.

In the financial industry the Basel Committee started to consider the financial strength of financial institutions in the light of the risks related to their assets. The banks were required to weight the risks of an asset. Different kinds of risks must be offset against the financial position of the bank, such as market risk, credit risk, investment risk, interest rate risk, exchange rate risk and concentration risk.[10] In addition, accounting standards and guidelines, such as the Market Risk Amendment and FRR 48, required the disclosure of information on market risks.

---

[10]   Basel Committee 1988, pp. 8 and 13.

It was also agreed that the standard should be set at a level that was consistent with the objective of securing sound and consistent capital ratios for all international banks. Accordingly, the Committee confirmed that the target standard ratio of capital to weighted risk assets should be set at 8% (of which the core capital element would be at least 4%).

Fair Value Accounting (FVA) was introduced to value financial instruments (FAS 107). The crisis stressed the importance of internal control systems. Regulators signalled that internal control weaknesses contributed to the crisis. Due to the 1991 FDIC, in the US this resulted in federally insured depository institutions (savings and loan banks) having to report on the effectiveness of internal control and on the attestation of the independent auditor. The publication of the COSO I Report by the Treadway Commission on fraudulent reporting opened the door to making standardization of the process of internal control possible. As early as 1980, the management of American corporations had to discuss and analyse material events and uncertainties pertaining to the reported financial information. The emphasis on preventing fraudulent financial reporting resulted in a new substance of internal control, one that was broader than the previous internal accounting controls. For example, in the UK the 1992 Cadbury report required directors to maintain an internal financial control system including procedures to minimize the risk of fraud. The referential document later became part of the London Stock Exchange listing requirements.

Approximately at the same time the US issued its sentencing guidelines. These guidelines were for a long time considered mandatory and articulated detailed and sophisticated criteria for identifying organizational law compliance programmes. The guidelines also provided a carrot for companies, as the fines for companies violating the law can be reduced by up to 95%.[11] Although the Supreme Court decided in 2005 that the sentencing guidelines were unconstitutional, their influence persists.

In the following years, multiple reports and guidelines on internal control were issued internationally. For instance, the UK Rutteman report recommended embedding the internal control statement in the corporate governance statement; the Dutch Peters Committee stressed that the board is primarily responsible for effective systems of internal control; and in the UK the Hampel Report and the Combined Code set out the board's responsibility for maintaining a sound system of internal control and the Turnbull Report provided guidance on how to apply, *inter alia*, the internal control provision of the Combined Code.

For the first time rules and regulations were issued that served as a

---

[11]   Fiorelli and Tracey 2007, p. 472.

basis for companies to internally structure their organizations. Although only a limited number of the rules were related to internal control or risk management, the requirements forced companies to organize frameworks for control activities which could relatively easily be transposed or expanded to other risk management fields. Table 6.3 provides a summarized overview of these developments between the late 1990s and the end of the millennium.

Table 6.3   Developments in stage 4: corporate governance movement

Date	Topic	Developments
Savings and loan crisis (Dow Jones from 2722 to 1738)		
1988	Basel I	Guiding Principles for capital adequacy
1991	FAS 107	Fair Value Financial Instruments
1991	FDIC	The Federal Deposit Insurance Corporation Improvement Act of 1991 required CEO, CAO and CFO to sign a report stating the responsibility for internal control
1991	US Sentencing Guidelines	Detailed criteria for identifying organizational law compliance programmes
1992	COSO I report	Sets out a definition of, and a framework for, internal control
1992	Cadbury report	Focuses on a system of internal control over the financial management of the company and provides recommendations, *inter alia*, on the role of directors and the audit committee
1994	Rutteman report	Proposed guidelines that were eventually superseded by the 1999 Turnbull report
1996	Basel	Market Risk Amendment, inclusion of market risk and the option to measure on internal Value at Risk Models
1997	FRR 48	Disclosure of market risk for public filers that use financial derivatives
1997	Peters Committee	The board is primarily responsible for effective systems of internal control
1998	Hampel report	The internal control system not only covers financial controls but also operational and compliance controls, and risk management
1998	Combined Code	The board should maintain a sound system of internal control to safeguard shareholders' investment and the company's assets
1999	Turnbull report	Set up to provide guidance on how to apply the Combined Code, especially the internal control provision

6.2.5   Stage 5: Codification of Internal Control and Risk Management

The burst of the Internet bubble and the attack on the World Trade Center coincided with the revelation of a series of accounting irregularities, which led to an increasing political demand for accountability and transparency. Many countries issued additional regulatory requirements. These requirements vary considerably in detail and prescriptiveness, partly because of the more rules-based US approach and the more principle-based European approach. Decisions were made to convert the US accounting standards and the international accounting standards. The aim is to complete the convergence in 2011. In the meantime, companies needed to restore public confidence, and risk management and internal control systems offer a framework to respond to market concerns and to reflect a sound business practice. The responsibility of supervisory board members for the broader scope of adequate internal control and risk management was stressed. The necessity of having checks and balances gained even more attention. Next to statements on the true and fair value of the company, internal control statements were introduced.

The best-known piece of *internal control* legislation is the 2002 US federal regulation for public companies, SOX. In Section 404 it requires the CEO and the CFO to report on and certify the effectiveness of the company's internal control over financial reporting. In addition, the role of the supervisory board and audit committee more often involved monitoring the internal control systems. Besides Sections 404, SOX contains other provisions dealing with internal control for financial reporting. Section 302 requires the CEO and the CFO to provide a certification both of the fairness of the financial statements and information in each quarterly and annual report and of their responsibility for establishing and maintaining internal controls regarding the disclosure.

The US, with its internal control requirements over financial reporting, its sentencing guidelines related to compliance programmes and its MD&A statement regarding future and influential events, has a relatively clear legislative schedule of internal control requirements and risk management processes. The legislative framework was further developed by the SEC and the PCAOB via, *inter alia*, SEC final rule 33–8238 of 5 June 2003 (Management's Reports on Internal Control Over Financial Reporting and Certification of Disclosure in Exchange Act Periodic Reports) and PCAOB Auditing Standard No. 2 of 2004 (An Audit of Internal Control Over Financial Reporting Performed in Conjunction with An Audit of Financial Statements). The additional audit activities, especially the amount of testing, which the latter standard prescribed, came at a significant cost. To alleviate this financial burden on public companies the

PCAOB released in 2007 Auditing Standard 5, which loosens some of these costly auditing requirements. For example, this standard takes a more risk-based approach, which reduces testing and gives the auditor some room to rely on tests that are performed by the company itself.

Other countries also introduced requirements of internal control frameworks and risk management systems, but many failed to appropriately define the different kinds of framework. In Europe, Directive 2006/43/EC on statutory audits stipulates that public-interest entities must establish an audit committee (or alternative body) to monitor the financial reporting process and to monitor the effectiveness of the company's internal control, internal audit where applicable, and risk management systems.[12] According to recital 24 of this directive, an audit committee and an effective internal control system help to minimize financial, operational, and compliance risks, and enhance the quality of financial reporting. The audit committee must monitor not only the effectiveness of the internal control system of financial reporting, but the effectiveness of *all* internal control systems. The statutory auditor must also 'report to the audit committee on key matters arising from the statutory audit, and in particular on material weaknesses in internal control in relation to the financial reporting process'.[13] For the latter, the range of application is explicitly limited to the financial reporting process. The MiFID Directive and the Banking Directive require companies in the financial industry to establish overall internal control and risk management systems, including all operational activities.[14] The monitoring role of the audit committee can be found in Directive 2006/73/EC, which prescribes specific and detailed risk management and internal audit procedures.[15] Senior management, the persons who direct the business, are responsible for compliance. The supervisory authority has specific powers and rights to assess the conduct of the business.[16] In addition to these requirements, Europe issued disclosure requirements in several directives. The 2006 amendment to the Accounting Directives demands an annual corporate governance statement that

---

[12] Directive 2006/43/EC, Article 41, paragraph 2, subparagraphs a and b.

[13] Directive 2006/43/EC, Article 41, paragraph 4.

[14] Equivalent requirements are given in other directives related to the financial industry. See, for example, Directive 2002/87/EC, Article 9. Financial conglomerates must have an internal control mechanism to identify and measure all material risks incurred and to appropriately relate their own funds to risks as well as sound reporting and accounting procedures to identify, measure, monitor and control intra-group transactions and risk concentration.

[15] Commission Directive 2006/73/EC, Articles 7 and 8.

[16] Directive 2004/39/EC, Article 63, paragraph 3, subparagraph a.

contains a description of the main features of the company's internal control and risk management systems for the financial reporting process. The 2004 Transparency Directive demands the annual report to include a description of the company's principal risks and uncertainties.

EU member states have to adopt these EU directive provisions, which generally focus on covering the financial reporting systems as well as the overall internal control and risk management systems. As a result of the implementation of EU directives, additional requirements have been laid down in national laws of EU member states. Before those requirements were implemented, member states had already started to develop legal internal control and risk management frameworks, mainly resulting in corporate governance codes. Such national corporate governance codes were also recommended by the EU Commission's Plan to Move Forward.

For instance, in the UK the 2003 Higgs report on the role and effectiveness of non-executive directors stated that one of the key elements of the role of non-executives is risk management. The 2003 Smith report on the role of the audit committees stressed the responsibility of the audit committee for assessing the scope and effectiveness of the company's internal control and risk management systems. As a result, in July 2003 the Combined Code was revised by integrating the recommendations of the Higgs and Smith reports.

In the Netherlands the Tabaksblat code emphasized that the company must have an internal control and risk management system, including instruments for risk analysis of the company's operational and financial objectives, as well as a monitoring and reporting system. In addition the code requires the management board to include in the annual report an *in-control statement*, in which the board declares that the systems are adequate and effective. This requirement of the in-control statements was later softened to reporting requirements of a more descriptive nature. The Dutch Corporate Governance Code of 2008 requires the board to declare in the annual report that the internal control and risk management systems provide reasonable assurance but only regarding the financial reporting risks. With regard to the overall internal control and risk management systems it is sufficient for the board to give a description of their design and effectiveness.

In neither the UK nor the Netherlands is internal control and risk management limited to the financial reporting process. The company should be in control. It was soon clear that the regulators were – probably unintentionally – *taking the lead* and required speeding up the implementation of general internal control and risk management frameworks that had not yet fully developed in practice. The COSO II framework offered relief as it identified four different categories for the achievement of an entity's objectives: strategy, operations, reporting and compliance.[17]

In addition to the development of internal control and risk management systems and the ensuring disclosure of information regulations, more elaborate guidelines and standards were developed on how to evaluate and audit internal control systems. The concept of enterprise risk management gradually replaced the concept of internal control in the corporate governance discourse. The importance of risk appetite and adequate risk analysis for organizations grew, which led to, for example, mandatory reporting on the principle risks and uncertainties an organization faces. This development was also supported by the publication of the COSO Enterprise Risk Management framework in 2004. The main developments of this stage can be found in Table 6.4.

Table 6.4   *Developments in stage 5: codification of internal control and risk management*

Date	Topic	Developments
Accounting and auditing development Internet Bubble / 9/11 (Dow Jones from 11723 to 7591)		
2002	IASB/FASB	Start of Convergence project to converge US and International Accounting Standards. The aim is to complete the convergence in 2011
2002	SOX	Prescribing mandatory reporting and audit of internal control over financial reporting. It also created the PCAOB to oversee the auditors and promote informative, fair and independent audit reports
2003	Higgs report	Report on the role and effectiveness of non-executive directors, stating that one of the key elements of their role is risk management
2003	Smith report	Report on the role of the audit committees stressing the responsibility of the audit committee for assessing the scope and effectiveness of the company's internal control and risk management systems
2003	European Commission's Plan to Move Forward	Recommending that member states designate a national corporate governance code for listed companies

---

[17] COSO II report, p. 3. For a more detailed discussion, see Chapter 2 of this book (Section 2.1.8).

Table 6.4   (continued)

Date	Topic	Developments
Accounting and auditing development Internet Bubble/ 9/11 (Dow Jones from 11723 to 7591)		
2003	Combined Code	The provisions of the 2000 Code and the Higgs and Smith reports
2003	Tabaksblat Code	The management board has to include an in-control statement in the annual report in which it declares that the systems are adequate and effective
2004	COSO II report	Sets out a definition of, and a framework for, the broader scope of enterprise risk management
2004	PCAOB-AS 2	Publication of Auditing Standards 2 for auditing the internal control over financial reporting
2004	Transparency Directive	The annual report must include a description of the principal risks and uncertainties companies face
2006	EU Audit Directive	Companies must establish an audit committee (or alternative body) to monitor the financial reporting process and to monitor the effectiveness of the company's internal control, internal audit where applicable, and risk management systems.
2006	EU Amendment to Accounting Directives	An annual corporate governance statement must be issued, containing a description of the main features of the company's internal control and risk management systems for the financial reporting process.
2007	PCAOB-AS 5	Publication of revised audit standards for internal control.
2008	DCGC 2008	Companies must have an internal risk management and control system including risk analyses of their operational and financial objectives and a monitoring and reporting system

6.2.6   Stage 6: Maturity or Reinvention of Risk Management

The subprime crisis and the subsequent financial and economic crises intensified the attention to risk management. The collapse of Lehman Brothers and the rescue of large financial institutions by governments all over the world highlighted the unwarranted trust in financial markets and management of risks. The systems were considered reliable, infallible even, and all kinds of risk were appropriately mitigated through a variety of financial instruments. However, not only did the systems fail to prevent the subprime crisis, although it certainly resembled the savings and loans crisis, but many instruments even aggravated the risks incurred. The level of systemic risk was also much higher than foreseen and the risk appetite of most financial institutions proved to be insatiable. The problem was no longer restricted to the reliability of financial reporting and the quality of internal control systems, but extended to the management of risks, including the use of risk-mitigating instruments to increase performance instead of limiting risks. It soon became apparent that many managerial incentives aimed to develop risk-increasing techniques; the instrument that fitted the risk strategy became an integrated part of the risk.

The systemic risk and financial institutions too big to fail meant that government intervention was necessary. In the US a relief plan (TARP) of over $700 billion was introduced and worldwide financial institutions such as ABN–AMRO, Royal Bank of Scotland and ING were (partly) nationalized. From a corporate governance perspective, these problems were not influenced by weak internal control systems and fraudulent reporting but by ineffective risk management. The shift in focus has evoked reports on the necessity of appointing Chief Risk Officers (CRO) as board members, the creation of risk committees (see for example the Dutch Bank Code and the UK Turner and Walker reviews) and the formalization of reporting on and monitoring of the risk appetite of organizations (see Table 6.5). In particular in the financial industry it is stressed that bonuses should not be unilaterally related to excessive risk-taking behaviour. This is an ongoing development and new regulation and governmental codes are being drafted. This will certainly lead to more disclosures on risk management practices, audits and standards. The question is: will it be more of the same? In other words, will it be more detailed regulation, reporting requirements and increased auditing, or will it lead to a reassessment of risk management? Before going into this challenge for risk management, the next section will first describe the interconnections in the risk management landscape.

Table 6.5   Developments in stage 6: maturity or reinvention of risk management

Date	Topic	Developments
Sub prime/financial crisis (Dow Jones from 13390 to 7062)		
2008	TARP	Government support of $700 billion to rescue financial institutions

Table 6.5   (continued)

Date	Topic	Developments
Sub prime/financial crisis (Dow Jones from 13390 to 7062)		
2008	Governmental support	Government support and nationalization of financial institutions (e.g. Royal Bank of Scotland, ING, and Fortis/ABN Amro)
2009	UK Turner review	Review of the financial crises and recommendations on the changes in regulation and supervision. Recommendation on risk management include investigation of necessary changes in governance structure to increase the independence of risk management functions and the skill level and time commitment required for non-executives to perform effective oversight of risks and provide challenges to executive strategies
2009	Dutch Bank Code	Risk appetite has to be approved on a yearly basis by the Supervisory Board, which also has to assess periodically if the activities of the company fit within the risk appetite. The launch of new products or services is subject to an approval process that includes a thorough risk analysis
2009	UK Walker review	The draft report of the Walker review contains a separate section on governance of risks, in which recommendations are made to establish a separate risk committee, to appoint a CRO to the board, and to publish a separate risk report

6.3   INTERCONNECTIONS

The history of risk management as described in this book shows developments within the disciplines of law, accounting and tax. These developments have contributed to the current concept of risk management. Some of the developments do not stand on their own but are (knowingly or unknowingly) influenced by developments of the other disciplines. Other developments are a reaction to irregularities on markets or in companies and do not take account of the developments in other disciplines. Either way, as this section will show, the disciplines of financial law, business law, accounting and tax are interconnected.

Figure 6.1 gives an oversight of the various elements that impact on the risk management landscape. Government-supervised branches of law are depicted on the left, market-based elements on the right. The latter range from best practices and frameworks such as corporate governance codes, COSO and corporate government initiatives to generally accepted accounting and auditing standards and professional bodies. As an alternative or supplement to governmental supervision by, among others, the SEC (USA), the FSA (UK) and the AFM (Netherlands), private monitoring or self-regulating bodies are included on the market-based side at the top. The interconnection between the different elements depends on the choices governments make between more or less government intervention. Making these choices is at heart a political process and does not rely solely on rational decision making.

The bottom elements are company features that interact with, and are regulated and influenced by, the other elements. Due to legislative and market-based developments, rules and standards now determine which information companies must report and outline the basic elements of corporate systems. Also, the interaction of the depicted actors has initiated or influenced both the structure of company boards and, more specifically, the role of the non-executives and the supervisory board, as well as the specific duties of the CEO, CFO, CRO and compliance officer. In this way, a framework for the internal structure of the organization has been created.

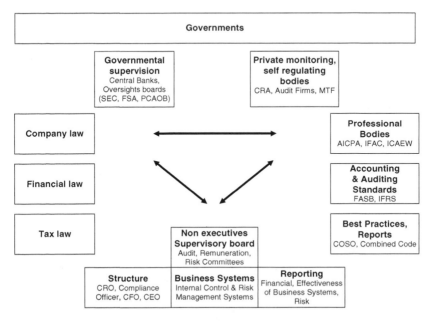

Figure 6.1   Interconnections: the risk management landscape

The interconnections in the risk management landscape of Figure 6.1 can best be described by linking them to the stages identified in the previous section of this chapter. Up to the birth of professional organizations, risks were more or less regarded as acts of providence. Throughout the development of risk management the interconnections between the various elements grew. First, companies were started, trading expanded and stock exchanges developed. Company laws reacted by making it possible to incorporate companies as separate legal persons with shareholders protected by limited liability. Meanwhile, corporate failures of, for example, the South Sea Company and the Mississippi Company had led to regulations such as the UK Bubble Act in order to suppress fraud. Thus company law (on the left of Figure 6.1) reacted directly to the developments on the markets and intervened when companies failed due to frauds. Over time, financial markets and company stakeholders called for more transparency and attestation; and more laws (on the left of Figure 6.1) were developed regulating the responsibility of directors for managing the company and regulating that accounts had to be kept and audited (influencing the bottom elements of Figure 6.1). In the years to follow, the elements on the right of Figure 6.1 grew as the accounting and auditing professions were established and that its members developed generally accepted principles.

As a reaction to the 1929 stock market crash and the ensuing Great Depression, mandatory reporting and safeguards to ensure reliable reports dominated both the legal and market-based elements in Figure 6.1, but they also had an effect on the top elements. For example, to restore public confidence after the stock market crash, US Congress passed the 1934 Securities Exchange Act that required disclosure and audit of financial information (from left to bottom elements). To enforce the law and protect investors, Congress established the SEC, which in its turn makes rules to ensure that the intent of legislation is carried out (from top to bottom elements). The elements on the right of Figure 6.1 countered these developments by establishing permanent committees on accounting and auditing that, although compliance was voluntary, standardized in more detail what information should be made transparent and how that information should be audited.

Codification of these standards intensified during stage three (see Section 6.2.3). The 1973 oil crisis, corporate scandals related to the bribery of foreign officials and fraudulent reporting led to, *inter alia*: (1) new committees in the accounting profession (on the right of Figure 6.1) to develop more rule based standards; (2) the establishment of the Basel Committee by central-bank governors (top of Figure 6.1) to encourage convergence towards supervisory standards and guidelines in the banking industry;

(3) the US Foreign Corrupt Practices Act (left of Figure 6.1) requiring companies to maintain a system of internal accounting controls in order to control management activities; and (4) the Fourth European Company Law Directive (left of Figure 6.1) harmonizing reporting standards in Europe. From all directions, the organizational activities of companies were being regulated and influenced.

The AICPA, a professional accounting association on the right of Figure 6.1, initiated the Cohen Commission on auditor responsibility and the Minahan Committee to provide guidance on internal control for management and boards among others. On the basis of the Cohen report (right) the SEC (top) proposed, but later withdrew, rules for mandatory management reports on internal accounting control systems (bottom). In addition, the SEC (top) gave an interpretation of the MD&A (left) and clarified that financial reporting (bottom) should also cover known trends and uncertainties, which requires a risk assessment regarding financial reporting. In line with the SEC (top) the Treadway Commission (right) also focused on assessing risks that could induce fraudulent financial reporting (bottom). This commission later issued the COSO I report, which provides a framework standardizing the basic elements of the internal control process.

In the UK, too, the concept of internal control became broader. The Cadbury Committee, set up by the Financial Reporting Council, the London Stock Exchange and the accounting profession (right of Figure 6.1), required directors to make a statement in the annual report on the effectiveness of the internal control system. The auditors should report on this statement. Slowly, focus shifted from preventing fraud to the effectiveness of systems. Moreover, the Cadbury report (right) recommended the establishment of audit committees with at least three non-executives (bottom). The London Stock Exchange (top) introduced a provision in the Listing Rules demanding a statement of (non-)compliance with the recommendations of the Cadbury report (influencing the reporting element at the bottom of Figure 6.1). On the basis of the COSO I report, the Rutteman Committee and later the Turnbull Committee of the ICAEW, a professional accountants association, issued their reports. Both stressed the directors' responsibility for reviewing the effectiveness of the systems and the latter underlined the need for an internal audit function.

The IASB, an independent and privately funded accounting standard-setting body in the UK, developed international financial reporting standards (IFRS). These standards, including the IAS, are principles-based standards (on the right of Figure 6.1) that influence the reporting and accounting element of the company (at the bottom of

Figure 6.1). Since the EU IAS Regulation these standards can undergo a process of endorsement and thereby become EU law (see the left of Figure 6.1).

Another element of the company, in addition to board responsibility and reporting, gained attention with the Higgs report describing the role of non-executives for the risk management systems and the Smith report describing the role of audit committees for the risk management systems. Due to the 2006 European Audit Directive (on the left of Figure 6.1) the other EU member states followed by requiring an audit committee with a monitoring role for risk management systems (see the bottom of Figure 6.1).

From the beginning of the new millennium onwards corporate and financial law had an increasing influence on how risks are mitigated. In addition to the regulations described above covering the role of audit committees and supervisory bodies, laws prescribed aspects of the business systems (bottom of Figure 6.1). For example, on the left of Figure 6.1 SOX demands companies to establish and maintain an adequate internal control structure and procedures for financial reporting (influencing the business systems element at the bottom of Figure 6.1). It also requires codes of ethics and obliges companies to develop more formal mechanisms to report on and handle internal shortcomings in business practice. The COSO I framework – devised by a committee composed of members of five professional accounting and auditing associations (on the right of Figure 6.1) – is used for implementing SOX (left) into companies' business (bottom). In the Netherlands, company directors are responsible by law for the proper performance of the duties assigned to them. Dutch business law (left) does not specify what proper performance entails and what these duties are. The law does stress that it is the duty of directors to ensure that accounts of the company are kept. The Dutch corporate governance code provides more specific guidance to companies and its directors. The code (right) received a legal basis (and was thus integrated with elements on the left of Figure 6.1). This code also refers to COSO I (right) as a framework for internal control.

To further develop the legislative framework given by SOX (left), the SEC (top) issued rules, such as Final Rule 33–8238 that deals with management reports on internal control (influencing elements of the company at the bottom of Figure 6.1). In this rule the SEC refers to SAS no. 78 for the definition of internal control, which is derived from the definition in the COSO I report (on the right of Figure 6.1). The final SEC definition of internal control, however, only encompasses the financial reporting objectives, not the elements operations and compliance, except for compliance with laws and regulations that are directly related to the preparation of financial statements.[18] Because of the increased attention of regulators and policymakers (left) to the business systems, companies called for principles-based guidance in order to implement risk management (bottom). The Treadway Commission (right) reacted to this need and issued its COSO II report on enterprise risk management.

SOX also established the PCAOB in order to provide independent oversight of public accounting firms. The PCAOB has issued Accounting Standard 5 that deals with how auditors should assess the effectiveness of internal control over financial reporting. In addition, not only accounting principles and standards (right) are integrated in the legal framework (left) but with the PCAOB, which is in its turn subject to SEC oversight, the oversight of the accounting profession itself entered the legal framework.

At EU level, a series of directives influence the bottom four elements of Figure 6.1. The sector-specific directives, especially, regulate the internal structure of companies by demanding certain duties to be performed and even by requiring the persons that perform them to have certain qualities. As mentioned above, the Basel Committee, established by central-bank governors, issued the Basel I Accord, a set of minimum capital requirements for banks, which were implemented in the laws of ten countries (known as the Group of Ten or G-10 countries). The 2004 Basel II Accord strives to promote greater stability in the financial system by focusing on minimum capital requirements as well as on supervisory review and market discipline. The EU has enforced the Basel Accords (at the top of Figure 6.1) through the EU Capital Requirements Directives (on the left of Figure 6.1).[19] It outlines, *inter alia*, senior management's role regarding the rating systems and the risk-control process and influences the internal organization of the financial company (at the bottom of Figure 6.1) by demanding that the persons who direct the business are 'of sufficiently good repute and have sufficient experience to perform those duties'.[20] EU member states have to implement the provisions of the directives in their national laws and regulations.

To harmonize regulation for investment services, the Markets in Financial Instruments Directive (MiFID) was issued (at the left of Figure 6.1). The MiFID level 1 Directive[21] sets out a framework for legislation and the MiFID level 2 Directive[22] enables investment firms and exchanges to operate throughout the EU and requires investment firms to have risk

---

18   SEC Final Rule 33–8238 of 2003.
19   Directive 2006/48/EC, Directive 2006/49/EC and Directive 2009/111/EC.
20   Directive 2006/48/EC, Article 135.
21   Directive 2004/39/EC.
22   Directive 2006/73/EC.

management policies, procedures and systems. This directive influences company features at the bottom of Figure 6.1 because it requires the establishment and maintenance of an internal audit function and stresses the responsibility of senior management and the supervisory functionaries for ensuring compliance with the obligations of the MiFID level 1 Directive. The directive also prescribes the creation of a compliance function and specifies the function's responsibilities and requires investment companies to ensure prescribed conditions to enable the function to work properly. This is clearly an intervention in the internal structure of the company (at the bottom of Figure 6.1).[23]

Insurance companies must have an effective system of governance that ensures sound and prudent management of the business in line with the Solvency II Directive.[24] This directive regulates the bottom elements of Figure 6.1 as it demands the persons that run the company to (1) have adequate professional qualifications, knowledge and experience and (2) be of good repute and integrity. The insurance companies must also have written policies relating to, *inter alia*, risk management, internal control and internal audit. Without specific requirements for the substance of these policies, best practices are needed to provide guidance.

Apart from the interconnections of business law and financial law to the market-based side of Figure 6.1, tax law has also begun to interact more with that market-based side. Originally, tax accounts either have or do not have a formal dependency on commercial accounts. In practice all systems have elements of both and the balance varies for each country. Thus, tax accounts do not need to have a clear connection with commercial accounts. In addition, COSO I is used for tax control frameworks. In recent years, more interconnections between tax law and the other elements of the risk management landscape have developed. For example, risk management is used not only by companies in determining their tax policies, but also by tax authorities to determine which companies to submit to a tax audit (known as horizontal supervision).

The financial crisis directed more attention to risk management and increased regulatory and other impacts on the internal structure of companies. This combination is shown by several reports, such as the Dutch Banking Code, the UK Turner report and the UK Walker review that underline the importance of establishing risk committees and appointing CROs.

Originally, risk management practices aimed at standardization and

---

[23]　Directive 2006/73/EC, Articles 6 and 7.
[24]　Directive 2009/138/EC.

attestation of companies' financial reports. As a result of the corporate government movement, risk management practices have also influenced the conduct of business and have led to the codification of reporting processes. The attention span of risk management is not limited to reporting and business processes but also extends to the structure of the company. In addition, as this and the previous chapters have shown, risk management practices differ greatly between countries and cultures and are too complex to offer normative one-size-fits-all solutions.

From the above it can be concluded that business law, financial law and accounting have a history of interconnections which is expanding over time. In recent years, tax law has also started to interconnect with certain aspects of the risk management landscape. The influences of these disciplines on risk management call for alignment, because companies are facing a landscape that has grown substantially through the years and is still developing rapidly. Whether alignment alone is sufficient for the further balanced development of the risk management landscape remains to be seen. There are some tensions between the different perspectives due to the inevitably narrow point of view of the individual disciplines. A multidisciplinary approach to risk management might therefore be in order to ensure well-functioning markets and companies.

In general, the recent focus on risk management systems and the companies' internal organization has led to an increasing number of detailed provisions from both the financial and business law areas. Meanwhile, the accounting and auditing standards, as well as the profession, are gaining a foothold in the legal framework. Quite a few company features are influenced or regulated by these disciplines, and this could lead to a negative spill-over. This holds the risk of obstructing economic prosperity instead of improving the economic condition. For example, accounting and auditing provisions aimed at improving the reliability of disclosed information may well have unforeseen negative side effects. For instance, the pro-cyclical effect of FVA impacts the capital adequacy of the Basel agreements. Another example is that the standardization of the internal control and risk management systems could overemphasize the actual risk and crowd out the agility of organizations and the entrepreneurial spirit needed for the continuity of organizations. At the same time, legislative movements regarding the internal audit function, compliance function and risk committees still have to prove beneficial. In addition, the overall focus is on effectiveness rather than on efficiency.

Besides this risk of a negative spill-over, the disciplines do not seem to have pinpointed a direction. The development of risk management shows a shift in focus from preventing fraud, establishing internal accounting controls to regulating parts of the internal structure of the organization and codification of internal control and risk management. In addition, regulations and other influences on the supervisory perspective have expanded from supervision of the board and company by internal auditors, external auditors and non-executives or supervisory boards to supervisory authorities. Will all these rules and all this supervision be able to detect black swan events early? If the goal remains that of preventing fraud and retaining public trust, a focused development within all disciplines, while taking into account the other disciplines in the broader risk management landscape, may lead to an appropriate balance of the overall economy's costs and benefits.

At this point in time, the risk management landscape faces several issues that might be better dealt with from a multidisciplinary perspective. In the following section some of these challenges and problems will be analysed.

6.4   ANALYSING RISK MANAGEMENT

Over the years, internal control has evolved from internal accounting and auditing principles to a growing attention to the internal organization and functioning of firms. The substance of internal control has evolved into a broader concept than the previous internal accounting controls. This was first done by including operational and compliance controls and later by extending its scope to corporate risk management and including strategic controls. The development of the accounting and auditing profession, as well as that of internal control and risk management laws and regulations, is for a large part linked to financial shenanigans and crises and the ardent wish to prevent corporate failures and frauds, such as those that surfaced between 2000 and 2003. The more recent financial crisis has even bolstered the risk management profession. From academic publications to newspaper articles, the emphasis now seems to be on the broader management of risks rather than on the quality of the internal control system. The financial scandals show that even the legal risk management framework of the 21st century could not prevent these risks. It also raises questions as to the different approaches to the business law framework of the US, the EU and the EU member states, as none of these approaches seems to have detected these failures and frauds early. To be sure, the development of business control frameworks is aimed at improving risk management in organizations. These frameworks are prescriptive and describe how companies should act. Does enterprise risk management live up to its promises? Developments are often based on best practices and only loosely predicated on the scarce outcomes of empirical research on risk management practices. The intentions of companies and the ways in which they actually adopt, implement, and use risk management systems could diverge widely from the assumptions of the business control framework.

6.4.1   Risk Society

According to Beck, in the risk society the exceptional condition threatens to become the norm.[25] Possible negative consequences of uncertain future calamities dominate the debate and colour, or some say determine, the perception of reality. In the risk society a focus on risks determines the political discourse and often leads to indecisiveness, and non-intervention will increase the negative consequences of the existing problems. Risk management instruments such as COSO have an impact on people's perception of risk and influences their assessment of the feasibility of activities. Although COSO aims to support the achievement of objectives, which includes taking advantage of opportunities, risk management practices may stress and overvalue the attention to threats. A study by LaSalle, for example, shows that 82% of students who had been taught the COSO method concluded that the risk of misappropriation would be high compared to 54% who had studied the fraud triangle.[26] The experiment was based on a case where asset misappropriation was known to be quite low: that of a talented group of street artists selling CDs without explicit accounting controls.

As risk management discussions continue, it is important to keep focused on its objective. Organizations must take risks on a regular basis to enhance stakeholder value and managing those risks can even result in strategic advantages. In other words, 'the goal of effective ERM is not solely to lower risk, but to more effectively manage risks on an enterprise-wide, holistic basis so that stakeholder value is preserved and grows over time.'[27] Risk management models and risk management regulation do not aim to prevent risk-taking behaviour. Rather, it seems to aim at heightening awareness of the risks and responding to them – for example by avoiding, reducing, sharing or accepting them – in order to fit corporate risk appetite. Information on risks and the functioning of risk management systems have to be disclosed in order to inform the shareholders and other stakeholders.

The current financial crisis drives home the momentousness of internal control and risk management systems for the financial industry. For a

---

[25]   Beck 1992, p. 24.
[26]   LaSalle 2007, pp. 74–87.
[27]   COSO 2009, p. 3.

number of years companies have been obliged to have sound risk management systems in place, especially companies within the financial industry.
Yet even with an excellent risk management system and a dedicated legal
environment in place (including disclosure of meaningful information and
proper ways of enforcement) failures cannot be averted. Before changing,
or adding to, the regulatory framework, the debate should home in on
interconnections between the legal internal control and risk management
environment and the high complexity of the financial products that might
have caused the credit crunch. As will be discussed later in this chapter,
someone who wants to deviate from the regulations or accepted behavioural codes will search for a *facilitating* approach. True though this may
be, it would be unfortunate to overlook the basic idea of risk management
– managing the company's risks within its risk appetite – and the limitations of human abilities. A company can decide to take a risk expecting
large profits and with such a low failure probability that it is within bounds
of the company's risk appetite. But even an acceptable risk is still a risk.
Taking such a risk willingly can be based on good business judgement even
if in a rare case the risk occurs. If the decision turns out poorly, but the
risk was properly understood and within the company's risk appetite, risk
management failure need not be the obvious or inevitable explanation.[28]

6.4.2   Role of Directors and Managers

Nevertheless, executive directors, non-executive directors and senior management are receiving increased scrutiny regarding their role in the crisis.
It will therefore be interesting to discuss their regulatory duty in the risk
management process, especially since the group of persons involved in risk
management is expanding. Risk management provisions in the UK and the
Netherlands provide that it is the board's duty to maintain a sound internal
risk management and control system. In the US, management is responsible for maintaining an adequate internal control structure and procedures
for financial reporting. The oversight duties of the non-executive directors
or the supervisory board regarding the management board extend to the
risk management systems. EU member states are required to mandate
audit committees for public interest entities (2006 Audit Directive).[29]
Such an audit committee is to be composed of non-executive directors or
members of the supervisory body. In the EU member states it is the audit

---

[28]   Stulz 2008, p. 2. On these issues and fields of regulatory concern, see
Goodhart 2008.
[29]   See also Chapter 3 of this book (Section 3.2.2).

committee's role to monitor the effectiveness of the company's internal control, internal audit where applicable, and risk management systems.

The turmoil in the markets during the past years has emphasized the importance of effective board oversight practices, especially with regard to risks. This focus on risk management now leads to discussions about, *inter alia*, the necessity of appointing – and even mandating – a CRO.[30] The CRO is not a new board position. In 1993 James Lam was appointed CRO at GE Capital, claiming to be the first to hold a formal position with that title.[31] Nowadays, the CRO is becoming part of a standard managerial solution to implement, and to stress the importance of, risk management in organizations. The Dutch Maas Committee on the future of the banking industry in the Netherlands recommended that the CRO should be a member of the board.[32] Combining the positions of CRO and CFO can be acceptable under certain circumstances. Although appointing a CRO signals organizational commitment to risk management, questions can be (and have been) raised. Is it possible to impose the responsibility for risk management on a single officer? Does creating a separate position not open up the possibility for the CEO and other board members to shift responsibility to the CRO? Ultimately decisions on the level of risk appetite, risk strategy and safeguarding a healthy internal environment are managerial decisions.

Legislative movements regarding risk committees have also sprung up. For example, in addition to the New York Stock Exchange's corporate governance rules that require audit committees to discuss the guidelines and policies governing the process of risk assessment and risk management,[33] legislation has been introduced in Congress to mandate risk committees for publicly traded companies.[34] More precisely, in May 2009, Senator Charles Schumer introduced a bill in the US Senate to enhance shareholders' authority. The bill, entitled 'Shareholder Bill of Rights Act of 2009', would, if passed, require publicly traded companies to establish risk committees. The role of these risk committees, which are to be composed of independent directors, is to be responsible for the establishment and evaluation of the risk management practices of the issuer.[35]

---

[30] See Section 6.2.6 of this chapter.
[31] Power 2007, p. 82.
[32] Maas 2009, p. 15.
[33] Section 303A of the NYSE Listed Company Manual.
[34] COSO 2009, p. 2.
[35] Shareholder Bill of Rights Act of 2009, Section 5. The bill proposes to amend the Securities Exchange Act of 1934 (15 U.S.C. 78a et seq.) by inserting Section 14A, which includes subsection (e) 'Corporate Governance Standards', (5) 'Risk Committee'.

As in the US, in the Netherlands the idea of demanding companies to have a risk committee is gaining ground. For instance, the Dutch self-regulatory Banking Code requires banks (both listed and unlisted), though not insurance companies or pension funds to have a risk committee.[36]

6.4.3   Enhanced Transparency and Shareholder Power

According to the SEC, shareholders have in recent years expressed the desire for additional information to enable them to make informed voting and investment decisions. The call for enhanced transparency – especially regarding activities that materially contribute to a company's risk profile – has been reinforced by the troubled markets. For that reason, in July 2009, the SEC issued a set of proposed rules in order to enhance the corporate governance disclosures that registrants are required to make about, *inter alia*, their overall compensation policies and their impact on risk taking and the board's role in the risk management process.[37] According to the SEC, disclosure about the board's involvement in the risk management process should provide important information. With that information shareholders can gain a better understanding of how a company perceives the role of its board in managing the material risks facing the company. It also gives insight into the relationship between the board and senior management in managing the company's risks. The SEC points at the pivotal role that risk and the adequacy of risk oversight have played in the recent financial crisis and that it is therefore important that investors have a clear understanding of the board's or board committee's role. The SEC highlights that with such disclosure investors are able to better allocate capital to companies they believe in and the board will be adequately focused on risks. This will also result in increased market efficiency.[38] An interesting question here is whether a US federalized structure of corporate governance is needed to supplement state law and SEC rules.[39] The above-mentioned Shareholder Bill of Rights Act of 2009 should enhance shareholders' authority, because

---

[36]   *Code Banken* 2009, Section 4.2, p. 10. This self-regulatory code will most likely receive a legal basis in 2010.

[37]   SEC Proposed Rule 33–9052 of 2009.

[38]   SEC Proposed Rule 33–9052 of 2009, pp. 25–29. On 1 August 2009, a few weeks after the SEC had proposed these rules, several important amendments to the Delaware General Corporation Law became effective, such as amendments incorporating proxy access procedures. See State of Delaware House Bill 19 of 2009.

[39]   Phillips 2009, p. 1.

of the lack of accountability of boards to shareholders for causing loss of shareholder value. Unfortunately, it is not clear whether shareholders can play a positive role in resolving the crisis. According to Bratton and Wachter, there are no plausible grounds for stating that prior to the crisis increased shareholder power would have resulted in more effective risk management.[40]

6.4.4 The Risk of Fraud

Clearly, the financial crisis has resulted in an increased focus on risk management and the lower confidence of stakeholders has led them to demand more disclosure. However, it is not clear whether stakeholders will be better protected with enhanced disclosure. Information on the board's oversight role and the audit committee's role will most certainly contribute to a stakeholder's understanding of how the company's risks are managed. But is it enhanced risk disclosure that is needed in order to lower the possibility and impact of a next crisis? As mentioned above, risk management models and risk management regulation do not – and should not – aim to prevent risk-taking behaviour. An interesting question in this context is whether the risk of fraud should be treated as a separate legal issue. Put differently, should the aim be to regulate both frauds and risks and also to the same extent? For most risks, such as financial, operational and strategic risks, it makes sense to manage them within the companies' risk profile or risk appetite. Regarding compliance risks it is easy to imagine that companies first focus on the most pressing risks, as it can be complicated, for multinationals in particular, to comply with every law and regulation at any given time. The risk of fraud, however, is of a very different nature as it relates directly to a company's integrity. If someone within the company – in any position – can get away with a little fraud at no significant cost to the company, that person is more likely to commit another fraud: the line has been crossed, and successfully so. In other words, reasonable assurance or minimizing the risk of fraud does not seem to be enough, because once bounds have been overstepped, fraudulent behaviour is more likely to accumulate. Treating the risk of fraud as any other risk could be the reason for – or at least contribute to – the fact that the internal control and risk management framework does not seem to properly detect severe fraudulent behaviour in an early stage.

---

[40] Bratton & Wachter 2009, p. 8.

6.4.5   Zero Fraud Tolerance Policy

Should companies have a *zero fraud tolerance* policy? And if so, what will be the role of the board or oversight body? According to the SEC, the overall purpose of internal control over financial reporting is to foster the preparation of reliable financial statements. Because the financial statements must be materially accurate, material weaknesses that can lead to material misstatement in the financial statements need to be identified.[41] It goes without saying that material financial frauds dilute the reliability of financial statements. The 1999 COSO report on fraudulent financial reporting states that '[f]or the first time, we have a clear understanding of who, why, where and how of financial reporting fraud'.[42] Unfortunately, an analysis of the occurrences of fraudulent financial reporting among US public companies for the 1997–2007 period, updating the 1999 monograph, has not yet been published. However, the 1999 report does yield some interesting insights. For example, it shows that the frauds investigated went to the very top of the organizations, since the CEO appeared to be associated with the fraud in no less than 72% of the cases. In addition, in 43% of the cases the CFO was associated with the financial statement fraud. The report shows that, when considered together, in 83% of the cases either the CEO or the CFO or both appeared to be associated with the fraud. Other officers were also named in the investigated fraud cases, for example the controller (21%).[43] It is noteworthy that more than half of the fraud cases involved overstating revenues by recording revenues prematurely or fictitiously.[44] In addition, the report stresses that the committed frauds had severe consequences next to the financial penalties imposed, such as bankruptcy, significant changes in ownership and delisting by national exchanges.[45] The upshot is that although the 1999 report states that the who, why, where, and how of financial reporting fraud were clear, this understanding did not lead to changes in the legal and accounting environment that adequately prevented fraud.

The 1999 report also points out that it is COSO's mission to improve the quality of financial reporting through internal controls, governance and ethics.[46] Over the last ten years, more focus on frauds and ethics might

---

[41]   SEC 2005, under B.
[42]   COSO 1999, p. 1.
[43]   COSO 1999, p. 5 and pp. 19ff. The report clearly states that most of them admitted no guilt of any kind.
[44]   COSO 1999, p. 6.
[45]   COSO 1999, p. 7.
[46]   COSO 1999, p. 1.

have been needed to improve the control environment or the sense of commitment at the top, especially since it is the top that was most often associated with the financial statement frauds between 1987 and 1997 and is still involved with fraud. To what extent does or can the increased regulation prevent such frauds?

Future analysis of the costs and consequences of frauds as well as of risk management failures would further the governance debate. The results of such an analysis can indicate the future role of oversight and clarify what might be of greater use: a *fraud prevention committee* or a *risk committee* such as recently introduced by the Dutch Code for Banks and in a legislative proposal to the US Congress.

6.4.6   Enterprise Risk Management as Legitimization

To start with a provocative example, Kenneth Lay argued that Enron not only had the best risk management system in their line of business, it had the best in the world. Enron also stated in its *Code of Ethics* – a 64-page booklet – that it had a reputation for fairness and honesty,[47] and it highlighted that 'Enron stands on the foundation of its Vision and Values. Every employee is educated about the company's Vision and Values and is expected to conduct business with other employees, partners, contractors, suppliers, vendors and customers keeping in mind respect, integrity, communication and excellence.'[48] Clearly having a risk management system in place as well as a code of ethics does not guarantee ethic behaviour and acceptable risk management practices. Institutional sociologists argue that adoption of management practices is also based on legitimacy concerns.[49] The adoption and use of risk management systems serves to convince the institutional environment rather than to mitigate risks. The ongoing standardization and structuring of risk management has a negative side effect: they may obscure actual risk management practices. The standards are used to convince interested parties that risk management is at a high level. Companies using COSO ERM comply with different corporate government codes, have auditing and risks committees and fall under a strict regulatory regime. The actual effectiveness of these risk management practices will depend on the internal environment and the quality of the risk assessments and controls that are implemented. The effectiveness of the internal control environment depends on soft controls, such as trust,

---

47   Enron Code of Ethics 2000, p. 2.
48   Enron Code of Ethics 2000, p. 4.
49   DiMaggio and Powell 1983, pp. 147–160.

leadership style and fairness. Porter claims a negative interaction between trust and standardization; the standardization of accounting standards has led from an ongoing decline of trust in the auditing profession to an increasing trust in the accounting standards.[50] Examples of creative compliance and treating form over substance that have been mentioned in previous chapters point in the same direction. For effective governance the level of transparency, amounts of standards, and the applicability of auditing has to be weighted against these negative side effects.

6.4.7 Complexity of Actual Behaviour

One of the other assumptions of formal risk management systems is that information on risks provides clear signals that can and will be used. However, deep-seated organizational assumptions may prevent readily available information from being assembled and acted upon.[51] Diana Vaughan studied the tragedy of the launch of the Challenger STS–51L on 28 January 1986, which resulted in the death of all seven crew members. An O-ring of the solid rocket booster failed because of unusually cold temperatures. At the centre of the analysis of the tragedy is a recommendation of the supplier to postpone the launch in a final teleconference meeting on the night before the scheduled flight. Halfway through the meeting, the people assembled at the supplier's location asked for a short break to hold an off-line discussion. Four administrators reversed the original recommendation and went back-on-line, announcing that they had re-examined their data, reversed the decision, and recommended a launch.[52] It was common wisdom, and this was reaffirmed by the report of the Rogers Commission, that the accident was ultimately caused by production pressures to meet launch schedules, which has led managers to violate internal NASA rules. According to Scott Sagan, this common wisdom is 'perversely comforting, for it suggests that if we try harder, organize more intelligently and follow rules more closely, similar accidents can be prevented in the future'.[53] A study made by Vaughan argues convincingly that the calamity had structural and cultural causes, which are not so simple to address. The engineering charts contained inconsistencies and did not live up to NASA standards. The recommendation was based on a temperature of 53° Fahrenheit, which caused most damage to

---

50 Porter 1995, Chapter 5.
51 Vaughan 1997, p. 86.
52 Vaughan 1997, p. 93.
53 Sagan 1997, pp. 401–405.

the O-ring, but the second-worst damage occurred at the hottest launch. The recommendation ultimately was not based on quantitative data but on qualitative data. The technical culture required quantitative, scientific data for every launch recommendation. The role of quantitative, scientific data in the technical culture had been of great importance for assuring safety. Absence of quantitative data had previously resulted in postponements of launches. The managers and engineers followed the usual rules and norms, which hindsight shows were inappropriate. One of the recommendations of Vaughan's study highlights the importance of studying rule-violating behaviour in normal work situations: 'How to install a rule following mentality that will assure coordination and control in a crisis, and at the same time teach people [. . .] to recognize the situation for which no rules exist and for which the existing rules do not apply.'[54]

6.4.8 Corporate Ethics

As discussed above, a zero fraud tolerance policy and risk management systems are only pieces of the puzzle. Research conducted by the US Ethics Resource Center shows that whistleblower hotlines and formal internal control mechanisms – though important – give an incomplete picture of the amount of misconduct that occurs.[55] In addition, it reveals that public companies' ethics risk is higher for most types of misconduct.[56] The report emphasises that '[m]ore than five years after Enron and other corporate ethics debacles, businesses of all size, type, and ownership show little – if any – meaningful reduction in their enterprise-wide risk of unethical behaviour. The situation is ripe for another major corporate scandal.'[57] Though SOX Section 406 requires public companies to disclose whether they have codes of ethics – and, if not, their reasons for not having them – it brought little or no change to the ethics risk environment of businesses. That, in combination with the abovementioned outcome of the 1999 COSO report that the corporate top is often extremely associated with the financial statement frauds, might point to a major future problem. For that reason, incorporating a strong enterprise-wide ethical culture into the business and having well-implemented ethics and compliance programmes are likely to be essential future tasks.

---

54 Vaughan 1997, p. 98.
55 Ethics Resource Center 2007, p. 26.
56 Ethics Resource Center 2007, p. 22.
57 Ethics Resource Center 2007, p. 1.

6.4.9 Remuneration

One way of mitigating management acting in its own interests is to make a portion of its compensation dependent on the company's profits. Shareholders stand to gain when profits are high (payable as dividends). Managers, entrusted with the day-to-day business, are paid to manage the company. It is not necessarily in their interests to realize high profits. They might be more in favour of, for example, having a flashy business car or state-of-the-art office furniture. The incentives of management and shareholders become better aligned when managers have a large stake in the company's equity – and in this way also become major shareholders themselves – and/or receive bonuses that are based on the profits of the company during their time of control. At least, that has been argued by financial economists for decades.[58] The familiar discussion on outrageous compensation systems does show that bonuses also have a downside. It has even been said to be one of the underlying problems that contributed to the current crisis, as these bonuses provide management with incentives to engage in practices that increase the company's risks. Taking huge risks can be tempting if it drives up reported corporate income and thereby secures tremendous salary increases for managers.[59] The incentive to drive up reported corporate income can even become so strong that managers condone or even conduct fraudulent behaviour. But it is not only the managers who may stray too far from the straight and narrow. There are many examples of investors pushing management to maximize shareholder value. Private equity funds and hedge funds are almost routinely accused of doing that.

6.5 CONCLUDING REMARKS

Adding to the disclosure laws and regulations on risk management might not be the answer. As the previous chapters show, requiring additional disclosure of information in order to restore public confidence has been done a couple of times before. Still, corporate failures, opportunistic behaviour, and inadequate management occur. This raises legitimate doubts as to whether confidence can once more be restored with disclosure requirements. Also, additional rules will increase compliance costs and lawmakers may wish to tread carefully for the sake of entrepreneurship and economic growth in the long run.

---

[58]   Stulz 2008, p. 7.
[59]   Black 2007, pp. 14–27.

Currently, there is a shift from focusing on the prevention of fraud to prevention of bad, especially overly risky, management. Traditionally, assessment of the quality of management decisions has been left to the market. Ideally, informed investors can assess the quality of management if they possess reliable and relevant information. In this light, financial reporting and attestation by independent auditors should guarantee the functioning of an efficient market. The quality of management will be reflected in the financial reports and the market will value these qualities. Ultimately, bad management will force the company to replace managers or file for bankruptcy. The numerous crises and frauds have led to more disclosures to inform investors. Financial results and positions are accounts of past behaviour and have limited predictive value. The attention to internal control and risk management can be seen in this perspective. Statements and disclosures on the management processes – such as internal control statements and risk reporting – and deficiencies in these processes and auditing help to better inform investors. From a corporate governance perspective, the current trend of risk management shows signs that more standards will be developed on what should be disclosed and audited.

This raises still more questions. Will more transparency, standardization and attestation prevent corporate failures due to bad management? Does the market really work? Will information on risks and the way management assesses and monitors those risks inform the public about the quality of management and will the market reward and punish? Are institutions not too big to fail and do government interventions undermine the functioning of the market? A look at recent regulation and regulation that is being drafted confirms that mechanisms other than transparency are being applied: audit and risk committees, appointment of CROs, solvency ratios and penalties and prison sentences if (members of) organizations do not comply with regulation. The financial crisis triggers extensive new regulation and amplifies the role of oversight bodies. Many of the regulations will be helpful, but whether a new equilibrium has been or indeed can be reached remains to be seen.

REFERENCES

Beck, Ulrich (1992), *Risk Society – Towards a New Modernity*, London: Sage Publications.

Black, William K. (2007), '(Mis)Understanding a Banking Industry in Transition', available at http://www.ssrn.com/abstract=1103942 (accessed 26 January 2010).

Bratton, William W. and Michael L. Wachter (2009), 'The Case Against Shareholder Empowerment', available at http://ssrn.com/abstract=1480290 (accessed 26 January 2010).

DiMaggio, Paul J. and Walter W. Powell (1983), 'The iron cage revisited:

Institutional isomorphism and collective rationality in organizational fields'. *American Sociological Review,* **48** (2), pp. 147–160.

Fiorelli, Paul and Ann Marie Tracey (2007), 'Why comply? Organizational guidelines offer a safer harbor in the storm', *Journal of Corporation Law*, **32** (3), pp. 472–490.

Gevurtz, Franklin A. (2004), 'The historical and political origins of the corporate boards of directors', *University of the Pacific, McGeorge School of Law*, working paper, pp. 41–58.

Goodhart, Charles A.E. (2008), 'The Regulatory Response to the Financial Crisis', available at http://ssrn.com/abstract=1113002 (accessed 26 January 2010).

Hines, James R. (2001), 'Corporate Taxation', *University of Michigan and NBER*, Working Paper, available at http://unpan1.un.org/intradoc/groups/public/documents/UNPAN/UNPAN002493.pdf (accessed 25 January 2010).

LaSalle, Randall E. (2007), 'Effects of the fraud triangle on students' risk assessments', *Journal of Accounting Education*, **25** (1–2), pp. 74–87.

Phillips, Arden T. (2009), 'Can congress cure corporate governance? The Shareholder Bill of Rights Act of 2009, in imposing a rigid structure, could have negative consequences', *The National Law Journal*, ALM Media Inc., available at http://law.com/jsp/cc/PubArticleCC.jsp?id=1202432221252 (accessed 26 January 2010).

Porter, Theodore M. (1995), *Trust in Numbers*, Princeton, New Jersey: Princeton University Press.

Power, Michael (2007), *Organized Uncertainty – Designing a World of Risk Management*, Oxford: Oxford University Press.

Sagan, Scott D. (1997), 'The Challenger launch decision: Risky technology, culture, and deviance at NASA'. *Administrative Science Quarterly,* **42** (2), pp. 401–405.

Stulz, Rene M. (2008), 'Risk Management Failures: What Are They and When Do They Happen?', available at http://ssrn.com/abstract=1278073 (accessed 26 January 2010).

Vaughan, Diane (1997), 'The trickle-down effect: Policy decisions, risky work and the challenger tragedy', *California Management Review*, **39** (2), pp. 80–102.

CODES AND GUIDELINES

Adviescommissie toekomst banken (Commissie Maas) (2009), *Nederlandse vereniging van banken*, available at http://www.nvb.nl/scrivo/asset.php?id=291556 (accessed 26 January 2010) (Code Banken).

Basel Committee on Banking Supervision (1988), *International Convergence of Capital Measurement and Capital Standards*, available at: http://www.bis.org/publ/bcbsc111.pdf?noframes=1 (accessed 26 January 2010) (Basel I).

Basel Committee on Banking Supervision (2004), Basel II: International Convergence of Capital Measurement and Capital Standards: a Revised Framework, http://www.bis.org/publ/bcbs107.pdf?noframes=1 (accessed 26 January 2010) (Basel II Accord).

Cadbury Committee (1992), *Report on the Financial Aspect of Corporate Governance*, London: Gee, (Cadbury Report).

Cohen Commission (1978), *Commission on Auditors' Responsibility: Report, Conclusions, and Recommendations*, New York: AICPA Inc., (Cohen Report).

Committee of Sponsoring Organizations of the Treadway Commission (COSO) (1992), *Internal Control – Integrated Framework*, New York: AICPA Inc., (COSO I Report).

Committee of Sponsoring Organizations of the Treadway Commission (COSO) (1999), *Fraudulent Financial Reporting: 1987–1997 – An Analysis of U.S. Public Companies*, New York: AICPA Inc.

Committee of Sponsoring Organizations of the Treadway Commission (COSO) (2004), *Enterprise Risk Management – Integrated Framework*, Executive Summary, New York: AICPA Inc., (COSO II Report).

Committee of Sponsoring Organizations of the Treadway Commission (COSO) (2009), *Effective Enterprise Risk Oversight: The Role of the Board of Directors*, New York: AICPA Inc.

Committee on Corporate Governance (2000), *The Combined Code – Principles of Good Governance and Code of Best Practice* (Combined Code 2000).

Corporate Governance Code Monitoring Committee (Frijns Committee) (2008), *The Dutch Corporate Governance Code – Principles of Good Corporate Governance and Best Practice Provisions* (2008 DCGC).

Department of Trade and Industry (2003), *Review of the role and effectiveness of non-executive directors* (Higgs I Report).

Enron Code of Ethics (2000), available at http://www.thesmokinggun.com/enron/enronethics1.html (accessed 26 January 2010).

Ethics Resource Center (2007), *National Business Ethics Survey: An Inside View of Private Sector Ethics*.

Financial Reporting Council (FRC) (2003), *Audit Committees – Combined Code Guidance* (Smith Report).

Financial Reporting Council (FRC) (2003), *The Combined Code on Corporate Governance* (Combined Code 2003).

Hampel Committee (1998), *Committee on Corporate Governance – Final Report*, London: Gee (Hampel Report).

IOSCO (2003), 'General Principles Regarding Disclosure of Management's Discussion and Analysis of Financial Condition and Results of Operations', *Internal Organisation of Securities Commissions*, available at http://www.sec.gov/about/offices/oia/oia_corpfin/genprinc.pdf (accessed 26 January 2010).

Maas, Cees (2009), 'Naar herstel van vertrouwen', *Adviescommissie Toekomst Banken*, available at http://www.nvb.nl/scrivo/asset.php?id=290352 (accessed 26 January 2010).

Minahan Committee (1979), *Report of the Special Advisory Committee on Internal Accounting Control*, New York: AICPA Inc., (Minahan Report).

Nederlandse Vereniging van Banken (NVB) (2009), *Code Banken* (Dutch Banking Code), Dutch and English version available at http://www.nvb.nl/index.php?p=291464 (accessed 26 January 2010).

Peters Committee (Committee on Corporate Governance) (1997), *Corporate Governance in Nederland – De Veertig Aanbevelingen* (Corporate Governance in the Netherlands – Forty Recommendations) (Peters Report).

Rutteman Working Group (1994), *Internal Control and Financial Reporting*, London: The Institute of Chartered Accountants in England and Wales (ICAEW) (Rutteman Report).

SEC (2005) (Division of Corporation Finance, Office of the Chief Accountant, US

Securities and Exchange Commission), *Staff Statement on Management's Report on Internal Control Over Financial Reporting*, available at http://www.sec.gov/info/accountants/stafficreporting.htm (accessed 8 February 2010).

Tabaksblat Committee (Corporate Governance Committee) (2003), *The Dutch corporate governance code: Principles of good corporate governance and best practice provisions* (Tabaksblat Code).

Treadway Commission (1987), *Report of the National Commission on Fraudulent Financial Reporting*, New York: AICPA Inc. (Treadway Report).

Turnbull Committee (1999), *Internal Control: Guidance for Directors on the Combined Code*, London: The Institute of Chartered Accountants in England & Wales (ICAEW) (Turnbull I Report).

Turner Review, (2009), *A regulatory response to the global banking crisis*, FSA, available at http://www.fsa.gov.uk/Pages/Library/Corporate/turner/index.shtml (accessed 26 January 2010).

Walker Review (2009) *A review of corporate governance in U.K. banks and other financial industry entities – Final recommendations*, available at: http://www.hm-treasury.gov.uk/walker_review_information.htm (accessed 26 January 2010).

US LEGISLATION AND DOCUMENTS

Shareholder Bill of Rights Act of 2009 (S. 1074) of 19 May 2009 to provide shareholders with enhanced authority over the nomination, election, and compensation of public company executives.

State of Delaware House Bill 19 of 10 April 2009, An Act to Amend Title 8 of the Delaware Code Relating to the General Corporation Law, available at http://delcode.delaware.gov/sessionlaws/ga145/Chp014.pdf (accessed 8 February 2010).

SEC Final Rule 33 – 8238 of 5 June 2003 on Management's Reports on Internal Control Over Financial Reporting and Certification of Disclosure in Exchange Act Periodic Reports, 68 FR 36636.

SEC Release 6231 of 2 September 1980 on Amendments to annual report Form, related forms, rules, regulations, and guides; integration of Securities' Acts Disclosure System, 45 FR 63630.

SEC Proposed Rule 33 – 9052 on Proxy Disclosure and Solicitation Enhancements of 17 July 2009, 74 FR 136.

SEC Interpretation 33 – 6835 of 18 May 1989 on Management's Discussion and Analysis of Financial Condition and Results of Operations; Certain Investment Company Disclosures, available at: http://www.sec.gov/rules/interp/33 – 6835.htm#P74_13103 (accessed 10 February 2010).

EU LEGISLATION AND DOCUMENTS

Regulation (EC) No. 1606/2002 of the European Parliament and of the Council of 19 July 2002 on the application of international accounting standards, OJ L 243 of 11 September 2002 (IAS Regulation).

Directive 78/660/EEC of the Council of the European Communities of 25 July

1978 on the annual accounts of certain types of companies, OJ L 222 of 14 August 1978 (Fourth Directive)

Directive 2002/87/EC of the European Parliament and of the Council of 16 December 2002 on the supplementary supervision of credit institutions, insurance undertakings and investment firms in a financial conglomerate and amending Council Directives 73/239/EEC, 79/267/EEC, 92/49/EEC, 92/96/EEC, 93/6/EEC and 93/22/EEC, and Directives 98/78/EC and 2000/12/EC of the European Parliament and of the Council, OJ L 35 of 11 February 2003.

Directive 2004/39/EC of the European Parliament and of the Council of 21 April 2004 on markets in financial instruments amending Council Directives 85/611/EEC and 93/6/EEC and Directive 2000/12/EC of the European Parliament and of the Council and repealing Council Directive 93/22/EEC, OJ L 145 of 30 April 2004.

Directive 2004/109/EG of the European Parliament and the Council of 15 December 2004 on the harmonisation of transparency requirements with regard to information about issuers whose securities are admitted to trading on a regulated market, OJ L 390 of 31 December 2004 (Transparency Directive).

Directive 2006/43/EC of the European Parliament and of the Council of 17 May 2006 on statutory audits of annual accounts and consolidated accounts, amending Council Directives 78/660/EEC and 83/349/EEC and repealing Council Directive 84/253/EEC, OJ L 157 of 9 June 2006.

Directive 2006/46/EC of 14 June 2006 of the European Parliament and of the Council amending Council Directives 78/660/EEC on the annual accounts of certain types of companies, 83/349/EEC on consolidated accounts, 86/635/EEC on the annual accounts and consolidated accounts of banks and other financial institutions and 91/674/EEC on the annual accounts and consolidated accounts of insurance undertakings, OJ L 224 of 16 August 2006 (Amendment to Accounting Directives).

Directive 2006/48/EC of the European Parliament and of the Council of 14 June 2006 relating to the taking up and pursuit of the business of credit institutions (recast), OJ L 177 of 30 June 2006.

Directive 2006/49/EC of the European Parliament and of the Council of 14 June 2006 on the capital adequacy of investment firms and credit institutions, OJ L 177 of 30 June 2006.

Commission Directive 2006/73/EC of the European Parliament and of the Council of 10 August 2006 implementing Directive 2004/39/EC as regards organizational requirements and operating conditions for investment firms and defined terms for the purposes of that Directive, OJ L 241 of 2 September 2006.

Directive 2009/111/EC of the European Parliament and of the Council of 16 September 2009 amending Directives 2006/48/EC, 2006/49/EC and 2007/64/EC as regards banks affiliated to central institutions, certain own funds items, large exposures, supervisory arrangements, and crisis management, OJ L 302 of 17 November 2009.

Directive 2009/138/EC of the European Parliament and of the Council of 25 November 2009 on the taking-up and pursuit of the business of Insurance and Reinsurance (Solvency II) OJ L 335 of 17 December 2009.

Communication from the Commission to the Council and the European Parliament, Modernising Company Law and Enhancing Corporate Governance in the European Union – A Plan to Move Forward, [COM(2003) 284 final], 21 May 2003, (Commission's Plan to Move Forward).

Index

ABN–AMRO 205
accounting 7–12, 48–51, 207–16
  capital and revenue expenditure 29
  fair value 19, 28–9, 35–7, 49, 200,
    215
  generally accepted accounting
    principles 12, 37, 145, 193, 195,
    210
    convergence 30, 35, 202
    principles-based approach 33–5,
      49, 50–51, 82, 88, 91, 202,
      211, 213
    rules-based approach 18, 30, 33–5,
      50–51, 196, 202, 210
    standards 49, 196, 215, 224
    US *see under* United States
  historical cost 18–19, 36
  off-balance sheet debt 28, 30
  profession 8–9, 181, 193, 210, 211,
    213, 215, 216
  risk
    accounting measures 13–14, 32
    standards and regulation 17–24
adverse selection 116, 122, 192
agency problem 62
Ahold 180
Aicher, R.D. 148
Allen, F. 134
Allen, W.T. 62
Amato, J.D. 154
American Institute of Accountants
  (AIA) 12, 17, 193, 194
American Institute of Certified Public
  Accountants (AICPA) 9, 18, 33,
  197
  Cohen Commission 63, 65, 72, 197,
    199, 211
  Minahan Committee 63, 72, 197,
    199, 211
Andersson, K. 186
Anson, M.J. 150, 151, 153

Arsenal Football Club 3
Asselt, M. van 47
Asset Backed Securities (ABS) 147, 149
audit committees 39, 103, 212, 221, 227
  EU 80–82, 96, 203, 212, 218–19
  Netherlands 85, 86–7
  UK 68, 90, 92, 204, 211, 212
  US 24, 64, 76, 202, 219
auditing 7–12, 45, 48–51, 103, 131, 227
  audit requirement 9, 49, 193, 194,
    197
  generally accepted auditing
    principles 193, 195, 210
  internal *see* internal audit
  internal control systems 49, 194, 195,
    197, 198, 205
    assessment and attestation on
      20–21, 24, 29, 49, 62, 63, 65,
      68, 76–7, 87–8, 200, 211
    PCAOB 29, 202–3, 213
    risk and 14–17
    Securities Act (1933)(US) 61–2,
      76–7
  non-compliance report 18, 195
  PCAOB 29, 39, 40, 75, 77, 202–3,
    213
  peer review 33
  power to obtain information 90–91
  profession 8–9, 33, 39–40, 193, 210,
    215, 216, 224
  quality 39–41
  scope and limitation of audits 37–9,
    50
  Securities Exchange Act (1934)(US)
    61, 194, 210
  standards 16, 18, 38, 49, 63, 205,
    215
  taxation 40, 165, 174, 175, 176,
    178–9, 184
    authorities 179–80, 182, 184, 214
Avi-Yonah, R. 178

Baker, N. 41
Bank of International Settlements 194
banks 14, 20, 32, 110, 114, 171, 213
    effectiveness of internal control
        statements 42–5
    European Union 124, 203, 213
    fair value accounting 36, 37, 215
    Netherlands 207, 208, 214, 219, 220
    operational risk 121
    ratio of capital to weighted risk
        assets 19, 124, 198–200
    risks of deposit 119–20, 134–6
    securitization 136–49
        subprime crisis 32–3, 49, 205
    supervision 123, 129, 131–2, 196,
        210
    systemic risk 119–20
    US *see under* United States
Banner, S. 58
Barings Bank 20
Barlev, B. 19, 35
Barmentlo, D.G. 183
Barth, J.R. 122
Basel Committee on Banking
    Supervision 19, 36, 121, 123, 124,
        196, 198–200, 210, 213, 215
Batten, J.A. 150, 152, 153
Bear Stern investment bank 32
Beck, U. 2, 46–7, 217
behaviour
    complexity of actual 224–5
    soft controls 48, 50, 223–4
Belgium 194
bell curve 3, 47
Bellingwout, J.W. 183
Benston, G.J. 12, 18, 34, 35
Bentham, Jeremy 47
Berle, A.A. 60, 100
Bernstein, P.L. 2
Bhattacharya, S. 134
Bindenga, A. 39
Black, W.K. 226
Black–Scholes model 3, 13
Blokdijk, H. 16, 17
boards *see* directors
Bonham, M. 146
Bowler, T. 151
Bratton, W.W. 221
Brazil 39–40
Breeden, Douglas 19, 35

Bretton Woods system 194
Brewer, R.B. 145
bribes, foreign 21, 62, 196, 199, 210
Brown, M.E. 48
Buhariwalla, A. 48
Burgert, R. 12, 18
Burmeister, R. 147
business law 56, 102–4, 125, 216
    comparison of EU and US 81–2,
        83
        Netherlands 88, 89, 92–4
        United Kingdom 92–4
    historical development 56, 71–4
        EU in 20th century 65–6, 70
        Netherlands in 20th century 66–7,
            70–74
        pre-20th century 57–9, 210
        UK in 20th century 9, 67–71,
            73–4, 192, 193
        US in 20th century 60–65, 71,
            72
    incomplete framework 102–3
    interconnections 207–16
    level of disclosure and enforcement
        100–102
    twenty-first century 74–5, 94–9,
        216
        EU 78–82, 83, 88, 89, 92, 93–4,
            96–7, 103–4, 216
        Netherlands 82–8, 89, 92–4, 97–8
        UK 88–94, 98–9
        US 75–8, 79, 81–2, 83, 88, 89, 92,
            93–4, 95–6, 216
business risks 49, 117

Camfferman, K. 9, 10
Caprio, G. 110
Chandler, R.A. 10, 15
Cheffins, B.R. 114
chief accounting officers (CAOs) 24
chief executive officers (CEOs) 24, 76,
    202, 219, 222
chief financial officers (CFOs) 24, 76,
    202, 219, 222
chief risk officers (CROs) 207, 214,
    219, 227
Choi, S.J. 101
Chorafas, D.N. 20
Choudhry, M. 151, 152
civil liability 29, 63

Clikeman, P.M. 9, 11, 12, 19, 24, 38
Coase, R.H. 62
Cohen, J.R. 48
collective investment schemes 129,
    154–6
companies legislation *see* business law
complexity of actual behaviour 224–5
compliance officers 127, 130
compliance risk 175, 221
concentration risk 119, 199
concept of risk management 2–4
conflicts of interests 129
consolidated accounts 81, 82, 84,
    145–7, 169–70, 197
controlled foreign companies (CFCs)
    164
corporate income tax 163–4, 166,
    167–70, 195
    deferred tax 169, 170, 175
    EU: CCCTB 180, 184–6
COSO *see* Treadway Commission
Cox, T. 164
credit crunch 218
credit default swaps (CDS) 150, 151,
    152–3
credit derivatives 149–54
credit linked note (CLN) 150, 153
credit rating agencies 14, 131, 142–3
credit risk 13, 119, 199
Cressey, D.R. 38
criminal liability 29, 33, 63, 76
Crockett, A. 142
crowding out 47–8, 215
Cunningham, L.A. 76
Cushing, B.E. 16
customs duties 163, 180

Daelen, M.M.A. van 62, 63, 64, 75, 82,
    103, 128
Daníelsson, J. 13, 45, 46
de Moivre, Abraham 3
Deacon, J. 138
Dechow, P.M. 141
deferred tax 169, 170, 175
definitions of risk and risk
    management 4–5
Diab, N.A. 134
Diamond, D.W. 135
Dijker, R.A. 10–11
DiMaggio, P.J. 223

direct taxes 166
    income taxes 163, 195
        companies *see* corporate income
            tax
directors 56, 71, 103, 210
    Netherlands 66–7, 71–4, 85–7, 88,
        101, 212, 218, 219
    non-executive 68, 85, 90, 91, 204,
        211, 212, 218
    role of 218–20
    supervisory board 39, 67, 85, 86–7,
        165, 202, 218
    taxation 165, 177, 178
    UK *see under* United Kingdom
    United States 21, 63, 202, 218, 219
disclosure of information 3–4, 9, 49,
    103, 193, 218, 226–7
    costs 101
    credit rating agencies 131
    European Union 66, 80, 84, 203–4
    fair value 19, 37
    financial instruments 19
    financial market participants 119,
        128, 131
    initial public offerings (IPOs) 130
    level of 100–101
    Netherlands 66, 82, 84, 85, 86, 87,
        92–4, 100, 101
    non-compliance with GAAP 18,
        195
    on risks 7, 32, 50, 64, 71, 80, 82, 84,
        86, 91, 128, 205
        and risk management 32, 50, 81,
            86, 217
    Sarbanes-Oxley Act 76, 100, 225
    Securities Act (1993)(US) 61
    Securities and Exchange
        Commission 19, 199, 220
        Securities Exchange Act (1934) 61,
            100, 194
    supervisory agencies 194
    taxation 174, 176, 178
    transparency and 7–8
    United Kingdom 9, 59, 67–70, 91,
        92–4, 101
dividends 101, 168
    withholding tax (DWT) 171–2, 176
Dombrecht, M. 135
double dip 180
Duff, D.G. 177

Dutch East India Company (VOC) 7,
57, 110, 111, 192
Dzinkowski, R. 36

East India Company 57, 110
economic value added (EVA) 14
employees 3, 48
wage withholding tax (WWT) 172–3,
174
Ende, E.M.E. van der 165, 183
Endres, D. 172
enforcement 101–2
Engel, E. 41, 42
Enron 24–9, 34, 75, 131, 180, 223
enterprise risk management *see under*
Treadway Commission
Epstein, B.J. 30
Ericsson 24, 25–8
Ernst & Ernst 11
Essers, P.H.J. 168, 182, 184, 185
ethics 10, 22, 31, 48, 222–3, 225
SOX 76, 212, 225
taxation 177, 179, 181
European Union
credit rating agencies 131
audit committees 80–82, 96, 203,
212, 218–19
audit partner rotation 39
business law 78–82, 83, 88, 89, 92,
93–4, 96–7, 103–4, 216
20th century 65–6, 70
Directives 66, 88, 103–4, 213
accounting 81, 87, 96–7, 203–4
audit 81, 87, 96, 203, 212, 218
banking sector 203, 213
collective investment schemes
155–6
Fourth Company Law Directive
81, 84, 197, 211
MiFID 126–8, 203, 213–14
parent-subsidiary 172
Seventh Company Law Directive
81, 84
solvency II 125–6, 214
transparency 80, 84, 96, 204
VAT 170–71
financial institutions 122–3, 124,
125, 145
investment firms 126–8, 203,
213–14

supervision 132–3
IFRS 82–4, 145, 185, 211
internal control systems 66, 70,
80–82, 203–4, 214, 218–19
comparison with US 81–2, 83,
88, 89
taxation 172, 180, 184–6
VAT *see* value added tax
events after reporting period 197
exchange rate risk 194, 199
externalities 122
Exxon 21

Fabozzi, F.J. 138, 139, 141
fair value accounting (FVA) 19, 28–9,
35–7, 49, 200, 215
fairness 48, 50, 224
Fayol, H. 60
Fernald, H.B. 61
Financial Accounting Standards Board
(FASB) 18, 19, 30, 35, 36, 196, 200
financial crises 49, 74, 111–13, 114,
122, 205–7, 218
financial industry 14, 207
see also banks
financial instruments 19–20, 118
EU Directives 126–8, 203, 213–14
fair value accounting 19, 200
securitization 13, 20, 136–49
subprime crisis 32–3, 49, 205
financial law 109–14, 156
collective investment schemes 129,
154–6
credit derivatives 149–54
dark pool 128
definitions
financial sector 114
financial system 114–15
interconnections 207–16
as risk mitigating mechanism 122–3
business organization 125–7
capital requirements 123–5
compensation schemes 125
conflicts of interests 129
financial market organization and
disclosure 127–9
insider information 128–9, 130
supervision 129–33
risks of traditional deposit bank
134–6

risks of and within financial system
116–22
securitization 13, 136–49
cash collateral pool 144
credit enhancement 141–3
credit insurance and guarantees
145
excess spread 143–4
influence of accounting rules
145–7
legal position of investors 147–8
secured lending 139–41, 148
true sale overview 137–9, 148–9
Financial Reporting Council (FRC) 41,
91, 211
financial risks 45, 117, 119, 174, 221
financial system 33, 192
Fiorelli, P. 200
floating rate 151–2
Fortis/ABN Amro 33
Foucault, M. 47
Frankel, T. 155
Fraser, R. 178
fraud 8–9, 11–12, 20, 33, 58, 74, 100,
103, 210, 216, 227
Cadbury report (1992) 200
enforcement 101–2
reporting, fraudulent 64, 71, 196,
198, 200, 210, 222
risk of 221
Sarbanes-Oxley Act (SOX) 75–6
scope and limitation of audits 37–9
triangle 217
zero tolerance 222–3, 225
Freedman, J. 164, 183
Frentrop, P. 58, 114
Frey, B.S. 48
Friehling & Horowitz 33

G-10 213
Gaastra, F.S. 58
Gagné, M. 48
GE Capital 219
Geiger, M.A. 40
Geld, J.A.G. van der 183
General Electric 20
Germany 168
Gevurtz, F.A. 193
Gillan, S.L. 28, 30
Goodhart, C.A.E. 218

Goodman, L.S. 13
Gorton, G. 138, 149
Grant, John 41
gravity and probability 2, 47
Gribnau, H. 183
Grossmann, R. 147
Grotenhuis, A. 165
Gwilliam, D. 29

Hamme, K. van 33
Hanlon, M. 170
Happé, R.H. 177, 180, 181, 183
Harris, R. 58
Hartman, W. 15
Hartnett, D. 181
Hassink, H. 38
Hayre, L. 13
hedge funds 32, 226
Heier, J.R. 63, 65, 77
Heijer, H.J. den 57, 58
Hen, P.E. 15
Henderson, J. 137
Herdman, R.K. 30
Herwijnen, P.A. van 183
Hickey, L. 181
Higgs Report 212
Hines, J.R. 195
historical cost accounting (HCA)
18–19, 36
history in stages
birth of regulated markets 192–4
reporting to stakeholders 194–6
codification of reporting
requirements 196–8
corporate governance 198–201
codification of internal control and
risk management 202–5
maturity or reinvention 205–7
Hoeven, R. ter 35
Hof, K. van der 8
Hofstra, H.J. 166
Holton, G.A. 116
Hood, C. 2
Hoyng, R. 175
Hudson, A. 150
Hughes, J. 41

ICAEW 9, 211
income taxes 163, 195
companies *see* corporate income tax

indirect taxes 163, 166
VAT 166, 170–71, 175, 180
information
asymmetry 49, 60, 100, 115, 116,
121, 122, 127, 128, 192
auditors: power to obtain 90–91
COSO I and II frameworks 23, 32
disclosure of *see separate entry*
ING 32, 33, 46, 205
initial public offerings (IPOs) 130
insider information 118, 128–9, 130
insurance companies 125–6, 129, 214
VAT: exempt businesses 171
internal audit 92, 211, 215
EU 81, 126, 203, 214, 218–19
outsourcing 40, 41
internal control systems 49, 56, 197,
198, 200–207, 215, 216, 225
audit *see under* auditing
COSO I and II Reports *see under*
Treadway Commission
effectiveness of 7, 47–8, 50
statements 42–5, 227
EU *see under* European Union
example of reporting on 24, 25–8
financial intermediaries 130
fraud, risk of 221
insurance companies 126
Netherlands 67, 70–74, 85–8, 89,
101, 212
risk society 217–18
taxation 175
UK *see under* United Kingdom
US *see under* United States
International Accounting Standards
Board (IASB) 30, 35, 185, 211
International Accounting Standards
Committee (IASC) 196
International Federation of
Accountants (IFA) 18, 197
International Financial Reporting
Standards (IFRS) 34–5, 37, 82,
145, 145–6, 185, 211
International Monetary Fund (IMF)
181
International Standards Organization
(ISO) 4
investment services 213–14
Isaac, William 36
Italy 39–40

Jackson, A.B. 40
Jager, J.C. de 183
Jain, P.K. 42
Japan 122
Jeffrey, P. 145
Jensen, M.C. 62
Jett, Joseph 20
Jobst, A.A. 152
Johnston, A. 165
Jong, A. de 71, 101

Karaoglu, E. 141
Kastein, J. 182
keiretsu 122
Kerviel, Jérôme 33
Keynes, J.M. 60
Kidder Peabody 20
Kiff, J. 150
Kinney, W.R. 16
Kirkpatrick, G. 45
Knechel, R. 4, 16, 17
Knight, F.H. 4, 60
Kohn, M. 120
Kolb, R.W. 154
Kothari, V. 139
KPMG 41
Kraakman, R.R. 62
Kravitt, J.H.P. 148
Kreuger case 11, 49
Krishnan, J. 41
Kuiper, J.G. 178

La Porta, R. 102
Laan, R. van der 173, 174, 175, 182,
183
Lam, James 219
Landolf, U. 181
LaSalle, R.E. 217
Laux, C. 35, 36, 37
Lay, Kenneth 24, 223
leadership 48, 224
Leeson, Nick 20
legal risk 121
legitimacy: standards hiding actual
practices 223–4
Lehman Brothers 33, 42–5, 49, 205
Levant Company 110
LIBOR 152
Limperg Jr, T. 10, 15, 41
Lincoln, Abraham 195

liquidity risk 13, 121–2
Lockheed 21
Lodewijk Pincoffs case 8–9
Luhmann, N. 4

Maas, C. 219
McCahery, J.A. 66
Macdonald, G. 170
McKesson & Robbins fraud 11–12, 49
Macours, K. 144
Madoff, Bernard 33, 49
Makridakis, S. 45–6
managers 60, 63, 65, 100, 226
  role of 70, 218–20
market risk 13–14, 118–19, 199
Marrisson, C.I. 14
Masters, B. 132
Mastroeni, O. 139
materiality 29, 38, 174
Mayer, R.C. 48
Meisner, N. 139
Mikes, A. 13, 14
modelling of risk 3, 13–14, 45–6
Moeller, R.R. 63
Moloney, N. 154
moral hazard 116, 125, 192
mortgage-backed securities (MBS) 13, 20
  subprime crisis 32–3, 49, 205
Moye, J.E. 59
Mulder, L.B. 48
multinational corporations 221
Munro, J.H.A. 110

Neale, T. 185
Netherlands 8–9, 33, 34–5, 220
  audit committees 85, 86–7
  auditing 15–16, 39, 87–8
  banks 207, 208, 214, 219, 220
  business law 66–7, 70–74, 82–8, 89, 92–4, 97–8
  Corporate Governance Code (2008) 204, 212
  directors 66–7, 71–4, 85–7, 88, 101, 212, 218, 219
  disclosure of information 66, 82, 84, 85, 86, 87, 92–4, 100, 101
  Dutch East India Company (VOC) 7, 57–8, 110, 192
  financial law 110, 114, 130
  Frijns code/DCGC 2008 85–7, 97
  Peters Committee (1997) 67, 70, 72–3, 101, 200
  Tabaksblat code 85, 97, 100, 204
  taxation 168, 172, 173, 174, 179
    horizontal supervision 180, 181–4, 186
Niu, F. 141
non-executive directors 68, 85, 90, 91, 204, 211, 212, 218
Norton, J.J. 143

off-balance 28, 30, 147, 152
operational risk 13, 121, 175, 221
opportunism 3, 48, 49
outsourcing 40, 41, 126
over the counter (OTC) 150

Paape, L. 45
Parmalat 180
Partnoy, F. 143
PCAOB (Public Company Accounting Oversight Board) 29, 39, 40, 75, 77, 202–3, 213
pension schemes 3, 129–30
Perignon, C. 19
Pheijffer, M. 41
Philips 174, 176, 178
Phillips, A.T. 220
Poolen, T.W.M. 181, 184
Porter, T.M. 224
Poulain, A. 148
Power, M. 2, 4, 15, 50, 219
Price Waterhouse 11, 12
principal–agent problem 62
principles-based approach 33–5, 49, 50–51, 82, 88, 91, 202, 211, 213
private equity funds 226
probability and gravity 2, 47

quantitative risk management 45–6, 50
  value at risk (VAR) 13–14, 19, 46

Raaijmakers, T. 57, 66
Rabenort, M. 164, 173, 176
Ramsey, F.P. 60
Rappaport, A. 14
Rayton, B.A. 69
real estate transfer tax (RETT) 167, 172

Rebonato, R. 45, 46
recourse 100, 147–8, 149
remuneration 207, 226
Rentokil 41
reputation risk 40, 121, 130, 149, 173, 175
Ribstein, L.E. 76
Ricklefs, M.C. 57
risk appetite 5, 7, 30, 31, 32, 205, 207, 217, 218, 219, 221
risk assessment, limitations of 46–7
risk committees 207, 215, 219–20, 223, 227
risk society 217–18
risk-adjusted return on capital (RAROC) 14, 32
Robinson, D. 40
Romano, R. 41, 75
Rosenblatt, M. 146
Royal Bank of Scotland 33, 42–3, 44, 45, 205
Royal Mail case (1931) 9–10, 49
Ruiz-Barbadillo, E. 40
rules-based approach 18, 30, 33–5, 50–51, 196, 202, 210
Ryan, S.G. 36, 37

Sagan, S.D. 224
Salomon v. Salomon 58
Sarbanes-Oxley Act (SOX) 29, 40, 45, 75–6, 95, 122, 212
  codes of ethics 76, 212, 225
  costs of and effectiveness of 41–2
  internal control systems 29, 41–2, 45, 49, 75, 76, 77–8, 202, 212
  PCAOB *see separate entry*
Savage, L.J. 60
Schep, A.W. 181
Schipper, K. 34, 149
Schmidt, R.H. 114, 115
Schmit, T.P.M. 184
Scholtens, B. 134, 137
Schrans, G. 134, 137
Securities and Exchange Commission (SEC) 20, 30, 61, 132, 194, 197–8, 210, 211, 213, 220–21
  final rule 33–8238 (2003) 202, 212
  internal control 12, 62–3, 212
  principles-based accounting system 34, 35

risks 64
  Market Risk Amendment and FRR 48 19, 199
  Sarbanes-Oxley Act (SOX) 77
securitization 13, 20, 136–49
  subprime crisis 32–3, 49, 205
Self, H. 177
Shapiro, B. 18, 20, 21, 24
share value 181, 182
shareholders 3, 60, 71, 85, 100–101, 102, 103, 149, 226
  transparency and power of 220–21
Simonis, P.H.M. 177, 186
Skeel, D.A. 4
Smith Report 212
social construction of risks 46–7
Société Générale 33, 49
soft controls 48, 50, 223–4
Sommer, J. 32
South Sea Company 58, 111, 114, 193, 210
Spain 40
special purpose vehicles (SPVs) 28, 30
stakeholders 3, 45, 102, 103, 164, 193, 194–6
Starreveld, R.W. 16
Stevens, L.G.M. 181, 182
Stewart, G.B. 14
Stulz, R.M. 218, 226
subprime-mortgage crisis 32–3, 49, 205
swap 150, 151–2
Sweden 11
systematic risk 117, 118
  see also market risk
systemic risk 119–20, 124, 205

Talbot, L.E. 59
Taleb, N.N. 47
Tanzi, V. 181
Tavakoli, J.M. 13, 138
taxation 34, 163–7, 186, 195, 214, 215
  accountant, internal 173–4
  arbitrage 180
  auditing 165, 174, 175, 176, 178–9, 184
  authorities 179–80, 182, 184, 214
  non-audit tax services 40
  authorities
    advance rulings 178, 182, 183

horizontal supervision 180, 181–4
tax audit 179–80, 182, 184, 214
avoidance 177, 178, 182
board decisions 165, 177, 178
corporate income tax *see separate entry*
disclosure in accounts 174, 176, 178
dividend withholding tax (DWT) 171–2, 176
double dip 180
participation exemption 168, 169, 171, 172
penalties 174, 179
planning 177–8, 180–81
real estate transfer tax 167, 172
recent developments 179–86
risks 165–6, 173, 175, 176–7, 178, 183
strategy 177
tax assurance providers 178–9
Tax Control Framework (TCF) 166, 173–9, 182
tax department of company 164–5, 169–70, 171, 172, 174, 177
tax havens 180, 181
transfer pricing 172, 176, 185, 186
VAT 166, 170–71, 175, 180
wages: WWT 172–3, 174
Taylor, F.W. 60
Thakor, A.V. 135
Tilly, R.H. 110
time limits: taxation 173, 174
total return swap (TRS) 150, 151–2
transfer pricing 172, 176, 185, 186
transparency 7–8, 30, 50, 103, 124, 202, 210, 224, 227
disclosure of information and 7–8
non-audit services 40
shareholder power 220–21
taxation 183
see also disclosure of information
Treadway Commission 64, 65, 72, 198
COSO report: fraudulent financial reporting 222, 225
enterprise risk management
COSO II Report 5, 30–32, 78, 95–6, 99, 204–5, 213
internal controls
COSO I Report 21–4, 64–5, 70, 71, 72, 78, 99, 200, 211, 212

study of COSO risk management method 217
Tribunella, H. 35
true and fair view 35, 164, 197
trust 45, 48, 50, 121, 223

Ugur, A. 144
uncertainties 50, 176, 205
annual reports 80, 82, 84, 91, 128, 204
risk and 4–5, 46–7, 60, 116
SEC financial reporting 64, 65, 198, 211
Undertakings for collective investment in transferable securities (UCITS) 129, 155
United Kingdom 9–10, 33, 34–5, 58–9, 195
audit committees 68, 90, 92, 204, 211, 212
auditors 9–11, 39, 90–91
internal 92, 211
business law 58–9, 88–94, 98–9, 210
20th century 9, 67–71, 73–4, 192, 193
Cadbury report (1992) 68, 70, 73, 90, 101, 200, 211
Combined Code 69, 73, 90, 91, 92, 101, 200, 204
directors 58–9, 91, 101
information to auditors 91
internal control 42, 68, 69–70, 90, 92, 101, 200, 211, 218
non-executive 68, 90, 91, 204, 212
financial law 110
Financial Services Authority 92
Hampel report (1998) 69, 73, 90, 200
Higgs Report 90, 91, 204, 212
internal control systems 68–71, 73–4, 200–201
audit committees 204
directors 42, 68, 69–70, 90, 92, 101, 200, 211, 218
London Stock Exchange 68, 114, 200, 211
Rutterman report (1994) 68–9, 73, 200, 211
Smith Report 90, 204, 212
Turnbull report 68, 69–70, 73–4, 91, 200, 211

Turner review 207, 208, 214
Walker review 207, 208, 214
United States 9, 195, 200, 219, 224–5
    AIA 12, 17, 193, 194
    AICPA *see* American Institute of
        Certified Public Accountants
    audit committees 24, 64, 76, 202,
        219
    auditing 11, 16, 33, 38, 41, 202–3
        standards 12, 18, 38, 63
    banks 120, 122, 131–2, 136
        savings and loan 18, 21, 24, 38, 49,
            132, 198, 200
    boards 21, 63, 202, 218, 219
    bribes, foreign 21, 62, 196, 199
    business law 59, 75–8, 79, 81–2, 83,
        88, 89, 92, 93–4, 95–6, 216
        20th century 60–65, 71, 72
    credit rating agencies 131
    FASB 18, 19, 30, 35, 36, 196, 200
    financial institutions 35, 122, 131–2
        banks *see above*
    generally accepted accounting
        principles (GAAP) 8, 12, 34–5,
            37, 145–6, 147, 194–5
        convergence 35, 202
        financial instruments 200
        standards 17–19, 35, 199
    internal control systems 60–65, 71,
        72, 79, 195, 197, 202–3, 218
        comparison with EU 81–2, 83,
            88, 89
        Foreign Corrupt Practices Act
            (1977) 21, 62–3, 65, 196,
            210–11
        Sarbanes-Oxley Act (SOX) 29,
            41–2, 45, 49, 75, 76, 77–8,
            202, 212
    savings and loan banks 21, 200
    Securities Act (1933) 61–2, 76–7
    Securities Exchange Act (1934)
        194
    Treadway Commission *see*
        separate entry

    law compliance: sentencing
        guidelines 63, 77, 200
    Sarbanes-Oxley Act (SOX) *see*
        separate entry
    SEC *see* Securities and Exchange
        Commission
    Securities Act (1933) 11, 61–2, 75,
        76–7, 100, 122
    Securities Exchange Act (1934) 11,
        61, 75, 100, 122, 194, 210
    TARP 33, 205

Vaassen, E.H.J. 16
value added tax (VAT) 166, 170–71,
    175, 180
value at risk (VAR) 13–14, 19, 46
Van der Elst, C. 62, 63, 64, 75, 82, 103,
    104
Van der Hof, K. 8
Van Hamme, K. 33
Vaughan, D. 224, 225
Ven, A.C.N van de 41, 45
Verbakel, R. 182
Verburg, J. 164
Vermilyea, T.A. 149
Vermeulen, E.P.M. 66, 105
Véron, N. 36
Vries, J. de 9, 58
Vries-Robbé, J.J. de 137, 138

wage withholding tax (WWT) 172–3,
    174
Webber, L. 143
whistleblowers 225
Williamson, O.E. 4
Wood, P.R. 137, 138, 141, 145
WorldCom 24, 29, 75, 131, 180
Wyckoff, J. 33

Ydema, O.I.M. 163

Zeckhauser, R.J. 60
Zhang, I.X. 41, 42
Zwemmer, J.W. 183